Passwords Primeval:
20 American Poets in Their Own Words

Passwords Primeval
20 American Poets in Their Own Words

Interviews by

Tony Leuzzi

American Reader Series, No. 18

BOA Editions, Ltd. • Rochester, NY • 2012

Manufactured in the United States of America

First Edition
12 13 14 15 7 6 5 4 3 2 1

Publications by BOA Editions, Ltd.—a not-for-profit corporation under section 501 (c) (3) of the United States Internal Revenue Code—are made possible with funds from a variety of sources, including public funds from the New York State Council on the Arts, a state agency; the Literature Program of the National Endowment for the Arts; the County of Monroe, NY; the Lannan Foundation for support of the Lannan Translations Selection Series; the Mary S. Mulligan Charitable Trust; the Rochester Area Community Foundation; the Arts & Cultural Council for Greater Rochester; the Steeple-Jack Fund; the Ames-Amzalak Memorial Trust in memory of Henry Ames, Semon Amzalak and Dan Amzalak; and contributions from many individuals nationwide. See Colophon on page 350 for special individual acknowledgments.

Cover Design: Sandy Knight
Interior Design and Composition: Richard Foerster
Manufacturing: McNaughton & Gunn
BOA Logo: Mirko

Library of Congress Cataloging-in-Publication Data

Leuzzi, Tony.
Passwords primeval : 20 American poets in their own words : interviews /
by Tony Leuzzi. — 1st ed.
p. cm. — (American readers series ; 18)
ISBN 978-1-934414-95-8 (pbk. : alk. paper)
1. American poetry—21st century. 2. Poets, American—21st century—Interviews. 3. Poetry—Authorship. I. Title.
PS617.L48 2012
811'.608—dc23

2012014240

BOA Editions, Ltd.
250 North Goodman Street, Suite 306
Rochester, NY 14607
www.boaeditions.org
A. Poulin, Jr., Founder (1938–1996)

for Jessica, Peyton, Sophie and Stephanie;
the poets included herein;
and Ai and Rane Arroyo, who should be here

Contents

Introduction

"Someone once asked Robert Frost to explain one of his poems, and Frost said, 'Oh, you want me to say it worse?!'"
—Billy Collins, October 10, 2011

Robert Frost didn't like to explain his poems—and for good reason: to explain a poem is to suck the air from its lungs. This does not mean, however, that poets shouldn't talk about their poetry, or that one shouldn't ask questions about it. Rather, it suggests that any discussion of poetry should celebrate its ultimate ineffability and in so doing lead one to further inquiry. I think of that wonderful scene from Elie Wiesel's memoir, *Night,* where Mosche the Beadle of the local synagogue, in dialogue with the young, precocious author, explains: "Every question possesses a power that does not lie in the answer." It is my hope that the discussions in *Passwords Primeval: 20 American Poets in Their Own Words* illuminate these poets and their poems in such a way that one may access valuable insights into the magic and mystery of their works, and be compelled to ask more questions.

"Each poem is an instance of possession," Robert Glück confides. "When you read someone in a deep way your thoughts and your rhythms are taken over." After six years of intense reading and serious engagement with the works of these writers, I've come to understand Glück's words in ways even I could not predict. While sequencing the discussions for this book, I realized certain relationships between a number of the writers that were previously obscured by my knowledge of movements and schools. Bin Ramke and Scott Cairns may hold vastly different aesthetic notions but many of their poems are shaped by an intimate knowledge of scripture; Arthur Sze and Nathalie Handal possess very different artistic temperaments, yet they both understand the complex ways in which world and national literatures inform each other—and how, in fact, the distinctions between them are ever shifting; Glück and Carol Frost's views on narrative may at first seem oppositional, yet some of their statements about it are surprisingly similar. These are just a few examples.

But the most conspicuous and pervasive commonality among these poets is a shared respect for and allegiance to the father of American poetry, Walt Whitman, with whom many in these pages have come to terms. Gary Young says, "Whitman's propulsive verse was one of the catalyzing agents that led me toward a notion of a 'horizontal poetry.'" Michael Waters cites Whitman's "blab of the pave," in which colloquialisms, slang and vulgarity are accepted into poetic utterance, as an influential strategy for contemporary poets. Martín Espada credits Whitman with establishing the traditions of political poetry and radical democracy in Anglo and Latin American letters, traditions that Espada, Gary Soto, and Handal have absorbed through Pablo Neruda and others. Gerald Stern acknowledges his Whitmanlike tendency to "embrace everything." Mark Doty is one of countless authors working on a book about Whitman. Kevin Killian embodies Whitman's inclusiveness, and like Whitman, finds inspiration in the "low" as well as "high" elements of the culture. Whitman's presence was so pervasive in these discussions that, midway through the process, I realized that through him I could tie the collection together. Not surprisingly, then, a passage from "Song of Myself"—alluded to by Espada in our discussion—furnishes this book's title:

> I speak the pass-word primeval, I give the sign of democracy,
> By God! I will accept nothing which all cannot have their counterpart of on the same terms.

Indeed, all the poets in *Passwords Primeval* speak their passwords to mysteries linked with the world's oldest secrets. Perhaps the greatest of these involves our own mortality. Whitman certainly thought so. In "Out of the Cradle, Endlessly Rocking" he calls death, "The word final, superior to all." With forceful candor, Billy Collins echoes that sentiment when he says, "The theme of my poetry is basically me . . . and death." Dara Wier is a bit more philosophical: "We are all in the same boat when it comes to the fact that we are creatures with an expiration date. The fact that we are still able to have love in our lives and are sometimes happy is all mixed together with this knowledge of our eventual death."

Ultimate though death may be, it is not the only mystery the poets in *Passwords Primeval* explore. Jane Hirshfield contends, "What you see in the development of poetry over the millennia is an ever-widening range of subjects being investigated in ever-widening ways . . . the thrill is not only beautiful speech, but beautiful speech that makes a discovery." Related to Hirshfield's notion of discovery is what Soto apprehends as the search for truth beyond words: "There is something symbolic groping underneath the language in a poem," he says. No matter how transparent or opaque that language may be, poets and readers of poetry must attune themselves to the deeper questions nesting beneath a poem's surface. Some poets set out in search of large questions. Others find answers in their own familiars: "I think we spend so much time looking for the huge answers right in front of us," Patricia Smith says. "We think there's an answer that comes from high up that will trickle down to us and solve everything. It doesn't exist."

But whether the poets in *Passwords Primeval* consider poetry an apt medium for exploring universal themes or a means to record and transform the particulars of their environment, it is clear that these authors possess an intellectual curiosity that gives their work rigor and texture. Mark Doty explains, "I'm interested in how we make our knowledge, how we map the world, constructing a sense of our relation to what it is . . . this action of meaning-making." For Doty and the rest of the poets here, this act of meaning-making, though subjective, is anything but solipsistic: it requires concentration, an understanding of the nature of reality and existence beyond one's self. "I don't see how poems could be other than steeped in intellectual matter," Ramke insists. Poets like Ramke, Sze, and Hirshfield engage the discourses of science and philosophy on a routine basis; Glück digests the language of critical theory; Killian and Frost look with relish to the visual arts; Handal and Espada respond with mind and heart to the language of politics.

In addition to the breadth of their interests, these poets are conscious of a literary tradition that rewards formal innovation. Waters' work with syllabics has lent strength and dignity to a process too often trivialized by poets and critics. Young's prose poems share structural affinities with Petrarchan sonnets, a centuries-old verse form Karen Volkman celebrates and deconstructs. Likewise, Frost's invention of conceptual forms demonstrates her ability to blend new ideas with preexisting structures. Sze and Wier use unrhymed couplets to create linguistic and visual space, and reduce syntactic clutter. Dorianne Laux and Doty build images through enumeration and lush details. Clearly poets adopt certain composition strategies that speak to individual temperament; the diversity of approaches discussed in this book demonstrates the accommodating nature of American poetry. So much is possible. All seems permitted. Whitman's legacy persists in the twenty-first century.

The interviews in *Passwords Primeval* are not typical in the sense most people understand the medium. Instead of a series of quick-fire questions that call for equally quick, breezy responses, these are closer to heightened discussions—well-formed dialogues emerging through sustained development and negotiation. Thus they are also collaborations. In each instance, I tailored questions specific to individual participants based primarily on their published works. This meant months of preparation were required for each interview. It was a labor of love, for what poetry enthusiast *wouldn't* want to immerse oneself in the works of poets as fine as these? "It's like you're taking a course in each writer you interview," Laux observed at the end of one of our phone discussions—and she was right.

In positioning myself as a self-motivated student, I had to master the art of humility. Too many interviewers use the medium as a prop for their ideas. I wanted my presence in these discussions to prod the interview subject towards a greater articulation of his or her poetics. This meant allowing myself to risk occasional moments of professed ignorance, and to posit misreadings at others. In such cases, I did not edit my blunders from the discussions because the poets' responses to them helped clarify their own views more effectively.

These discussions, conducted between 2006 and 2012, were collated and reshaped from several conversations using different mediums for communication. Face-to-face interactions were always preferred but not always possible; even when they were, almost all of the poets received my questions in advance of our meeting. In every case, an in-person encounter was followed by further edits and clarifications during ensuing e-mail exchanges.

Many poets preferred to write their answers. This initially surprised me, since doing so required of them a lot more commitment. I soon realized that poets, perhaps even more than writers of fiction, are afraid of being misunderstood and therefore welcome the chance to present themselves as they wish to be seen. While this approach was useful, I augmented each poet's written responses with an hour-long discussion via telephone, which I then transcribed and inserted carefully into the prepared portions. In this way, I was able to ensure a healthy dose of spontaneity and surprise, and to tease from each participant certain observations that might not have surfaced if the discourse wasn't improvised.

"Cursed be the writer who first allowed a journalist to reproduce his remarks freely!" Milan Kundera laments in his essay "Sixty-three Words." No matter how these interviews were conducted, each poet featured in *Passwords Primeval* was given the opportunity to observe the finished result and make sure all elements of it met with his or her approval. This pleased me as much as it did the poets, for it now means this anthology collects official documents.

Not every interview found its way into this book. For reasons of space, BOA Publisher Peter Conners and I limited the collection to 20 writers. The writers were selected based on many factors, including aesthetic difference, thematic variety, gender identification, and, most crucially, the strength of their interviews. The result is a unique mix of the usual suspects with less-expected voices. I'm quite certain, for example, this is the first anthology to feature Laux, Ramke, and Killian alongside one another. But then any anthology must be seen as a subjective compilation of its editor: ultimately, I chose these poets because I admire their work.

Contemporary American Poetry is a vast, evolving entity that does not cohere in some neat, manageable form. Although *Passwords Primeval* does not pretend to fully represent the diversity of poetry written by Americans in the last 40 years, a front-to-back reading of the book will demonstrate an astonishing interconnectedness, as if each voice echoes another from opposite ends of the same canyon.

Kundera, Milan. "Sixty-Three Words." *The Art of the Novel*. Trans. Linda Asher. New York: Grove, 1986.

Whitman, Walt. "Song of Myself." *Leaves of Grass: 150th Anniversary Edition*. New York: Oxford University Press, USA, 2005.

Wiesel, Elie. *Night*. Trans. Marion Wiesel. New York: Hill and Wang, 2006.

Writing by Ear: An Interview with Michael Waters

In his autobiographical essay, "The Bicycle and the Soul," Michael Waters recalls his memorable encounters with Allen Ginsberg and Robert Lowell, two Post-War poets of very different temperament whom Waters has understood and absorbed. Like Ginsberg, Waters writes bold, fiery poems that challenge oppression and celebrate one's right to sexual and political freedoms. Like Lowell, Waters can be intensely personal yet formally strict. In his earlier poems, he used traditional procedures to achieve remarkably subtle, individual rhythms, an approach he later exchanged for the equally demanding rigors of syllabic verse. In this second phase, Waters has achieved his greatest distinction, for poems like "Black Olives" (from *Darling Vulgarity)* and "Mrs. Snow White" (from *Gospel Night)* rank among the best examples of syllabic verse in English. A consummate craftsman, Waters also edits the widely used anthology *Contemporary American Poetry.* A passionate teacher and mentor to countless emerging writers, he demonstrates time and time again that the best poets embrace their influences and transcend them. He has received many prizes and honors, including three Puschart Prizes and a fellowship in Creative Writing from the National Endowment for the Arts. He currently teaches at Monmouth and Drew Universities.

You once told me that a reviewer of The Burden Lifters *(1989) observed that the book displayed a "dizzying" variety of forms and styles. The implication here was that you favored eclecticism over a consistency; but even a superficial perusal of* Parthenopi: New and Selected Poems *(2001) proves that you persist in a handful of classic stanzaic forms—couplets, tercets, quatrains—and syllabic, non-stanzaic poems that accumulate anywhere from 25–50 lines. Can you speak about the importance of form in your verse?*

I seem to need some sort of form to ground my free verse, and believe that any good free verse contains formal gestures. Robert Bly refers to his own poems as "free verse with distinct memories of form." Without form, poetry is often, if not always, prose. Many hold up William Carlos Williams's "The Red Wheelbarrow" as an example of a good free verse poem. But there's really nothing free about this poem. It's broken into short-lined couplets. Each first line of the couplet has a precise number of words: three. Each second line of the couplet has a precise number of words: one. Each of those one-word lines consists of two syllables. The poem has a formal shape, though it's still considered free verse.

Williams invents the poem's shape for this occasion using "nonce" form.

Yes. I began writing in rhyme and meter. The first poems I published were rhymed-quatrain imitations of Richard Wilbur, the poet I most admired when I was 19 and 20. Earlier, in high school, I'd begun reading the Beats: Allen Ginsberg, Lawrence Ferlinghetti, Gregory Corso. But I went to college in 1967, and my first English class was "Contemporary Literature," taught by Gregory FitzGerald, who had just come from the University of Iowa's Writers' Workshop. He used Donald Hall's *Contemporary American Poetry* as well as Donald Allen's *The New American Poetry*. Hall's anthology opened me to poets like Wilbur and W. D. Snodgrass. I was fascinated by the way they were able to give shape to their poetic narratives. So I began writing in form, mainly to give shape to my own narratives, otherwise my poems were just sprawling all over the place; all the word-spewing I had taken from Ginsberg needed to be reined in. Wilbur, for example, showed me to do that. Despite his influence, despite my early use of rhyming quatrains, the poems included in my first book, *Fish Light* (1975), still seem to me to be rather shapeless. I was aware of this. I was so concentrated on the image as the central element of the poem, and believed that the poem could stand on images alone. But I remember sending some poems to a journal, and the editor responding, "These poems have many wonderful images, perhaps too many." I thought, "What does *that* mean?" I thought of the editor's remark later when I watched the film *Amadeus*. Do you remember when the emperor tells Mozart that his compositions are filled with too many notes, and Mozart replies, "Which notes?" Still, I was struck by the editor's remarks. He was complementary of my verse, but he was responding to something I hadn't spent enough time considering. That first book was not as crafted or attentive to language as my others. When I moved *toward* forms in my second book, *Not Just Any Death* (1979), I slowed down, and began working more consciously with quatrains, often unrhymed or loosely rhymed.

I have noticed in those poems quite a bit of slant and internal rhyming.

Exactly. I learned slant rhyming from Emily Dickinson and Shakespeare, whom I, now in college, began reading seriously. "Ways" and "grace," or "God" and "cloud"—those sorts of rhymes from traditional verse. Vernon Watkins, the English poet and critic, wrote, "Poetry rhymes all along the lines, not only at the ends." *All along the lines:* this idea stayed with me, especially when I discovered John Logan's poetry in 1969 or 1970. Logan was doing precisely what Watkins required. So, for me, working with quatrains became a way of organizing not only the narrative materials, but also the sounds of the poems. I continued to use tight stanzaic structures—quatrains, couplets, and tercets—through successive books, especially *Anniversary of the Air* (1985) and *The Burden Lifters* (1989), becoming comfortable with that structure so that, eventually, I again needed to break away.

Some of the newer poems in Parthenopi, *such as "God at Forty" and "Cognac," and the title poem in* Darling Vulgarity, *are written in syllabic verse. More precisely, you adapt a variation of decasyllabic meter, where your lines alternate between thirteen and seven syllables each. What are some of your reasons for working in this form?*

When Brad Leithauser reviewed Richard Howard's *Inner Voices: Selected Poems* (*New York Times Book Review,* November 21, 2004), he wrote, "As systems go, syllabic verse has little to recommend it, except for one puzzling thing: It works. With some frequency, the eccentric discipline it imposes seems to push everyday utterance into memorability." After my first few books, I found myself moving toward the syllabic verse that I had noticed in John Logan's poetry. The syllabic system you see in "God at Forty," for example, became a means for me to break up the quatrain while not always relying on a precise decasyllabic line, which occurs in some of my poems. The alternation between thirteen- and seven-syllable lines enables me to cast out a long line, adding three syllables to the decasyllabic line, and then pull back by three syllables in the next seven-syllable line.

It creates a tension between expansiveness and compression.

The interplay between the thirteen- and seven-syllable lines allows me to adopt a more conversational tone. This syllabic system enabled me to think not only vertically as the poem moves down the page, but horizontally as the language flows across the page. The integral unit of poetry is the line itself: the line as a unit unto itself, that requires its own context and which, out of the context of the rest of the poem, needs to remain interesting. Each line requires balance and heft, and needs to express certain tactile qualities. Writing in syllabic forms was not inhibitive in terms of my thinking; in fact, I found it liberating. After writing this way for several years, I found myself thinking naturally along syllabic lines. I could hear people in conversation speaking lines of thirteen and seven syllables! Half of my next book, *Darling Vulgarity* (2006), consists of poems written in this strict syllabic system or some variation of it.

A poet working in syllabics faces some significant challenges. One of the challenges is to avoid a prosy sounding line. Another is to create a line-ending that is both consistent with the syllabic pattern and aesthetically pleasing in itself. When you write in syllabics are you conscious of using a variety of sound and rhythmic patterns that will bolster the line?

Very much so. Any verse is weak when it is not attentive to sound work, to tactile qualities divorced from literal meaning. Williams talks about this in his *Autobiography*: "the words themselves beyond the mere thought expressed." I've read so many interviews with or critical articles by twentieth-century artists who talk about the importance of composition in paintings and photographs. Henri Cartier-Bresson takes a postcard of a painting to the museum, then turns it upside down in front of the painting to compare images: "You can see it more clearly this way." The subject is no longer emphasized. In an undated, unpublished article titled "What Is the Use of Poetry?" Williams mentions the pleasure of reading backward, "from somewhere near the end back to the beginning and thus finishing. I find my own sensual pleasure greatly increased by so doing. I am much better able to judge the force of the work in this way."

Reversing not word sounds but syntax?

I like to do this just to hear the sounds that exist on the page. I remain aware of the way words clamor against each other or with each other, the musical phrasings, the chiming effects that occur. Such sound work takes the place of the more traditional metrics of my apprenticeship, and becomes a means of keeping the entire poem in the foreground. Each line of poetry should bring forward all of the lines before it, and it can do this through rhyme, through chiming devices, and through what Norman Dubie in a recent interview called "rhythmical contracts." The line should be attentive to sounds that occurred in previous lines, and should anticipate, even require, in terms of such sounds, lines that follow. So if there is revision—and I'm constantly revising poems while I'm writing them—it's like the effect betting has on a tote board. Suddenly *all* the numbers have flipped. "One might imagine that in order to make a painting it's simply a question of placing one detail next to another," Alberto Giacometti stated. "But that's not it. It's a question of creating a complete entity all at once." The whole poem must be reexamined syllable by syllable to see if other changes are required.

Let's see how some of this sound work can be evinced in a poem like "God at Forty." One of the qualities I like about this poem is the respect you have for the end of the line, which is one of the major problems I see with syllabic poems. Lesser poets working in this form tend to get sloppy towards the end of the line and are primarily concerned with making sure the syllabic count is consistent. Line endings like "the," "of," or "and," for example, better be justified. But in "God at Forty," you are clearly aware of the important position of information at the end of the line. This integrity is evident even when you end with a conjunction like "but," as you do in the following line:

He never answers prayers, but

That "but" is crucial to an understanding of the line as its own unit of meaning and in terms of its relationship to other lines. The line begins with an absolute statement, "He [God] never answers prayers," which gets negated or undercut in the final word. This negation is particularly potent here because, within the line, the negation of the absolute reveals the persona's complicated relationship to God and to faith.

And yet the lack of concern for line shape and sound that you speak of is not endemic to syllabic verse alone. While line endings are crucial, there are many poets—Sharon Olds, for example—who end lines with words like "of" and "the" because they are more concerned with the vertical thrust of the poem, the progression of the narrative, than with the horizontal thrust of the language. I admire the intensity of Olds's work and its commitment to forward movement, but I don't think she crafts an interesting line. She is able to write a powerful poem while not attending to the line as carefully as she might. This is possible for her. Louis Simpson is a master of tone and humor. But that's not what I'm interested in doing with my own work. "You can only get to do anything," Giacometti also stated, "by limiting yourself to an extremely small field." Ultimately, we must play to our strengths.

"God at Forty" means to be a playful poem. The line you quoted that ends with "but"—which *is* an unusual line ending for me—means to be a playful line. It does what you say it does: states an absolute that then is immediately undercut by the "but," which also anticipates the information on the next line. In terms of end rhyme—and this is not a fully end-rhymed poem, of course—"but" leads a few lines down first to "lost," then to "shut," "that," and "out."

While poets often pay attention to how a line ends, too many poets begin a line in weakness, as if they're taking a breath, then struggling uphill. The more interesting language tends to appear—if it appears at all—toward the end of the line. At the beginning you find mostly prepositions, conjunctions, or pronouns. In the right hands, such as Seamus Heaney's, you can avoid such words or integrate them into the poem, making them absolutely essential, equal in importance to any other words; you can bring such words into the foreground. This intrigued Williams. His compositions on the page were meant, in part, to move all the language of the poem into the foreground. In doing this, he was influenced by modern art, by those paintings in which the canvas, having traditionally featured a foreground subject against a background, was suddenly shattered. The distinction between foreground and background was lost. The painting was no longer a window into the world. When you viewed such a painting, you were stopped, made aware of the textures of the painting, its colors and shapes. Williams attempted this with language. In any poem I write, syllabic or otherwise, I'm conscious of trying to balance the line by giving it a beginning, a middle, and an end. In "God at Forty," words such as "into," "to," or "of" begin a few of the lines, but more often words such as "noodle," "slabbed," "late," "predict," "traditional," and "postmodernists" start each line.

Or the wonderful line:

Rain quickens the white dwarf pines.

The first word, "Rain," determines the heavily-stressed rhythm for the rest of the line.

That observation leads me to something that I try to teach. If we choose two symbols—not the ictus or breve to signify stressed or unstressed syllables—one to denote a word that seems crucial and the other a word that somehow seems less crucial, I would like a line of poetry to contain more of the former. So when I consider the line you just quoted, five of those six words—"Rain," "quickens," "white," "dwarf," "pines"—seem necessary and interesting.

But even in the context of rhythm, the "the" is crucial. In "Rain quickens the white dwarf pines," the line is heavily stressed with sprung rhythms. The article "the" is an unstressed or, in Hopkins's terminology, a riding syllable that sweeps the latter half of "quickens" and itself from two heavily stressed and slower syllables ("Rain" and "quick") into three more heavily stressed syllables ("white," "dwarf," and "pines"). You need the "the" there.

We can't write without those articles. Otherwise our English will sound like the phony Indian language in old Westerns! Here's another line from the same poem:

Rain spatters the cabin roof.

Four of the five words in the line are crucial. I want my students—those beginning writers—to think, "I'm winning this ballgame four-to-one." Not only are four of the five words in the line essential in terms of content, they're crucial in terms of sound: the alliteration of "rain" and "roof"; the slant-rhyme of "rain" and the last syllable of "cabin." I'm conscious of the way the line sounds. Here's one more:

> One hushed breeze freshens the crab apple blossoms upstate

Again, there are thirteen syllables and twelve of them seem to me to be crucial. I'm not taking anything away from the article. The idea of democracy in language is important. Democracy was the great subject of Walt Whitman; for William Carlos Williams, who was influenced by Whitman and who was, by the way, his contemporary for nine years, democracy was an essential idea in terms of form. I think of the craft that he brings to the poem. *All words are created equal* has been important to me. What I see happening in contemporary poetry is that the subject matter is often more important than the language used to express that subject. Such poems lack balance. There are poets who lean in the other direction, who give themselves over fully to matters of craft while not having much to say.

The poem is a piece of music. Those writers who place content over form—as if the two can be separated—are treating the poem the way one might treat a newspaper article or a piece of expository prose. A poem may, for example, communicate through its sound-work elements that cannot be effectively represented by ordinary means of explanation.

One of the things I learned from poets such as John Logan, Isabella Gardner, Seamus Heaney, and Robert Lowell is that there's a way of *writing by ear* rather than writing solely by image or idea. I let the sounds of words suggest other words. I move forward in the poem not simply by rational thinking, but by allowing sounds to suggest other sounds, to suggest words that will make use of those sounds. In this way, I'm constantly surprising myself in terms of direction. So many of my poems have narratives imbedded in them, yet when I begin to write I don't have that narrative in mind. It's in the process of writing the poem where I find out what will happen. I'm always surprised and pleased when people talk to me about the personal element in my work and how this element has managed to touch them. It surprises me because I didn't set out to talk about a particular aspect of emotional life, but, in the poem's process of becoming, this personal element announced itself.

For some, the idea of writing by ear is frightening because it forces them to surrender any preconceived notions of how a poem will look or develop. Many poets deliberately set out to transcribe personal experiences, for example, and if their primary aim is to get the experience on the page, they are not as attuned to discovering through auditory associations the real poem underneath the surface poem.

This is unfortunately true. And yet, while writing by ear can suggest the direction the work will take, this process is not a restriction. There is an expansiveness that can occur within strict form. Our American-English language is endlessly inventive, especially when writers use what Whitman called the "blab of the pave," bringing into poems our colloquialisms, slang, vulgarities—those words we wouldn't ordinarily consider as poetic language. The publication of Ginsberg's *Howl* and Lowell's *Life Studies* in the 1950s opened up the possibilities for such words. Before these books, there was merely lip service given to opening up the language; a certain self-censorship persisted. Poetry was associated with higher education. In the latter half of the twentieth century, though, an elasticity of language asserted itself. I don't think of working by ear as limited. If anything, it opens up a whole other set of options, allows you to develop a different palette with which to work.

You mention how self-censorship or the refusal to embrace the "blab of the pave" could be limiting. One of the more interesting elements of one of my favorite poems of yours, "Horse," is your decision not to name the horse's genitalia. You signify it with a long dash. What led to this narrative decision?

Robert Bly read that poem in manuscript and said, "Ah, you're just afraid to say *cock.*" I replied, "Robert, that's only one word. Other words also come to mind if I don't state it." We have so many slang words for "penis," many of them with that harsh consonantal sound. Part of the humor of the poem is in it's being spoken by someone remembering who he was as a young boy, and recalling that moment when the word and the object it signified became distinct. Suddenly word and object were separate. The word that signifies the world is not the world itself; the world itself can offer so much more in terms of sensory experience. The boy he's remembering might place his hand over his mouth the moment he realizes what he's seeing. He might think: "I know this word, but I'm not supposed to say it."

What I like about "Horse" is that, though there is an absence in the decision not to name, the unnamed object is everywhere. The horse's penis, cock, dick, or whatever, is no longer merely a body part, but a phallus. For example, you write, "Under the enormous belly, his ——" followed immediately in the next stanza with four lines of ample description:

swung like the policeman's nightstick,
a dowsing rod, longer than my arm—
even the Catholic girls could see it
hung there like a rubber spigot.

Yes. I set up the reader in a number of ways. The poem opens with that off-rhyme of "saw" and "furniture," then moves to "flies" and "eyes," and "noon" and "fume." The word that's *not* there may rhyme or off-rhyme with "stick." That was meant to be slyly humorous as well. "Horse," like so many of the poems in the first section of *Parthenopi*, is about becoming a writer. The boy's sudden awareness of the distinction between word and object is part of this process.

Towards the end of the poem, the persona says, "Horse, I remember thinking." He understands now what the word is. He knew the word before, but did not know the enormity of what it signifies.

Right. Now, and forever after, that word will convey scent, will convey eroticism, and so many more things. There's a deepening of the language.

The boy comes to this awareness through first-hand observation, but the reader is also aware that "horse" is an archetypal symbol of eroticism. So there are two paths of knowing here: the boy's coming to knowledge through observation; and, perhaps, the adult voice's sophisticated conjuring of an erotic symbol he knows his audience will already understand. There is the autobiographical component and the mythological one.

The poet Jack Myers once told me, with affection, that the titles of my poems were boring. I objected. Here's a poem simply called "Horse." By the time you work through the poem, you can go back and see that the title has expanded and deepened in many ways. In an odd way, the entire poem becomes an extended definition.

That's funny because, when I was looking at the table of contents, I saw the title "Horse" and went to the poem right away. I thought, "This poem will define horse for me in an unexpected way." I knew something essential was going to be clarified through it.

I was pleased some years ago when Ted Kooser reviewed one of my chapbooks in *The Georgia Review.* He mentioned the deceptive simplicity of my work.

Many of your poems flaunt a deceptive simplicity. "Horse," for example, can be enjoyed as a coming-of-age narrative, where a boy discovers the complex relationship between an object in the world and the language we use to designate it. But so many other elements are at work within it. This leads me to another observation about this same poem. The end rhymes you pointed out earlier often cut across stanzas: "noon" and "fume," "bed" and head," "hair" and "there," and even the very slant feminine end-rhyme of "urine" and "junkman." These across-stanza end-rhymes, as well as the sentences that are carried from one stanza to the next, suggest that the poem might have been organized in another way. In Poetic Meter and Poetic Form, *Paul Fussell insists, for example, upon the autonomy of the stanza, that each stanza should be justified as its own logical unit within the larger structure of the poem. He often illustrates this concept by citing those poems where sentences and end-rhymes are contained within the stanza. However, if we look at the first two stanzas of "Horse," we see a far less restrictive sense of organization at work:*

The first horse I ever saw
was hauling a wagon stacked with furniture
past storefronts along Knickerbocker Avenue.
He was taller than a car, blue-black with flies,

and bits of green ribbon tied to his mane
bounced near his caked and rheumy eyes.
I had seen horses in books before, but
this horse shimmered in the Brooklyn noon.

The first sentence is three lines long. The second stanza, introduced in the fourth line of the first stanza, is then carried over into the next two lines of the second stanza. You could have chosen tercets to demonstrate autonomy between stanzas here. Why did you work with quatrains?

I didn't want to stop the reader at the end of the first stanza with a period. I organized the lines and stanzas for their flow, weaving lines together so that the language remains in the foreground.

And yet I can see that you want the quatrain to stand as independent as well.

I do.

I can see this because, in terms of sense, the first stanza does communicate an autonomous truth. Though the second sentence continues into the next stanza, the juxtaposition of the fourth line with the previous three is, on one level, complete and self-contained. You are at once pushing the reader forward beyond the stanza and asking the reader to consider the stanza in itself.

In *The Pound Era,* if memory serves me well, Hugh Kenner was trying to make sense of Williams's notion of the variable foot and the triadic line. He was, I guess, trying to understand the theory behind the form. Williams himself wrote a good deal about his reasons for developing what he thought of as forms, but I've never been able to make sense of those essays. Kenner comes up with something so simple and possibly brilliant: after his stroke, Williams, who at that time composed on a typewriter, had a hard time, visually, locating his lines; breaking them up on the page made it easier for him to find and revise them. For me, in terms of telling stories, it was helpful to organize the narrative details initially in stanzaic verse, then later in a strict syllabic system, because these shapes helped me to remove any clutter from the poem, to sweep clutter from each line. By "clutter," I mean unnecessary words and syllables. I wanted the sentences to be sleek—even though I'm not thinking in terms of sentences, but in terms of lines. The lines, gathered together, comprise sentences, so I wanted this sleekness as the narrative moved down the page.

My early work, based on idea or image, paid less attention to tactile language. To my ear, those poems now sound a bit cluttered—a lot of language to make the image, let's say. What I found later was that rather than creating a clump of poem, which did not allow a sense of control, I moved in the second book towards simple stanzaic structures—quatrains, tercets, couplets. I was teaching myself to organize materials; in order to see those materials clearly, it was necessary to divide them into two-, three-, or four-line stanzas, then bear down fully, and sustain concentration on each stanza as a unit in order to do away with extraneous verbiage.

And in working with precise stanza lengths, you must consider how much detail is necessary, too. You don't want to overload the form. You can't put too much in the quatrains, for example.

I want every word to count. Working with stanzaic forms, I was forced to think first of the entire poem as a unit, then of each stanza as a unit unto itself, and then, finally, of each line as a unit unto itself. This helped me not only to organize materials, but to select language that would best convey the subject matter—the best words, syntax, and sounds. It interests me now to read aloud some of my early poems. I sometimes hear a different word press forward. A good example of this occurs at the end of "Shadow Boxes," which I published first in a journal (*The Missouri Review*), then, with slight revisions, in *The Burden Lifters* (1989). Later I included it in *Parthenopi: New and Selected Poems* (2001). I made small changes with each new publication. The poem is spoken by a boy who visits Joseph Cornell in his workshop on Utopia Parkway in Queens. The movement at the end of the poem opens it in a way that finally displeased me, but that I heard only when reading it aloud fifteen years after its composition. The penultimate line includes a word that I can't stand seeing in other poets' work: "everything." Here's the final stanza:

> in a world where nothing would be lost,
> where everything was given purpose,
> if only it could remain patient.

I wanted the end of the poem to have a precise focus; words such as "nothing," "everything," "someone," and "anyone" drive me nuts because they're too easy to plug in and they remain imprecise. Too many poets use them, perhaps thinking, "I'll find the precise word and revise later." This doesn't happen. When I'm reading a poem, even by a poet whose work I admire, I begin to anticipate that imprecise language toward the end of the poem because I see it occurring so often. I'm afraid that the poem is going to be ruined. So, for me to write a concluding stanza containing the word "nothing"—and that word seems to me to be the right word in that line—means I shouldn't follow it in the next line with "everything." That language is too general. I think, "What am I talking about here?"

And in the final line the all-too-general "it."

Yes, an impersonal pronoun. To what does "it" refer? Is it "everything?" That language is unsatisfying. So, I've once again revised the poem:

in a world where nothing would be lost,
where each button was given purpose,
if only it could remain patient.

I love ending the poem with a single button, which in a Joseph Cornell shadow box would be given significance and would connect in some odd compositional way with the other objects included in that box. I want that ordinary button to become extraordinary in the context of the poem.

It's an intelligent revision. Buttons are symbolically-charged objects; they hold bits of cloth together; they activate machines, ignitions, lights. Even in terms of sonic qualities, "each button" is superior to "everything." The first line of that final stanza features some closed vowel sounds: "world," "nothing," and "lost." This sound is again repeated in "only" and "could" from the final line. The effect is one of containment. But "everything" opens the sound in a way that is at odds with the rest of the words. "Button," on the other hand, condenses; the vowels are closed and surrounded by consonants.

Thank you. You know, some of this discussion reminds me of what Graham Greene says in his novel *Our Man in Havana*: "How long it takes to realize in one's life the intricate patterns of which everything—even a picture-postcard—can form a part, and the rashness of dismissing anything as unimportant." Who can tell what trivial item might suddenly begin to consume us? What sort of significance will be attached to it, because someone we love touched it? One thing I've attempted throughout the body of my work is to yoke together two disparate moments and try to find the connection between them.

And I see this yoking of two disparate elements successfully at work in "The Inarticulate":

Touching your face, I am like a boy
who bags groceries, mindless on Saturday,
jumbling cans of wax beans and condensed milk

among frozen meats, the ribboned beef
and chops like maps of continental drift,
extremes of weather and hemisphere,

egg carton perched like a Napoleonic hat,
till he touches something awakened by water,
a soothing skin, eggplant or melon or cool snow pea,

and he pauses, turning it in his hand,
this announcement of color, purple *or* green,
the raucous rills of the aisles overflowing,

and by now the shopper is staring
when the check-out lady turns and says,
"Jimmy, is anything the matter?"

Touching your face, I am like that boy
brought back to his body, steeped
in the moment, fulfilled but unable to speak.

This poem is a cleverly-arranged epic simile, where the voice of the poem articulates the present moment ("Touching your face") with the young-adult bagger's erotic linguistic awareness he (himself or any boy) comes to when he runs his hands over the woman's groceries. You have yoked the present with the past, and, within the time-frame of each, fantasy with reality.

This is, for the boy, the moment when he becomes a writer; he understands, as does the boy in "Horse," that the relationship between the object and the language used to describe the object is intense, magical. The tactile qualities of the vegetables in his hand also become the tactile qualities of words: *purple, green.* He experiences familiar words in a different way. There he is, staring down the supermarket aisles, "the raucous rills of the aisles overflowing"—overflowing now with sensuality. The sensory experience draws him, until the check-out lady brings him back to himself.

The boy "brought back to his body" in the final stanza has been changed through his experience with the objects he touches and his assignment of words to them. The poem has a circular structure, but it isn't a serpent swallowing his own tail.

This poem owes a debt to a poem by William Meredith called "The Illiterate," taking its cue from the opening line of that poem. It also owes a debt to John Updike's much-anthologized story, "A & P." Like the boy in Updike's story, Jimmy has come to a perhaps foolish but willfully decisive moment in his life. I must also acknowledge Elizabeth Bishop's wonderful poem, "In the Waiting Room," where she captures an ineffable moment when the young girl realizes that she is connected to a larger reality.

The tercets are expertly managed here. This is one of those poems that boasts, as others have recognized in your work, a deceptive simplicity. The poem can be enjoyed for the sheer force of its immediacy, for the boy's sudden and intense sensual experience; but it keeps yielding something new with each read.

I also see "The Inarticulate" as a love poem.

And that love is directed partially to language. Like all love poems here, desire cannot be fully sated. There remains a tension and a distance between the lover and the loved object. There will always remain something that is unfulfilled. And in the final line you write, "fulfilled but unable to speak."

That goes back to the nature of writing. I think for any creative artist—writer, visual artist, composer, choreographer—there is a sense of the ideal. What is the kind of poem I would like to write one day? Is it ever going to be possible for me to write that poem? And the answer is not only "No," but should be, "I hope not." I begin a poem wanting to reach that ideal, but by the time the poem is accomplished, it's not close to what I had in mind. The fact that I did not reach my ideal in the poem's composition leaves me unfulfilled. I'll have to write another poem, then another, that attempts to do that. So much art is involved with searching for that ideal. I don't know who invented 8.5 x 11 paper as the standard on which we impose our work. If our paper were longer or wider, as it is in other countries, would many of us who write the same sort of poem, shape-wise, and fill up the same amount of space, perhaps write longer, more vertical poems? If we turned that longer sheet on its side, would our poems have longer lines and a shorter vertical movement? Someone once suggested that we remove borders entirely. What would our poems look like then? Suppose we composed poems on air? This idea was helpful to me in reconsidering, as I mentioned earlier, horizontal thrust—namely, how language moves along the line. The language could still pay attention to itself, still convey information—still create the vertical thrust that tells the story. But out of the context of the poem, the line is caught up in itself, in its particular sound. I could consider the heft and balance of a single line, even though it's dependent on a context that brings language forward and anticipates additional language. This is, perhaps, the only way a poet can approach originality. In paying attention to the line as the integral unit, the poet is forced to place words together in ways that they have not been placed together before.

You're an avid reader. I can see the influence of many of your contemporaries on your work. Despite all of this apparent influence—conscious or otherwise—your poems are never derivative. In fact, your active engagement with contemporary voices enlivens your work and allows you to discover aspects of voice you might not have realized without encountering other writers' poems.

I am an avid reader. Other poets have been important in the shaping of my work. In his 1837 oration, Emerson insisted: "There is then creative reading as well as creative writing. When the mind is braced by labor and invention, the page of whatever book we read becomes luminous with manifold allusion. Every sentence is doubly significant, and the sense of our author is as broad as the world." By embracing other poets and allowing their work to influence you, you have a better chance of sounding like yourself.

Emerson, Ralph Waldo. "The American Scholar." *The Essential Writings of Ralph Waldo Emerson*. New York: Modern Library Classics, 2000.

Greene, Graham. *Our Man in Havana*. New York: Penguin Classics, 1957, 2007.

Leithauser, Brad. "Review of Richard Howard's *Inner Voices: Selected Poems. New York Times Book Review,* November 21, 2004.

Lord, James. *A Giacometti Portrait*. New York: Farrar, Staus and Giroux. Revised ed. 1980.

Waters, Michael. "God at Forty," "Horse," and "Shadow Boxes." *Parthenopi: New and Selected Poems*. Rochester: BOA Editions, Ltd., 2001.

Watkins, Vernon. "Vernon Watkins: An Encounter and a Re-encounter." Qtd. by Philip Larkin in *Required Writing: Miscellaneous Pieces 1955–1982*. New York: Farrar, Straus and Giroux, 1984.

Williams, William Carlos. *The Autobiography of William Carlos Williams*. New York: New Directions, 1967.

______. "What Is the Use of Poetry?" (Undated, Unpublished.) Lockwood Library, Buffalo. Quoted by Bram Dijkstra in *Cubism, Stieglitz, and the Early Poetry of William Carlos Williams*. Princeton: Princeton University Press, 1969.

Poetry:

Gospel Night, BOA Editions, Ltd., 2011
Selected Poems, Shoestring Press (UK), 2011
Darling Vulgarity, BOA Editions, Ltd., 2006
Parthenopi: New and Selected Poems, BOA Editions, Ltd., 2001
Green Ash, Red Maple, Black Gum, BOA Editions, Ltd., 1997
Bountiful, Carnegie Mellon University Press, 1992
The Burden Lifters, Carnegie Mellon University Press, 1989
Anniversary of the Air, Carnegie Mellon University Press, 1985
Not Just Any Death, BOA Editions, Ltd., 1979
Fish Light, Ithaca House, 1975

As Editor, a Selection:

The Pushcart Prize XXXVI: Best of the Small Presses (poetry ed., with Laura Kasischke), Pushcart Press, 2012

Contemporary American Poetry, Eighth Edition (with Al Poulin, Jr.), Houghton Mifflin, 2006

Perfect in Their Art: Poems on Boxing from Homer to Ali (with Robert Hedin and Bud Schulberg), Southern Illinois UP, 2003

Selected Poems by A. Poulin, Jr, BOA Editions, Ltd., 2001

Dissolve to Island: On the Poetry of John Logan, Ford-Brown & Company, 1984

Horizontal Poetry: An Interview with Gary Young

"My primary aesthetic tool . . . is elimination of the inessential," Gary Young states in the following interview. A poet whose oeuvre consists mainly of brief prose blocks, Young has spent years refining his aesthetic, ridding his work of the "hierarchical" devices associated with verse lineation to create a more rigorous, "democratic" prose poem. While poets like Michael Waters attend as much to the rhythmic force and imagery in a horizontal line as to the vertical thrust of the narrative down several lines, Young's understanding of horizontal poetry abandons lineation altogether. The poet explains: "In lineated verse you really do fall through the poem, moving from top to bottom. I want readers to move from left to right, to walk along the poem rather than fall through it." Young's work is informed by his knowledge of many sources, which he has synthesized and transformed into a modest yet distinguished poetry. At first glance, his prose seems deceptively transparent, but closer readings reveal it to be remarkably suggestive and elusive. A book artist and printer, as well as a teacher at the University of California at Santa Cruz, Young has earned many honors, including the prestigious Shelley Memorial Award in 2009. He became the Poet Laureate of Santa Cruz County, California, in 2010.

Days *begins with a four-line poem from the eighteenth-century Japanese poet Kobayashi Issa and a single line from Walt Whitman, both cited on the same page. Can you explain ways in which your poems—in this book and in others—are influenced by these seemingly disparate sources? Put another way, do you see your own work as drawing on features from both of these poets?*

Issa's haiku possesses much of what I admire in any poem: concision, clarity, and sentiment without sentimentality. These are certainly things I strive for in my own work. Issa's haiku is from *The Year of My Life,* a book in *haibun,* a form that combines prose and haiku, and chronicles a year in the poet's life. *Days,* besides being comprised of short prose poems that bear at least a passing resemblance to haiku (I conceived of them as long, one-lined poems), also takes place over the course of a year and is organized by the passing seasons. Whitman's long lines are one of many inspirations for my long-lined prose poems.

I see a definite connection between your work and the spare, imagist elements of haiku, but there is a distinct formal difference between Whitman's long-lined verse and your prose poems.

Whitman's propulsive verse was one of the catalyzing agents that led me toward the notion of a "horizontal" poetry. Whitman's preface to *Leaves of Grass,* and a good deal of his book *Specimen Days,* while written in prose, share more equivalence with his poetry than with his other prose works. Consider Whitman's "Cavalry Crossing a Ford." The poem is a single sentence, and its lines are spread extravagantly across the page. Although the line breaks are hardly arbitrary, the poem would lose little or nothing if it were set as prose. It might not be something of which he'd approve, but I've taken the democratic itinerary, the horizontal as opposed to the vertical trajectory of his poetry and translated, or appropriated it into the prose poem.

You speak of Whitman's democratic itinerary, his sense of the horizontal as opposed to the vertical trajectory of poetry. How does this notion of the horizontal relate to your work?

One of the things that provoked me to shift from lineated poems to prose poems was *The Geography of Home,* an artists' book I created with Gene Holtan and Elizabeth Sanchez. I produced half of the prints, and they split the other half between them. The prints—woodcuts, engravings, collagraphs—dealt with the natural and domestic landscapes of our homes on the California central coast. (I'm primarily a landscape artist. I've spent most of my summers in Wyoming since I was five, and I've had a couple of long artist's residencies there. I know and love that particular landscape intimately: long horizons interrupted by little eruptions of trees and mountains. There's something about those vistas. I love painting them, doing woodcuts of them.) In any case, we had this book of relief prints. It was 24 inches wide; a very wide book. I wrote a text for it, a manifesto in praise of the domestic. I was afraid the text would be overwhelmed by all of the images, and didn't know whether to place it in the front or in the back of the book as a block of text. Finally, we decided to print it on the back of the prints—and so the manifesto runs as a single line for 98 pages. Suddenly, a light bulb went off. I thought, "This is what I want my poems to do: begin, and move horizontally without interruption."

Since then, I have tried to rid my work of hierarchy. In lineated verse you really do fall through the poem, moving from top to bottom. I want readers to move from left to right, to walk along the poem rather than fall through it. I try to make my poems more democratic insofar as no single part of the poem is structurally more important than another. You don't have enjambment or end stops artificially inflating the poem. The language, in prose, has to sit there nakedly. This is why it's so difficult to write a good prose poem: there's nowhere to hide.

I have read much verse that would be impoverished if it weren't lineated. Oddly, your prose poems would be diminished if they were lineated as verse. Can you discuss why you turned to prose instead of verse, and how—in view of your work—the poems function best as prose?

I think the prose poem is the most rigorous poetic form. Consequently, if you can make your poem work in prose, you know you have something going. Ezra Pound's injunctive that "Poetry must be as well written as prose" suggests that a prose poem should be held to an even higher standard. I believe that's so. The prose poem is both supple and brazen, and it's subversive insofar as it doesn't look like a poem; the reader can be led to places he or she might ordinarily resist in a lined poem. My own attraction is personal and emotional. I want my poems to move horizontally rather than vertically, as I've said. I am drawn to the implausibility of the form itself, and to the humility it induces in me when I write.

If you see each of your prose poems as one long line of verse, how does this conception influence your composition?

I can't say that a conception of my verse as long, one-lined poems has had any particular effect upon my mode of composition, except insofar as any form will affect the ceremony of the poem as it's fit into a given architecture. I suppose I'm more aware of grammar, syntax, tone, and punctuation than I might otherwise be; those are your chief tools once you abandon the line.

A conspicuous feature of your work is its brevity. No single poem, for example, extends beyond a paragraph, and no paragraph reaches the midway mark of a page. Is brevity a conscious goal when you write? Do you, through a series of revisions, work to achieve it? Or is it the result of a more organic process by which you discover the poem as it is—a brief prose moment?

My primary aesthetic tool (and this is true of my writing, my printmaking and my typographic work) is elimination of the inessential. Concision, clarity, and immediacy are what I'm after, and I can't achieve that by filling my poems with fluff. Curiously, I've found that it's easier to cut down a short poem than it is to cut down a long one. Each poem in my first book of prose poems, *Days,* began as a one- to three-page, single-spaced, typewritten draft, which I then edited to the poem's final, abbreviated form. I've often thought that it would be interesting to go back and take those first drafts and expand them into short stories, but I'm too lazy for a project of that magnitude.

Have you ever written your poems out in some lineated form first before recasting them into prose?

I have written poems in prose and then broken the prose into lines, but I don't believe I've ever recast a lined poem as prose. There was a prose poem in my first book, *Hands,* but not one in my next book, *The Dream of a Moral Life.* My subsequent five books have all been collections of prose poems. The prose poem has become a habit, if not simply my natural inclination.

I appreciate that you don't place more than one poem per page, no matter how concise the poem is. This choice allows readers to see the ample white space on each page as part of the text itself.

Stéphane Mallarmé called that white space the "silence" around the poem. I spent two years hand-setting the type and printing D. J. Waldie's translation of Mallarmé's *Un Coup de Dés.* The book was never printed in Mallarmé's lifetime. I used Mallarmé's corrected proofs to design the book, and I became intimate with the text and with Mallarmé's negotiations with blank space. *Un Coup de Dés* is a poetic masterpiece of radical typography and penetrating silences, in which the poem can be read across the gutter as well as down the page. Somewhere Mallarmé says that he didn't violate the traditional uses of white space, he merely moved it around. In any case, my work as a fine printer has influenced my use of space (and silence) as much as anything.

Can you elaborate on the importance of white space/silence in terms of your texts?

If you believe, as I do, that every poem is a universe, an independent world, then the poem needs the relief of distance to establish itself. If all the poems in my books were run together as a single, long block of prose, it would be much more difficult to recognize the discreet ambitions of the individual utterances. Take this poem from my book *No Other Life:*

> I would live forever if I could, but not like this.

Or this one from my last book, *Pleasure:*

> Hunting mushrooms under the pine trees, I bend and brush needles from the brassy helmets of the dead.

These are very brief, very terse poems, and without the silence, the space around them, their significance, such as it might be, could easily be lost. This is true of graphic art as well. The space around a drawing or a print plays a significant role in the successful apprehension of the image. This is especially true in book illustration.

Your prose is crisp, vivid, and alive. However, you rarely use complex sentence structures or syntactical distortion. What are some considerations you undertake to make your prose original and fresh?

When you abandon the line in your poems, the sentence becomes your fundamental organizing structure, and sentences are primarily ordered by grammar and by syntax. I'm not particularly interested in tap dancing in a poem, and while I'm flattered that you think that I may be doing something new, all I'm really doing is trying to write with as much clarity as I can. I love long sentences (I'm thinking now of William Faulkner as much as I am of a poet like C. K. Williams) as much as I love short ones. I suppose all I really want a sentence to do is work. Of course, if it's also lovely, that's a plus.

Yet the sentences in your poems—long or short—are rarely grammatically tangled. Why is it that you chose a more direct utterance, and avoid the tap dancing you speak of?

I'm never smarter than I am when I'm writing a poem. The seductiveness of that intelligence, which seems to exist outside and independent of my own limited intellectual capacity, is best played out in my own mind by simple declaration. I don't think poems should be puzzles—the world is puzzling enough. I want my poems to be windows: as clear as possible.

On the surface it would seem your prose pieces could be arranged in a variety of ways. However, I sense the sequence is carefully considered. What factors determine how you arrange your poems in any single book?

All of my books are carefully sequenced, but they are also designed to be read randomly. Each of my last five books can be read as a single, long poem. That's one reason that I don't title my individual poems. They're meaningful utterances meant to travel horizontally across the page until they end. I also want the poems in my books to speak to one another. In my trilogy, *No Other Life,* the three separate books are themselves meant to be in dialog: questions asked in one book may be answered in another. This is how my own consciousness seems to work, and how memory plays out in my life. I order my books the same way I order any experience. The poems in *Days* were ordered in such a way as to chronicle a year; *Braver Deeds* follows the course of my lover's death from cancer and my mother's suicide; *If He Had* traces the failing health and ultimate death of a child. The poems in *Pleasure,* on the other hand, were organized almost entirely by tone. I suppose this is a long-winded way of saying that organization is important to me, but it tends to be eccentric and organic.

Can you elaborate on how the individual sections of the trilogy No Other Life *participate in a sort of dialogue or conversation with each other?*

There are several themes and signature events that are revealed and analyzed from different perspectives in all of my books, but it might be easier to give the example of the people who crop up regularly in my work. My mother first appears in *Days:*

> I last saw my mother a week after her suicide, in a dream. She was so shy; she was only there a moment. I'd called her stupid. How could you be so stupid? Eight years later she's back. What do you want, I ask her, what do you really want? I want to sing, she says. And she sings.

In later books we discover that she sang for soldiers during World War II when she was very young. We learn that she sang for soldiers again in Vietnam, and we learn a great deal more about her suicidal nature and her ultimate demise. We also see her again in a dream:

> My cousin had a dream last night about my mother. He said, I was sobbing, and she held me, and rocked me in her arms as I cried. She turned, and looked behind us at a room full of people, and I asked, do they know you're here? And she said, no, no they don't. My cousin said, I'd never dreamed of her before, and I woke up happy; I was still crying, but I felt all right. Then he stopped, and I asked, how is she? And he said, great, great. She looked great.

My brother appears in all of my books, depicted at various ages and in various attitudes; my dear friend and mentor, Gene Holtan, glides through my books, as do many other friends and characters.

Dreams play an important part in many of your poems.

I have never felt any great distinction between my waking life and my dream life, at least not experientially. Whenever I ask myself, "Where am I?" I'm no less confused, thrilled, awed, or satisfied to realize that I'm awake or dreaming. The two states certainly seem to inform one another, and my waking consciousness is often less cohesive than my dreaming mind. Memories often come to me unbidden. These are frequently random memories from childhood or adolescence. This happens more often as I've gotten older. Memories of certain dreams come to me the same way. The dreams I remember are very often from decades ago. The memory of an event, and the memory of a dream—in each case the memories (as I experience them) are identical.

Discussing any of your poems proves a bit problematic. On the one hand, they compel the active reader to name and interpret the silences, ideas, and emotions expressed in them. On the other hand, these very silences, as well as each poem's simplicity and directness, beg that they be left alone, free of the deadening rigors of analysis.

I like to think that my poems could stand up to some kind of rigorous critical analysis, and yet I find the idea slightly embarrassing. Like most lyric poets, my chief preoccupation is to stop time, to rescue a piece of the world from the uncountable, single instants moving irresistibly from the future, to the present, and forever into the past. What a maelstrom. It's hard to get a grip on anything. Ideally my poems offer the caring reader a spot outside the storm from which to take a bearing.

Your poems seem calm on the surface because of their careful, deliberate construction, but they are anything but precious. In fact, they often reference violence and illness in surprising ways. There seems to be a tension between the calm, meditative surface and the often-turbulent emotional content.

I suppose this is particularly true of my book *Braver Deeds,* which is specifically about violence—political, sexual, emotional, physical. It's difficult to write about violence (or pain, or the suffering of others) without pandering to your reader. Writing about violence, and I would certainly include illness as a kind of violence, easily becomes sensationalism. That's one of the chief problems with popular culture, and why movies and books are so full of mayhem—murder, random violence, explosions, and the like. It was important for me to find a way to write about violence without sensationalizing it. A calm voice was the only way, but of course the violence is still there, and violence is a violation, however it's portrayed or endured. Simone Weil says that violence is the only thing that can damage a soul. I suspect that's true. I love the world, and I love my life, but each is certainly a burden.

Discuss your decision to omit quotation marks.

I use dialogue frequently in my poems. I really do love what people say, the little poems they offer each other in their daily speech. Quotation marks create the impression that a new voice, a new consciousness has entered a poem. They also create a presumption in the reader that someone is being quoted faithfully and honestly. That may not always be the case. I may have fabricated the quote, or altered it, or remembered it wrong. The truth is that I almost never refine or modify a quote, but I might. I don't want the reader to forget that the voice of the poem is consistent. It's me talking, even when I'm quoting someone else.

Do you see yourself—Gary Young the writer—as the "I" in your poems, or do you make a distinction between author and persona?

When I say it's "me talking," I mean the voice of the poem. Insofar as I'm the author, it's my authorial voice. I don't want to surrender the authority for what's being said. Even if someone else is being quoted, it's my duty as an artist to take responsibility for its being allowed into the poem.

Your poems are remarkably powerful, in part because they seem so deliberately modest, so humble. They remind me of Charles Reznikoff's objectivist poems. He too is a remarkably generous poet who chooses to approach his craft with modesty. Have you ever seen a connection between you and him—or any of the objectivists?

I wouldn't presume to put myself in a continuum with Williams, Pound, Zukofsky, Reznikoff, and all the rest, but their poetry was, and continues to be both an inspiration and an aspiration. Pound's and Williams's translations from the Chinese were my introduction to the Imagists, and I still read their poems and their translations with delight and with amazement. I have to admit that of that group it's George Oppen who has had the greatest influence on me. I love his melancholy; his quiet communion with a world he loves, but recognizes is tarnished and imperfect. Stylistically, the prose sections of *Of Being Numerous* were profoundly influential. They make me weep.

So many prose poets seem to resort to irony and satire as hallmarks of the form. But your poems are almost entirely devoid of an ironic sensibility. When you say something, you mean it. Your tone is earnest.

Irony has its place, but I'm not interested in writing ironic poems. I'm not really all that interested in ironic art, either. You've hit it on the head: when I say something in a poem, I want to be believed. I can lie to the IRS or to my friends at the bar if I want to lie to someone. Why would I lie in a poem? I don't see the point in that. I see no purpose in mocking or satirizing a subject, either. There's something about irony that has always struck me as being snide. I don't see it as being very productive. What does it do? It doesn't do much other than make people feel bad, or obfuscate what is being discussed, talked about, or pointed out. I think one of the worst things about irony is that it tends to misdirect reasonable discord and legitimate rebellion. Why be ironic when you can be angry?

"Earnest" has become a pejorative term, and it shouldn't be. If I find something worthy of disdain, I would rather say, "I find this thing disdainful" rather than be ironic and pretend I like it.

There is such a rampant expression of irony in media, youth culture, in art, in literature. So much so that when I first read your work, I didn't know how to react to it. I was so disarmed by its earnestness, its honesty, its directness. I felt stripped naked. Initially, I was shaken. Such honesty and directness is what makes Whitman such an embarrassing figure for many people to read.

Of course! Whitman "see[s] through the broadcloth and gingham whether or no." He says, "Undrape!"—Strip off your clothes, baby! And you know he means just what he says. In contemporary culture we are so used to covering up. To be honest is to set yourself up for ridicule, which is, I think, pathetic culturally, damaging personally, and dangerous politically. And where are we emotionally if we can't say what we want to say? If we can't do that, we're dead.

Many of your poems introduce a situation or memory; then a concept is extracted from it. The concept then gets reworked and understood through another situation or context. I sense here the ghost of the sonnet form with its dualities of structure and surprising turns. Care to comment?

Somewhere in his book of prose poems, *The Bourgeois Poet,* Karl Shapiro says, "This is a paragraph. A paragraph is a sonnet in prose." There's no question that prose poems, at least the way I write them, are more like sonnets than any other poetic form. If the poet's intention, as I've already mentioned, is to stop time, to grasp some small part of the world—a concept, an image, a memory, person, or event—to render it precisely, and to suggest it's ramifications and infinite correspondences, the sonnet is the ideal model. Brad Crenshaw's book *My Gargantuan Desire* is a marvelous collection of prose poems, but each one was written as a Shakespearean sonnet. Crenshaw enjoys the rigors of the form, and relies on it as a method of directing his poetic intelligence, but once the poem is complete, he prints it out as prose. The meter, the rhyme, all the poetic rhetoric and intensity inheres in the form, even as it's disguised. He believes, and I agree, that the sonnet form on the page distracts from the apprehension of the poem, even though the form is necessary to birth the poem in the first place.

Have other poetic forms besides haiku and the sonnet influenced your conception of the prose poem?

My grandfather was a Methodist minister, so I was raised on the King James Bible. Certainly the verse cast as prose in the Bible was an influence and a model. I have to say that all the poetic forms and varieties of poems I've studied and loved have influenced my conception of the prose poem. The prose poem is simply a form; it will be useful to some, and useless to others. As I've said, form supports the ceremony of the poem. What that ceremony celebrates, mourns, witnesses or bemoans will ultimately be the burden and the treasure of the poet.

Do the occasional Buddhist references in your work emerge as an extension of your aesthetic or vice versa?

I think they're so completely wedded at this point. The way I decided, or rather found my vocation to write really began when I was an adolescent. I remember it very well. My junior high school had a book fair in the library. (My children's school still has them.) I was about twelve years old. For whatever reason, I bought Oscar Williams's *Immortal Poems of the English Language* and Witter Bynner's *The Jade Mountain,* his translations from the Tang dynasty. After reading those two books there was no doubt in my mind that I was going to be a poet. Of course, I wanted to be a Chinese poet. The truth is, that's what I've always wanted to be. But you can't be a Chinese poet if you're not Chinese, and you certainly can't be a Tang dynasty poet if you've been born 1,200 years after the fact. Still, the desire for that kind of rhetoric and clarity was born the moment I started reading seriously. Since then, I've done a lot of study in Buddhism, and read a lot of poems in translation, and have even done some translations of my own. But to say whether or not my aesthetic rose from my exposure to Buddhism or whether my understanding of Buddhism has been informed by my aesthetic, I can't really say or dissect at this point.

There seems to be a fascinating fusion of Christian and Buddhist thought in your work.

Well, I could never turn my back on Christianity. I am not a Christian, but I was raised as one. I was very close with my paternal grandmother, a devoutly Christian woman who lived until she was 98. She was married to my grandfather, who I've already said was a Methodist minister. So that was a huge part of my upbringing. I know the Bible well, and love much of it. Those biblical cadences, references, metaphors . . . my spirit is stained with it.

Interesting phrase!

I left the faith behind long ago, but it has influenced how I think. I believe in an incarnated world, even though I do not believe the spirit of Jesus Christ incarnates it. One of my ambivalences with Buddhism is that I believe the world exists. I cannot turn my back on matter. The world may be an illusion insofar as we are incapable, or too unevolved to see everything that is here —incapable of seeing what really is going on around us. To be honest, I don't worry too much about the notion of God *per se.* Simone Weil said, "There's a part of me that's not ready for God." Well, I think that most of us are not ready for God. We're smart monkeys, and we've figured out a couple of things, but the world is so much more complicated, and so much more transcendent than we're capable of comprehending. We cheat ourselves by thinking we know more than we do.

I believe in matter. I think this desk I'm sitting at is really here; it's not an illusion. And I believe some kind of spirit inheres in every object, every piece of matter. On the other hand, the whole idea of an afterlife I discount completely. I don't believe in immortality, though I do believe in eternity. I don't think what has happened can be taken away. That's one of the foundations of my belief: the things that have been, will have been forever, whether time stops or not. What has been will have been always. I take comfort in that.

So you're an Aristotelian Christian.

That works! I read of a lot of Thomas Aquinas, particularly through the works of Jacques Maritain. The Schoolmen were the first philosophers that I encountered who used language to describe the world in ways I could really apprehend. I might disagree with their conclusions, but I reveled in the language they used to parse the particulars of the world and our activities in it. So many of my Catholic friends couldn't stand to look at it anymore, but not having been raised a Catholic, I ate that stuff up.

It sounds as if it were more of a theological concern than a religious one.

Absolutely—and more philological. The Thomists had a language for particulars; they talked about different kinds of morality, virtue, and modes of aesthetics that I hadn't found anywhere else.

In what ways is Pleasure *different than your other books of prose poems?*

It's more mundane than any of my other books. I'm using that as a positive.

How so?

People tend to write about explosive, exciting, dangerous, or horrible things. We want some drama, whereas, in fact, we spend most of our lives in extremely undramatic circumstances. Who would want to live like Oliver Twist, or like a character in *Apocalypse Now*? No thank you. Most of our lives are filled with eating, sleeping, working, making love, walking the dog, and looking at the sunset. If we do not have such pleasures available to us, our lives are pretty shitty. I couldn't think of a book where such mundane things had been addressed exclusively. I wanted to dive into that. I'd always believed that pleasure was transitory, and relatively peripheral to our lives. As I began to write the book, I realized that pleasure was sustaining; it was a necessity. I also discovered that pleasure wasn't just having sex or winning the golden ribbon; it really was cracking eggs into the bacon fat, or finding a mushroom, or kissing my kids when they're asleep. I wanted to dig deeper into that.

Can you discuss your preference for print publications rather than online ones?

Like everybody else, I live on my computer. I'm not a Luddite, but I am an old letterpress printer. I love books. I love the feel of them. They're certainly the most intimate of human artifacts. The fact that we take books to bed is indicative of that. There aren't many things we crawl into bed with other than a partner or a book. Books have a body. The word on a computer screen is just light. That works, but it doesn't involve my hands. I want to hold a book the way I hold a lover. That's what books provide. As important as the computer is in our world, I don't see it ever fulfilling that function. I don't think the book will ever die.

Would you consider yourself a prolific writer?

Depending on my mood, I think I've published too much, or I've wasted my life and I could have written twice as many books—and should have. I think most writers vacillate between those two poles. I'm not a person who gets up everyday and writes for two hours. My life is much too chaotic. I have domestic obligations: children, my wife. I live in the mountains, which requires a lot of maintenance. I teach, I print, I have a life, I coach little league! There are things that go on that eat up the hours; they take time. Writing is not always a priority. For some, it has to be in order to write at all. For me it isn't. I only write those things that are necessary for me to write. I love to write, and when I'm not writing, I often feel as if I'm betraying my art, my gift, my calling, but that sensation is probably hubris or neurosis as much as anything else. The problem, and one of the joys of writing poetry, is that none of us can really count on entering the canon. The chances are that none of our work will survive long after we're gone. That's just the way it is. To feel otherwise is foolish. We write in competition with the dead for the attention of the unborn. We are all writing poems that are trying to take the attention of people away from Sappho, Shakespeare, Whitman, and Baudelaire. Good luck to you! There's a built-in failure to writing poetry that I find comforting.

How so?

If you know you're doomed to failure, then you can work freely. People who think their work is going to last, or that it matters, well . . . I always try to disabuse my students of their desire to write for fame. I ask them, "Who here has read Shakespeare?" Everyone raises his or her hand. We agree that his work is immortal, then I remind them: "he's still dead. He's as dead as he'd have been if you hadn't read him; and you'll be dead too someday, no matter how well you write." To sacrifice your life for your art is an appalling notion. On the other hand, I have been called to be a poet, and it's an unimaginably rich gift. Like every artist, I know that in order to be a moral, effective human being, I have to give myself wholly to my art. The trick is finding a balance. If you can't recognize that your art is no more, and no less, important than what you make for dinner, then you should find something else to do.

Shapiro, Karl. *The Bourgeois Poet*. New York: Random House, 1964.

Young, Gary. "I would live forever if I could," "I saw my mother a week after," and "My cousin had a dream." *No Other Life*. Berkeley: Heyday Books, 1997.

______. "Hunting mushrooms" *Pleasure*. Berkeley: Heyday Books, 2006.

Poetry:

Even So: New and Selected Poems, White Pine Press, 2012
Pleasure, Heyday Books, 2006
No Other Life, Heyday Books, 2005
Braver Deeds: Poems, Peregrine Smith Books, 1990
Days, Silverfish Review Press, 1997
The Dream of a Mortal Life, Copper Beech Press, 1990
Hands: Poems, Illuminati, 1979

As Editor (with Christopher Buckley):

One for the Money: The Sentence as a Poetic Form, Lynx House Press, 2012
Bear Flag Republic: Prose Poems and Poetics from California, Greenhouse Review Press/Alcatraz Editions, 2008
The Geography of Home: California's Poetry of Place, Heyday Books, 1999

Singing from a Wound: An Interview with Dorianne Laux

In 1990, Dorianne Laux burst onto the poetry scene with her stirring debut, *Awake*. The voice in those poems was earthy and direct, yet attuned to emotional and intellectual complexities lacking in some of the most seasoned poets. Two decades and four books later, Laux's work has lost none of that initial combination of raw energy and sophistication. Through unflinchingly honest testimony, she tackles hurt and loss without ever resorting to bathos or cheap sentimentality; and, although Laux's poems are distinguished by the richness of their narratives and their masterful amassing of details, they can often transcend storytelling-in-verse by seizing upon decisive lyric moments. One of America's most well-loved poets, she is a celebrated teacher of Creative Writing at North Carolina State University, and a contributing editor of *The Alaska Quarterly Review*. She has received many honors, including two fellowships from the National Endowment for the Arts, a Guggenheim Fellowship in 2001, and the Oregon Book Award in 2006. *What We Carry*, her second book of poems, was a National Book Critics Circle Award finalist in 1994.

In his by-now-famous "Foreword" to your first book, Awake, *Philip Levine writes: "If you've read* Awake *from the first poem on . . . you will have traveled through many lives, for this is above all a book of lives." Twenty years on this observation holds true for all of your books of poems. How early in your development as a poet did you realize you were inclined to write poems that honor many voices, many lives?*

Well, as I answer this question, we're into the evening of the first day after the announcement of Philip Levine's appointment as our 18th U.S. Poet Laureate. I'm so happy for him, and for our little country of poetry. There are really so few of us who care about poetry, who know how relevant it can be to our lives, and Phil will show many more of us the truth of that. One of the reasons I think Phil was drawn to *Awake* was because it was "peopled," something he values in poetry. I grew up reading adult novels with finely drawn characters, and I fell in love with the human. My mother was an emergency room nurse and would come home with stories about her co-workers and the patients she met, ordinary people in extreme situations. And I grew up in a large, loud family. We lived in military housing with people from all over the world. So, it would seem odd not to include them all in my poems. It was really a natural outgrowth of my very peopled life. Dostoevsky said, "We sometimes encounter people, even perfect strangers, who begin to interest us at first sight . . . even before they have spoken." I'm completely fascinated by strangers, maybe in a way similar to how Richard Hugo was fascinated by the anonymous towns he traveled through. The less I know about a person, the more I can simply describe them without judgment or preconception. Humans are complex, mysterious creatures, completely worthy of our attention.

What first struck me about your work was that many of your poems celebrate lives of working-class Americans, people without advanced degrees, people who do not live in glamorous urban areas, or by scenic vistas contemplating vegetation. While many male poets—Levine included—had been doing this, without condescension or false romanticisms, for years, you remain one of the most salient examples of a woman poet doing this. When you set out did you realize you were breaking ground in this way? Who were some of your models?

Early on, my models were the novels I had read: Dostoevsky, Saul Bellow, Betty Smith, James Agee, a few poets, Frost, Sandburg, cummings. But really, I was just looking around, more like a visual artist, and recording what I saw and heard. I didn't begin to read contemporary poetry until many years after I had begun writing, so Levine, Neruda, Ruth Stone, Olds, Forché, Li-Young Lee, and Lucille Clifton came along much later, after I had already sort of established my voice and vision. But they did show me how to become a better writer, how to express what I saw through imagery and metaphor, how to compress or expand, how to utilize a more elastic and memorable syntax.

And I don't think I was breaking ground as a woman writing about the working world. Certainly Tillie Olsen had been there before me, as had Betty Smith, Harriette Arnow, Ruth Stone, Gwendolyn Brooks, Lucille Clifton. That's partly why I was attracted to their work. What I can claim for myself is that life, the world I knew and found beauty in.

I suspect many readers of your work see your poetry as autobiographical. To some extent, this assumption is supported by the biographical sketch of you at the end of Awake, *where you are said to have "barely completed your education," where you "worked as a gas station manager, sanatorium cook, maid, and donut-holer." To what degree do you feel your poems are about you and/or the places you have lived?*

I had no other way to think about writing except as a mode of self-expression, for witnessing and recording what was happening to me, inside me, and around me. The poems I liked tended toward the autobiographical. I remember reading Robert Hayden's poem "Those Winter Sundays" and Carolyn Forché's "As Children Together" and thinking those were the kind of poems I wanted to write. I know now that the speakers in those poems are not exactly identical to Hayden or Forché, and that the poems represent aspects of them, small moments captured out of much larger and more complicated lives. Even so, I felt they spoke of their lives in ways that were honest, real, and included all of us. When I read Whitman, I understood we contained multitudes, but for me, when I was writing those early poems, I was intent only on capturing something of my own life, the truth of it, what it meant to be alive, aware, and awake.

In "Small Gods," from What We Carry, *I can see the influence of Hayden's "Those Winter Sundays." At a critical point in that poem you ask, "What did I know / of their terrors, their souls?" This echoes the final couplet in Hayden's poem.*

Absolutely. I loved those lines, that leap! Why *wouldn't* I use them?

And "After Twelve Days of Rain," from the same book, seems structurally and thematically reminiscent of Elizabeth Bishop's "In the Waiting Room."

I doubt it was a conscious borrowing, but I had read that poem many, many, many times and was completely struck by it, loved it. And so how could it not have been an influence? I didn't have it next to me and I wasn't thinking of it as I wrote "After Twelve Days of Rain," but certainly that poem had gotten inside my body. And, as it is with bodies, what goes in must come out! Any poem I've read over and over again, almost to the point of memorizing it, has been a great influence on my work.

This summer, a lot of what I was teaching was against Bloom's *Anxiety of Influence*, very broadly speaking, this anxiety of sounding too much like another poet, especially a firmly established poet, for fear of not sounding original. I kept telling my students, "Why wouldn't you want to be influenced by these poets! Why wouldn't you want to sound like Keats or Robert Hayden?" Pound and Eliot were influenced by Browning, and they influenced one another. James Wright—when he came on the scene, many of us were consciously imitating him, trying to do what he so gloriously did.

And James Wright imitated Rilke.

Exactly! He out and out stole from Rilke. I tell them not to worry about influence or imitation as long as you're emulating the best work, the work you love. How much imitation is too much? You'll know it when you see it. Or I will, and I'll tell you.

Some of the anxiety might come from the fact that too many people want to sound "unique."

And that's just a huge problem in general, especially in America. We're individuals. We're the one, not the many. We want to stand out from the crowd. Everyone is trying to differentiate themselves. The fact is we are one big organism. We belong together. We are a tribe. Not one of us can do something that doesn't affect the other, past or present.

One of the most consistently pleasurable features of your work is your ability to shape a finely-crafted poem—be it narrative or lyrical—from what some might consider unpoetic, homely contexts. In doing so, common and previously unvalued environments are transformed into beautiful worlds. To what degree do you see this dimension of your poetry as a sociopolitical act?

I think all good poetry, poetry that takes a reader beneath the skin and into the roiling guts and beating heart of another human being, revealing our similarities, our sorrow and suffering, our weakness and strength, our heroic spirits, is a poetry that allows us to see ourselves as part of a larger tribe, and therefore might be seen as somewhat of a sociopolitical act. I'm not sure if that's an intention of poetry, but it does seem to be a byproduct.

Who were some of your most important teachers? Who helped you see, for example, the value in poetic line, the power in vivid lists, the strength of a good simile?

Steve Kowit was my first poetry teacher, and he introduced me to the world of modern, contemporary, and international poetry. As a poet, Kowit is a list lover and maker himself, and I certainly followed along in his footsteps. Whitman was also a great influence there. My husband, Joseph Millar, is a poet who also employs the list. Often, when I'm stuck in a poem, he'll call out, "Make a list!" and it almost always helps me to get going again. B. H. Fairchild has a lovely little essay about lists called "A Way of Being: Some Observations on the Ends and Means of Poetry," which was published in *New Letters*. In speaking to the "syntax of the catalog" he says, ". . . a series of only four or five items may suggest completeness and totality, but anything exceeding that enacts the body's sense of loss of control, a sense of being overwhelmed, even of madness." I think this is true. A short list in a poem is a way toward establishing an order rather quickly and precisely. A longer list and things begin to fall apart, "the center will not hold," Li-Young Lee has written a wonderful poem that I have always admired for his use of the list. "This Room and Everything in It" begins with the narrator trying, as we all do at certain important times in our life, to memorize the moment. He decides to employ the trick of mnemonics his father taught him:

> I am letting this room
> and everything in it
> stand for my ideas about love
> and its difficulties.
>
> I'll let your love-cries,
> those spacious notes
> of a moment ago,
> stand for distance.

Your scent,
that scent
of spice and a wound,
I'll let stand for mystery.

Your sunken belly
is the daily cup
of milk I drank
as a boy before morning prayer.

The sun on the face
of the wall
is God, the face
I can't see, my soul . . .

This list, the woman's love-cries, her scent, her belly, the sun on the wall, creates order and we feel as comforted as the speaker feels capable. But soon the list gets away from him and confusion sets in:

My body is estrangement.
This desire, perfection.
Your closed eyes my extinction.
Now I've forgotten my
idea. The book
on the windowsill, riffled by wind . . .
the even-numbered pages are
the past, the odd-
numbered pages, the future.
The sun is
God, your body is milk . . .

Here we begin to feel that loss of control and being overwhelmed Fairchild speaks of in his essay. Eventually it all falls apart:

useless, useless . . .
your cries are song, my body's not me . . .
no good . . . my idea
has evaporated . . . your hair is time, your thighs are song . . .
it had something to do
with death . . . it had something
to do with love.

The too much here points to the impossibility of remembering not only the room and everything in it, but anything at all.

These lines are also worth talking about in terms of your questions about simile and poetic line. The similes here are subsumed into metaphor and the poem is stronger for it. In terms of the line, I love the way some of these lines break into discrete units of thought outside of the logic of the sentence. Look at lines broken to create subtextural images and ideas such as "is God, the face," a line that seems to ask a question. The line that follows sounds anguished, "I can't see, my soul." These line breaks set us up for the profusion and confusion to come.

I've learned so much by this kind of close reading, along with the memorization of poems I love and admire for their craft. Lee's poems have been my teachers, along with so many others, all of them challenging me to work hard at my trade, making every word, every image, every line count.

You are one of few women poets who write frankly about sex, often from a woman's perspective. Have you ever encountered—from editors, publishers, or other poets—resistance to this? Can you talk about the challenges you may have faced in addressing sex so honestly and openly?

Rarely have I run into resistance to my poems about sexuality. I think Anne Sexton and, later, Sharon Olds did a lot to pave the way for me in this regard. By the time I came along, they had blown the doors wide open. Even so, there was one funny encounter I had over my poem "The Shipfitter's Wife," which is possibly one of my least explicit erotic poems. Ed Hirsch was soliciting poems for the Labor Day issue of *The New York Times* and asked me for a poem. I sent him "The Shipfitter's Wife," a short lyric that details a husband coming home from work and his wife undressing him. At one point she opens his shirt and "takes the whole day inside" including "the clamp, the winch, the white fire of the torch, the whistle and the long drive home." Ed wrote me back to tell me the poem had been rejected by the editors because they felt it was "too racy" for their readership. I had to laugh. *The New York Times*? At any rate, I did get the last laugh because the poem was later published by a magazine called *DoubleTake*. Robert Bly saw the poem there and included it in *The Best American Poetry*. It's also probably one of my better-known poems, has been reprinted numerous times, and shows up all over the Internet. But that's about it. I do sometimes ask an audience if children are present before reading a sex poem, but of course that's self-censorship.

In your moving poem "My Brother's Grave," from Facts About the Moon, *you write, "what could I do but wander . . . I tried to see." This sentiment seems to be written underneath almost every one of your poems. What does wandering mean to you? For you, is it connected to the search for clarity? And if so, what kind of clarity?*

I think all poets are wanderers, restless, always looking for something we can't name, a place that feels like home. We're like children who keep asking foolish questions: How do trees make leaves? Where do we go when we die? Who created cruelty? Where does love come from? We try to see a way toward comprehending what we know is incomprehensible. We're failures before we begin, and every poem fails. So we wander, and we look, and we write down what we see, how it feels to be alone in a body that we know will someday die. Who are we? Why are we here? Not so much as individuals, though that's always a prime question, but as a species? What are we meant to accomplish? There is no real clarity, but there are times when we're so alive we can almost touch it, and we write toward that.

Why is it that poets so often ask the foolish questions?

We're the ones in the classroom that raise our hands and dare to ask, "Why do we need commas?" Personally, I don't know. I know nothing. I know less than nothing. But I do think—and Li-Young Lee says this, too—that we are all singing out of a wound. We've all been wounded, and it's poets who sing out of that opening. I think poets are often wounded children, children who never got enough attention, children who never got their questions answered sufficiently, children who were damaged in some way. So they're still stuck back there trying to figure things out. Now that's a very psychological kind of take, but I think it's pretty true. One could say poets are children who refuse to grow up, though I don't think we have that much control over it. I think we've been, in some way, arrested during this period and we're stuck there, trying to figure it all out.

Why set out if we know we are bound to fail?

That's what kids do, too. They know that to walk they have to fall. How many times do they stumble around? If they thought, "Well, I'm just going to fail," they'd never walk. It's the same thing with speaking. There are all sorts of grunts and sounds that come out of children's mouths when they're learning to speak. You can see the frustration and anger on their faces because they can't speak or communicate; they can't say the thing to their mother or father that they want to say. But they keep struggling with it, not knowing if they'll ever be understood, that it will all work out someday. But as children, we don't know this going in. This is what humans do. This is how we get anywhere.

"Laundry and Cigarettes" (also from Facts*) does what so many of your poems manage to do: transform the mundane into magic, by way of the imagination. By the time I finished reading this poem I had almost forgotten that the persona is waiting for her laundry to dry in her basement. Her act of concentration on the "tourist ashtray" is so penetrating. Can you talk about the importance imagination has upon you and the people you celebrate in your poems?*

Well, that persona was me, and the basement laundry room was at a writer's retreat in Redwing, Minnesota, I think, and there was this gaudy over-sized ashtray. I had my notebook and pen with me—tools of the trade—and began to do what any poet in her right mind (or in her requisite odd and fractured mind) would do: I described a thing in the world that had caught my attention. So yes and no to the imagination question. Yes, clearly I had to bring the thing to light, and I needed an imagination to do that, but more, I had to look closely, as a painter looks closely, and really see what I was seeing, or see into and beyond what I was seeing, and allow the thing to become significant in some way. It was around the time W. Bush was at the height of some idiocy or other, and so looking at that particular ashtray was more noteworthy for me than it might have been a few years prior. That final figure is a little caricature of W. Not exactly a celebration, but yes, a product of my imagination as the cowboy on the ashtray was too tiny to be anyone in particular. Other than that, there is nothing in the poem that is made up, except the adjectives: "dried blood," "pitiful," "casket-shaped," "shocked," and "strict." The word "heterosexually" was a suggestion my husband made, and I liked it. Only in Bush Country are we all heterosexuals in clean white shirts. The terrible truth is that I am not easily bored, and can find something of interest almost anywhere.

Why terrible?

Because some of the things I can find interest in seem, to me at least, to be rather foolish. Who would waste their time staring at an ashtray for hours? My husband says that being a poet seems a very undignified profession for an adult—not that you could even call it a profession. An undignified undertaking. It's like being a kid playing in a sandbox for hours on end entertaining herself. One could be out doing something more useful to the world, like giving blood.

The personal story in "It Must Have Been Summer" (again, from Facts*) takes place against the backdrop of a larger cultural context, a world of swiftly shifting values. In that poem, the adult voice reflects upon (her) body as a prepubescent girl and says, "In a few more years I'd have / breasts . . . and men / would be walking on the moon." Are such intersections between the private and public worlds important to you? If so, how and why?*

I would say that those intersections between the public and private are of interest to all of us, and poets are those among us that write it down. I just finished a short prose piece about the morning I watched the World Trade Center dematerialize on television. I think that was an extreme moment of the public and private intersecting. I was in my robe and slippers holding a coffee cup at what seemed to be the same moment thousands of people across the country were being burned and crushed to death. The three-hour time difference made it even more confusing for me—did this happen three hours ago, while I was sleeping? This was "live" footage, but what did "live" really mean? I was "dying" in my living room, alone, my hand to my mouth, my stomach and heart dropping, while others were actually dying, their mouths, stomachs, and hearts going down into the same earth I was standing on: pulverized. What is the meaning of one person, one private thought or action, when set against the history of the species? The cultures that species has developed? I don't know, but yes, that surreal intersection, which is also a chasm, is where poetry often resides.

In "Music in the Morning," you write: "luck and a love . . . that is what we sometimes get / if we live long enough. / If we are patient / with our lives." And in "The Job," the persona's friend who lost her finger in a work-related accident realizes "it was a small price to pay . . . to stay awake . . . to pay attention / to what's turning in the world." In both poems—and in fact, in many of your poems—you stress the importance of waiting and watching with patience. What are some of the reasons why this theme has emerged so strongly in your work?

Having grown up in a household that was often frightening, I learned to listen. I learned how to watch closely for any sign of impending violence. It was as if I could taste metal in the air and know a storm was on the way. And though I no longer need to employ this defensive posture in my present life, it remains a quality of my nature. As a child, I learned how to be still, how to wait, how to pay attention. While I waited, I looked at the rug, my shoes, a dead fly on the sill. I could hear a radio playing from the open window of a house at the end of the block. Not exactly a good Buddhist upbringing, but similar effects were nevertheless achieved. You might say I've recycled those psychological and behavioral traits and woven them into the materials of my particular brand of poetry.

In "Enough Music," from What We Carry, *you conclude: "Maybe it's what we don't say / that saves us." While the "rhythm of silence" you mention in that poem is acknowledged elsewhere in your work, your poems seem to say what they need to say in as clear a language as I can imagine. I don't see you withholding or pulling any punches. Do you feel omission—or, not saying—is an important part of your work? Can you give an example?*

I believe what's not said in a poem is more important than what is said. Poems, by their very nature, never tell the whole story. The best poems leave everything out except what is essential. And, they try to say the very thing that most would omit from polite conversation, the exact thing most of us would choose to leave out. Poems expose us. We read them silently to ourselves and recognize them as the silenced voices of our species. An example? I guess I could use the poem you quoted from, "Enough Music." I did not say the things I could have said, did not give the couple's history, or an example of an argument they had or a moment of closeness they shared, a betrayal, a kindness, a cruel thought, a good word. I left everything between them unspoken, and my hope is that in doing so, whatever tenderness hung in the air between them might be felt.

Many of your poems are driven by narrative. Yet, there are also a good number of them that are more conceptual, as if they began as a seed idea. I'm thinking of poems like "Face Poem," "What's Broken," and "Heart." Can you talk about the impetus for writing these kinds of poems?

With "Face Poem," I remember thinking there was just no way I could describe my husband's face, and how much I loved it. I wasn't even going to try—just leave it as one of those unwritten poems. His face is already a poem! How could I write a poem about a poem? Anyhow, I was mourning my inability to write it, and wishing I were a painter so I could simply paint it. That led me to thinking about the abstract painters, Picasso, Mondrian, Kandinsky, O'Keeffe, but especially Picasso, and how he could capture a face using a collage of geometric shapes, bold colors, and black lines. I thought about how collage artists would make a face using car parts or household items; a friend of mine makes collage portraits using cutouts from magazine ads—we have a lot of her work hung up on the walls in our house. So, I thought, maybe I could use those paintings and collages as a model for a poem. It was a way in. And music was an influence as well. If I could sing his face! Make it a song, or translate the song it is into language. Or sculpt it. Or dance it. Anything but poetry. I think all my admiration and envy for other arts helped make that poem.

"What's Broken" could have been subliminally influenced by Bob Dylan's "Everything Is Broken." I love that song, though I wasn't thinking of it at the time. At the time, I felt broken, and was trying to find a way out. I might have also had a song, recorded by Art Garfunkel, in the back of my mind called "Waters of March" written by a Brazilian named Antonio Carlos Jobim. It's a sweet little rhyme with a taint of darkness that I sing to myself when another March rolls around. I might have also been thinking of a poem by Laurie Duesing called "Wild and Blue"—a great poem. My poem is smaller, more of a lyric, closer to the Dylan and Jobim songs, and it simply asks the question,

What's broken? But I think Duesing's ideas were helpful in getting me going. I remember making that image of the cricket in the grass, and think I might have been turning over the Buddhist admonition: "Do not harm any living creature" and thinking how beautiful and impossible that was, for those who had harmed me, and for myself who would harm others.

I'm sure "Heart" was subtly influenced by Jane Hirshfield's heart poems, though I remember writing it as an exercise with the poet Steve Torre who had stopped by for a few days in Eugene on his way back from Canada and on his way home to Cedarville. When a poet sleeps over, Joe and I see it as a good excuse to write a poem in the morning. We'd had coffee and rolls, and I think Steve made up the exercise to write about the heart, Joe threw out a bunch of random words, said the poem must include a list, and off we went, Joe on the couch, Steve at the kitchen table, me on the porch. We wrote for an hour and came back to read to each other. We often give prizes for "best draft" and mine got the prize that particular morning.

Could you take a moment to describe The Book of Men, *your most recent collection of poems? In what ways does this book continue and extend your aesthetic? In what ways do you see this collection as different from the others.*

It's much of what the title promises, a book about men: a soldier, a slacker, a rock star, a football player going off to war, a superhero, monks, a detective, a singer/songwriter, poets, the Beatles, adolescent boys, a middle-aged man, a foster brother, an infomercial salesman, a husband. These are interspersed with poems about women and girls: a mother, a mother's best friend, a junkie niece, a superstar, a wife, a sister. It's pretty much in the same vein, I think: ordinary people living extraordinary lives, or extraordinary people with ordinary problems. I'm not sure what's different about it except that I've kept writing and reading and thinking and trying out new ways to get into the old obsessions, the old questions of who are we and why we are here. I used to ask the third question a lot, the "where are we going?" question. I ask that less at 60. We're dying, that's where we're going. I always knew that, but now I'm beginning to comprehend it, so I think that underlies the poems in a different way, maybe. It's hard to look at one's own work and know anything about what it's trying to do. I don't think I'll ever really know. I only hope I can keep writing poems.

One of your poems from that book that really spoke to me was "Bakersfield, 1969."

It's not very often that I remember writing a poem. I wake up from the experience of writing a poem and say, "Wow, where was I for the last 25 minutes or so?" I just get so lost in the process of writing it. I've looked back at many of my poems and simply can't remember where I was in the world when I wrote them. But I vividly remember writing "Bakersfield, 1969." I'd always wanted one of those goddamned La-Z-Boy type chairs. I'd just been promoted to full Professor and with my raise I went out and bought one. So I remember sitting in it, closing my eyes, being in that chair, feeling my life, and suddenly this image of the young man in the poem came into my mind. Luckily, I had my notebook right next to me. I just started writing. It's one of those few poems that just came out.

That's interesting. Let me cite the first few lines of it, for context:

> *I used to visit a boy in Bakersfield, hitchhike*
> *to the San Diego terminal and ride the bus for hours*
> *through the sun-blasted San Fernando Valley*
> *just to sit on his fold-down bed in a trailer*
> *parked in the side yard of his parents' house,*
> *drinking Southern Comfort from a plastic cup.*
> *His brother was a sessions man for Taj Mahal,*
> *and he played guitar, too, picked at it like a scab.*
> *Once his mother knocked on the tin door*
> *to ask us in for dinner. She watched me*
> *from the sides of her eyes while I ate.*
> *When I offered to wash the dishes she told me*
> *she wouldn't stand her son being taken*
> *advantage of. I said I had no intention*
> *of taking anything and set the last dish*
> *carefully in the rack. He was a bit slow,*
> *like he'd been hit hard on the back of the head,*
> *but nothing dramatic. We didn't talk much anyway . . .*

What can you share about this poem?

I was asked about it recently. Someone was asking me about the mother in the poem that the young couple play against. I was talking about the idea of threes and how I always stress this to my students. Three is a very powerful configuration. Think of pyramids! There's something about three people in a situation that creates tension. But again, I wasn't thinking of this at the time. The interviewer asked me if the poem was autobiographical and I said yes—except for the mother. I don't remember if the situation with her in the poem ever actually occurred. But it occurs in the poem. It could've happened. But it happened as I wrote the poem. And that moment between her and the narrator of the poem makes the poem.

It makes sense that the situation with her might not have happened because the tension the persona is feeling about the mother's son is really more in the persona's head. When you say, "she wouldn't stand her son being taken / advantage of. I said I had no intention / of taking anything" the lineation—particularly at the end of the second line and the beginning of the third—suggests the young woman in the poem is struggling with what she wants or does not want from this young man and that his mother is really just a mirror for her.

Yes, and it makes sense that I might make that mirror up so that I could say those things to myself in the poem. On the other hand, it might actually have happened. While writing that poem, I was so deeply into that moment from my past, maybe I was able to excavate what I had not remembered prior to writing the poem. I don't know which way it goes.

There's a marvelous ambiguity there. When you write, "she wouldn't stand her son being taken" one thinks the mother just doesn't want her son taken away by you.

That's right. That old, old conflict. The mother does not want her son being swept away.

And yet, when you continue with ". . . I said I had no intention / of taking anything" there is the suggestion that the young woman perhaps is taking advantage of the mother's son because the former doesn't want anything from him, other than sex, the trailer.

Exactly—to escape her own life for a while and not have anyone challenge her or anything expected of her.

This poem, like so many of your poems, straddles a line between the comic and the sad. Even when there are so many instances of violence or abuse in your harsher poems, there is often a comic element running through them.

I think comedy is what gets us through tragedy. Look at Shakespeare's plays. It's certainly how I got through tragedy as a child. My life was so absurd. If I looked at the life outside my household or read books about other people's lives, I would recognize how ridiculous my conditions were. I could have either succumbed to the tragedy or found some humor in it. Ultimately, my family was a very funny family. We loved joking and laughing, which can often be the case in tragic situations. So I somehow found a way to incorporate this in my poems. Actually, I don't think I found the way—I think it found me. It's just a reflection of how I got through my own life, and I think how many of us get through our lives. You really can't have tragedy without comedy if you want to reflect life on earth. In fact, those people who don't have a sense of humor are seen as tragic individuals. It's a sad person who can't laugh a little at herself or her circumstances.

In each of your books the poems seem to cluster around a concept.

Yes, but it only appears this way to me after the fact. I couldn't be thinking of a theme when I'm writing poems; it would be too limiting. Only after I have written so many poems that it becomes difficult for me to carry them around to readings do I sit down, spread them out on the floor and begin to see some larger theme or concept I've been struggling with.

Let me illustrate by talking about my second book, *What We Carry.* Al Poulin [Dorianne's first editor at BOA] called me one day and said he was applying for an NEA grant for BOA and needed the title of my next book for that application. I told him I didn't have a title yet, so he asked, "What was the last poem you wrote?" I told him it was "What We Carry." He said, "Okay, we'll make that the title." I said, "But, Al, I don't know if I want that to be the title!" He assured me it was just for grant purposes and that I could change it later. That was the first time I'd heard the phrase "working title." When I got off the phone I thought about *What We Carry* and began to consider what that book might look like. So I started spreading out my poems and putting them together in a way that made sense with that title. It was an evocative phrase. What *do* we carry? We carry love and death and betrayal, anger, sadness, and joy and more inside us. It seemed broad enough that I could look at the manuscript in this way. Once I started sequencing the poems I then began to think, "What words in certain poems could I change to 'carry'?" How can I use that word more in these poems? It all came together rather easily once Al had given me the title. It's interesting: it led me to believe one could arbitrarily pick a title then constellate the poems beneath it. On the other hand, the poem itself was titled by me and the poem contained themes that reverberated throughout the book, so it wasn't completely arbitrary.

In truth, I've come to see all of my books as one long project. For instance, my poem "The Lost," from *Facts About the Moon,* could easily have been in *The Book of Men*. It should have been! And in *The Book of Men* there is the "Dog Moon" poem, which would have filled out *Facts About the Moon*. My obsessions often bleed over from one book to another.

I love "The Lost." It's actually my favorite poem from Facts About the Moon.

Thank you. That poem was very much influenced by Mark Doty, his love of small, intimate details. How he can look so intently at a thing. I learned the power of that from him.

Both you and Doty are really skilled at amassing detail in your poems.

I love his work! One of the things I have my students do is what I call a first book project, where they read the first books of many well-known contemporary American poets. And sometimes it has to be a second book because the first one is no longer available, or that second or third book was the first book that really put the poet on the map. So, I always have Doty's *My Alexandria* on the list. One of my students read it and loved it. I suggested she read *Atlantis*. She read it that night during Hurricane Irene. Her power went out, halfway through so she finished it by candlelight. She could hardly see and was straining to read the print, but she kept on and was weeping by the end of the book. I understood her reaction. There's something about his work I want to emulate. I want to write poems as magnificent as his. Like him, I want to be able to see deeply into other people. In light of our earlier conversation about imitation, I think it's interesting because so much of how great poetry is written—and this is especially true of Mark—is by giving up the self to another human being. You enter another human being's aura and allow yourself to live in that space for an extended period of time. We have to let go of our egos for a time to do that.

Al Poulin and Philip Levine helped you get your start. Since you've become such an identifiable name in the world of poetry, you too have mentored and helped along the careers of many lesser-established poets, teaching, blurbing, etc. Is this a conscious effort to give back or do you feel your mentorship of others is part and parcel of your nature?

Yes, both. I was helped so much coming up, so many were so generous with their time and expertise, and so I feel it's my turn now to help whom I can. And I was an older sister, so yeah, I think it's part of my nature. There are so many good young poets out there and it's hard to catch a break. I remember how absolutely floored I was when I got a letter from Philip Levine, telling me he liked some poems of mine he'd seen in a magazine we had both published in. It was very early on and some of my first published poems, so you can imagine my surprise and delight. And when he asked if he could see a manuscript! I mean, really, how many established poets ASK to see a manuscript? My only explanation is that the poetry world was so much smaller then, and also Phil had been asked to forward a manuscript to BOA Editions, and so there I was, in the right place at the right time. Al was also a treasure. He would call me up and ask me to read him a draft of a new poem. Ask me! Then we'd go over it, line by line, tossing around ideas for how to revise it or enlarge it. I learned a lot from those late night, cross-country, one-on-one poetry workshops. I always hear Al's voice in my head when I revise. He's saying, "Do you really need that word, that line?" Or "Could this poem start later, end sooner? Could you cut out the middle here? This poem looks like an overweight man! Too much paunch!" Or, "This poem is anorexic. Put some meat on that poor girl's bones!" Phil has also always had input on my books, except for this last one, which made it a surprise when he saw I had dedicated it to him. I think he's had it with me sending him my manuscripts. He never says anything outright; he just ignores me, loudly. He commends my occasional individual poems when I send them his way, or not. It's the manuscripts I think he's done with. In a way, I feel he's pushing me out of the nest, telling me to go ahead and fly on my own, and that's just right. I find I have to do that for my own students as well. I've been lucky. I didn't get an MFA so I didn't have the training most young poets get, but I had two of the best teachers in the world for a good long while, and generous and talented poet friends, a supportive family, and I went to lots of conferences and took lots of workshops from the best poets out there, so I feel blessed. My own students have done well and I take no credit for that. They were talented when I met them. Mostly I channeled Phil and Al and my first teacher Steve Kowit who all knew that the secret to writing poetry is writing poetry. And reading poetry. Every day if you can, any way you can. They taught me that it was hard work, and I believed them, and I tell my students the exact same thing. No exceptions. No rules.

Dostoevsky, Fyodor. *Crime and Punishment*. Trans. Richard Pevear and Larissa Volokhonsky. New York: Vintage Books USA, 1993.

Fairhchild, B. H. "A Way of Being: Some Observations on the Ends and Mean of Poetry." *New Letters*: Vol. 74 No. 1, Fall 2007.

Laux, Dorianne. "Enough Music" and "Small Gods." *What We Carry*. Brockport, NY: BOA Editions, Ltd., 1994.

______. "My Brother's Grave," "It Must Have Been Summer," "Music in the Morning," and "The Job." *Facts About the Moon*. New York: W. W. Norton, 2006.

______. "Bakersfield 1996." *The Book of Men*. New York: W. W. Norton, 2011. (See Permissions Page.)

Lee, Li-Young. "This Room and Everything in It." *The City in Which I Love You*. Brockport, NY: BOA, Editions, Ltd., 1990.

Poetry:

The Book of Men, W. W. Norton, 2011
Facts About the Moon, W. W. Norton, 2006
Smoke, BOA Editions, Ltd., 2000
What We Carry, BOA Editions, Ltd., 1994
Awake, BOA Editions, Ltd., 1990

Nonfiction:

The Poet's Companion: A Guide to the Pleasures of Writing Poetry (with Kim Addonizio), W. W. Norton, 1997

To Write with Dark, Eternal Ink: An Interview with Gary Soto

Born and raised into a working-class family in Fresno, California, Gary Soto is one of the first poets of his generation to address the lives of Mexican-American migrant workers and tenant farmers with the richness they deserve. Time and again, in poems plain yet lyrical, Soto demonstrates compassion for people whose dignity and pride of place are greater than their ethno-economic marginalization. The struggles dramatized in these poems resonate with a broader audience because, though rooted in local imagery, they are understood in universal terms. Taking his cue from Pablo Neruda ("el maestro!"), Soto embraces humanity and sees larger political realities at work in the lives of individuals. Perhaps this is why his best poems achieve a delicate, microscopic precision typical of portrait painting. Prolific in all genres, he has written books for adults, adolescents, and children. He is the recipient of many awards, including the Nation Prize, the Levinson Award, and the Hispanic Heritage Award for Literature.

Dogs are a recurring image in your poems. What do dogs mean to you and why do you write so frequently about them?

In some of my poems, dogs represent sadness. In "Inferior Dog," for instance, the dog is a mangy mixed breed who can't run, frolic with other dogs, or wag its tail. There is more shame: stuff is coming out of its eyes. Obviously I see a parallel between this dog and me: inferior dog, inferior child. On the other hand, in my poem "Nelson the Dog"—which is based on Christopher Smart's "My Cat Jeoffry"—Nelson is a dog full of frolic, full of life. There's another poem called "True Story" where the dog represents a comic moment in life that changes a person from moodiness to happiness. I suppose, in short, dogs throughout my work represent a variety of moods, positions in life, and may be used for a variety of reasons.

And what do I like about dogs? If they weren't pinned behind fences or peeking out of front windows, they would roam, their snouts as compasses. Nowadays there are leash laws and such, but in my childhood dogs were able to roam free. If left to his devices, a dog will want to roam. I understand that urge since I myself have a strong urge to roam. In fact, it's a joke between my wife and me, as I'm seldom home at night. I'm either at a club, lecture, movie, or theater three or four nights out of the week. When I was a kid, I used to roam all over the place, mainly up and down the alleys poking my mug into boxes and behind garbage cans. Ah, to be a rascal again.

The dog is ever present in Mexican culture, too. How much of this tendency to use dogs in your poems is a conscious way of bringing the Mexican element into your writing?

I agree that dogs are ever present in Mexico. I've seen that in Mexico City and in some of the smaller Mexican towns and villages. But most of the time I'm not thinking of Mexican dogs, which have brief lives marked by sadness. When veterinary bills pile up, what's a poor Mexican going to do: feed his child and family, or take care of Pecas or Humo?

This reminds me of "A Simple Plan," a poem about how to get rid of a dog. In this case, a father has asked a son to get rid of the family dog. He and his family live in a culture of poverty and therefore can't afford to take the dog with them when they move. The boy thinks, "How do I go about doing that?" He decides to walk the dog as far as he can away from the house, so his pooch doesn't pick up the scent, a place beyond recognition, then throws him a stick and runs away. It's a sad situation. The boy realizes, "My goodness, I have to get rid of my pet, it must be done before we move because dad says I have to." He has a familial duty. Some might be able to abandon their dogs without remorse, but the boy in "A Simple Plan" is definitely struggling with the act. The poem is dedicated to "V. M."—a friend of mine who actually had to walk his family dog through an onion field, down and up a dry canal, and hurl that stick.

There's also something symbolic groping around underneath the language in that poem. I imagine the boy is 13 or 14 years old, coming of age and expected to perform his first bloody act. It's a kind of initiation into adulthood. How does a boy become a man? He could fall in love, learn through his father the power of the hammer and screwdriver, join the football team, and learn through practice about sex. But leaving the dog behind is an act beyond sexual gratification. The boy is learning to hurt another being.

The boy is learning certain social responsibilities, too, but at the cost of his innocence. He's confronted with a choiceless choice.

He's learning the importance of familial responsibility, which takes precedence in his poverty-stricken family over any bonds he may have formed with the dog. Some people are really troubled by this poem. I was troubled writing it, so troubled that I later wrote a short story version of this poem, also called "A Simple Plan." Still, this occurs more often than one realizes and is a subject worth reporting.

The terseness of its language is interesting. The narrative is bare, exposed. You don't try to romanticize or sentimentalize the material.

That poem and my handling of its subject reminds me of one of my short stories, called "The Chicks," which is about my brother and me, and three little hens. The neighbor's cat has come to sink his teeth into my little Easter chicks. The third one is mangled and just flopping about on the ground. Of course, I stare at the poor thing in fear. I was ten years old; my brother 11. What do you do to an innocent thing that is suffering? The hen's neck was bloody and one eye is gone. My brother says, "We should kill it." I stare at this hurt chick and tell my brother that, no, I couldn't kill it—we were going to slam it with a brick. He of course calls me a chicken, and complains that he has to do everything. So in the story he takes a shovel and with three sloppy strikes, the chick's head comes off. It's a gruesome ending. But it's that moment when *maybe* a child moves closer to becoming an adult, when he learns to strike something down for good.

But in that story, you didn't do the act. Your brother's swift violence there might have been the result of his anger at you for not doing it.

It could be. He picked up the shovel and then I was the one who buried it. There are initiations, moments when you stop something and move on to another set of experiences. That's what "The Chicks" and "A Simple Plan" are to me.

You place a lot of importance on male friendships in your poems, friendships such as those with Ernesto.

Whenever I think about a friendship and people who really meant a lot to me over the years, I can really name my friends on one hand: Ernesto, Jon Veinberg, and Christopher Buckley. Those were my three amigos. One of them, Ernesto, is gone. He died at an early age, 40 or 41, of cancer. He was the most dignified male I ever met. He made the rest of us look like slobs, even though we were trying to fashion ourselves into Robert Redford types in tweed jackets and faded (but not too faded) jeans. But Ernesto made us look really bad. I have written four or five poems in dedication to Ernesto. Everyone loved him. At his memorial service there was not a dry eye there. He was really honored and loved by the community of Fresno. Ernesto was Mexican. He came to the United States when he was a teenager and mastered English quickly. He was a very intelligent man, an economist by training—or at least his BA was in economics. He found poetry when he was a student at Fresno State. He wasn't going to be a prolific writer or translator, but he was gifted and lived for family, friends, and books.

In one poem, "Friends," you write about receiving a letter from Ernesto: "I held his letter to the light, a transparency."

Letter writing was and still remains important to me! In "Friends," Ernesto and his wife are in Mexico; my wife and I are in Fresno. We're all close and I have hunger for communication from him—god, how I used to wait for mail! I turn his letter over. It's on thin, transparent, bluish paper because the more the paper weighs the more it costs to send. I hunger so much for words that I examine every word on that letter from every angle—even the date in the upper right-hand corner and the signature at the bottom. In doing this, I actually *become* transparent, too, because, as the recipient of that letter, my hunger for love and communication is exposed.

Your vulnerability is revealed.

I think so. I used to hunger for letters from friends. Now we have e-mail and text-messaging, which is not the same as composing a letter. I receive personal letters once or twice a month. I receive a hundred fan letters weekly, but they're not personal: they're young readers and teachers who know me best through my writing. But with people I know, I hunger for their words. I once received a letter from a former student, which was, I think, a flirty letter. The paper was handmade, the writing done in fountain pen ink. The stamp was kind of cute, too. I found myself appraising all aspects of the letter—including the fabric of the paper—to discover the motive of the student who wrote it.

Do you see your poems as letters to people?

No, I don't. I see them as Dutch paintings, you know, those great works of the fifteenth century. Let me name a name: Jan Van Eyck. I love his paintings and his remarkable skill at rendering objects and people—his *Giovanni Arnolfini and His Bride* is of the highest order. The painting is clear, done with microscopic precision. In my poetry—and prose—I'm trying to achieve that same level of precision, but with some wackiness, I admit.

Like Ernesto's letter held to the light, your poems are transparencies. They're clear and accessible to pretty much everyone, and yet they possess all of the complexities and mysteries of great poetry. How do you strike this balance?

That's a really good question worth a private debate. Certainly my poems *are* transparent. Anyone who comes to my work will see a man, his moodiness, his jealousies, his love for people, his oddities. It's all on display. The reader will be able to count the dogs, the fruit, the rivers, the breasts behind bras, the skirts, the Nerudian seas—I'm pretty much visible in my desires.

How did you acquire your formal techniques? You write a lot of free verse, but you pay such close attention to lineation that even the freest of your poems are marked by craft.

I believe in this phrase—and I forget the smart aleck who said this—"poetry should be as well written as prose." We poets should pay as much attention to craft as novelists and short story writers. You can't argue, "It's poetry, it's how I feel, it's whatever I want to do." We poets have our end to keep up, which is to write well. I am aware of craft, but not overly concerned—it's natural, or should be natural. Although I don't labor over the poems, I am conscious of phrasing, lineation, and freshness of imagery as I'm writing and editing them. I really make that paramount in my work. I do this not only for readers who are aware of the history of poetry and its important place in the literary tradition; I also have to satisfy a friend of mine—Christopher Buckley who acts as my editor. If I send him a poem and it's not as good as the previous ones, he'll say, "You may be published, sucker, but this is a terrible poem." He'll then give me a line-by-line appraisal of what's wrong and how it can be improved.

Do you edit towards clarity?

I always edit towards clarity. I am by training and interest an imagist, so my function is—as I said earlier—to paint a strong sense of where the poem is. Whether it's narrative or lyrical I want people to see it.

Who were some of the writers who helped you shape your aesthetic?

I loved Edward Field for his comic nature, Robert Frost for his narratives, James Wright for his tenderness. But it was Pablo Neruda more than all the others. I have a book called *Neighborhood Odes* and the Great Master has one called *Elemental Odes*. A coincidence? I don't think so! He wrote *Canto General* and I have one called *Canto Familiar*. One pays homage. It's not that you're stealing from the master, but you are seeing what he's doing on the page and trying to do the same thing.

What was the impetus for your poem "Frost and Neruda"?

Early in my career I remember taking a course where we read Robert Frost, Wallace Stevens, William Carlos Williams, James Wright, and a poet I didn't quite like—George Oppen, a poet I admire now but when I was 20 years old thought a difficult fellow. I could see that Frost was working with metaphor: the apple tree, the birch, the mending wall, the sad farmer's wife . . . there's something beyond the literal lurking underneath the text. His strategy is a good strategy, and his efforts were conscious—he was making poems that would be studied for meaning. With Neruda, the process was different. He started a poem and I'm not sure he knew what he was doing or where he was going half the time. But there's that wonderful, spontaneous language that came out of him: it was either inspired language or language at the core of his being. Whatever it was, I was taken by his language. When I was 21, this was who I wanted to be—Neruda.

One was a craftsman, the other a shaman.

That's a good way of looking at it. And I think Frost was a little more calculating about his national recognition and what his work meant to the national literature, whereas Neruda was more aware of his political aspirations, what he meant to the world, what he meant to politics. I really admire Frost; he might be the greatest American poet of the previous century. But his letters and biographers show that he was focused on accolades and honors. Neruda, I think, really wanted to reach the world. Their motives were different.

Another difference between the two: Frost tried to become an ambassador for Kennedy, tried to solve this crisis with communism. Neruda *was* a communist: "There's no crisis to solve," he thought. "*We* are the answer to the world's problems." Frost was anti-communist. Neruda was in fact communist in his leanings and practice.

With whom do you align more closely?

Neruda, el maestro! I admired Frost and his duties as a fine stylist, but Neruda's humanity is much more telling. There are very few people who could do what he did. In my new book, *Human Nature,* there is a poem about Neruda's fountain pen—it was as large as a log, with dark and eternal ink, or so I describe it in my poem "Neruda's Fountain Pen."

Earlier you mentioned arranging a good deal of your early poems in very narrow lines, as a way of responding to Neruda's Elemental Odes. *Is that where you got the inspiration for poems like "At the Cantina"?*

Yes. I have a book called *Tale of Sunlight* and a section titled "The Manuel Zaragoza Poems." It features this Mexican protagonist, a dignified captain to his own earthly devices living in a small town. And he's doing this, he's doing that. I imagine him in his early 40s, which I thought in my youth, at 23, was two steps from the grave! Having passed 42 many years ago, I wonder, "What was I thinking then?" Anyway, in one of those poems, Manuel is telling his nephew about how he lost his finger.

What I like about that poem is that Manuel's explanation, his tale, says something beautiful without revealing the real reason why he lost the finger.

Yes, Manuel invents a story for the moment to explain the loss of his finger to his nephew. How he lost it is secondary. It's the act of telling a beautiful lie that is important. His story activates in the boy a sense of wonderment. I think if you go to small towns in Mexico, or even small towns in the San Joaquin Valley, there is still that sense of wonderment about where you are: what is this place? Where am I?

That poem takes the form of a dramatic monologue. Some of your most memorable poems are dramatic monologues.

Of course, when we think of dramatic monologues, we think of Robert Browning. I studied him in Victorian literature and found him a tad sweet for my liking; still, I understand what he was doing. His language was obviously different than mine, but understanding his approach helped me immensely. When I invented Manuel Zaragoza, I knew I was going to eventually write prose fiction.

Since the publication of 1994's New and Selected Poems, *I'm seeing an increasing attention to satire, to self-deprecating humor. Can you explain why this new element has gained prominence in your work?*

One of my most enjoyable poems by another poet is Edward Field's "Unwanted." It's about a young man who takes a tally of what he is physically: he looks at his hair and sees what used to be curly is now fuzzy; he was non-athletic in youth and called every name under our sky; nobody likes him . . . There is, too, in the poem an equation between the boy and a dog: "Don't call him or he will come." That poem combines a mixture of comedy and sadness that is brilliant—who needs Woody Allen or Larry David when you can have Edward Field? I'm trying to duplicate this combination in my work: I can write poems with a comic nature where underneath sadness sings like an out-of-tune accordion.

I taught a handful of your anthologized poems to a contemporary poetry class, all of them drawn from your work before 1994. Then, one day later in the course, I brought in your poem, "Sometimes It Takes a Long Time to Get Buried" from One Kind of Faith *(2003) and read it to the group without telling them who the author was. Most of them thought it was Stephen Dobyns. None of them guessed it was you.*

Stephen Dobyns! I'll take that as a compliment. That poem you mention comes from a group of poems called "Film Treatments for David Lynch," so yes, the imagery and subject matter are quite different than a lot of those earlier poems.

With A Simple Plan, *I see a kind of synthesis, a kind of mixture of the more serious, lyric poems of your youth and the edgier satire of your later years.*

Possibly, although once a book is finished, I really don't go back and investigate myself. I don't ask myself, "What was I doing in this period?" I'm pretty busy bouncing around from writing adult poetry, to middle-grade poetry, to fiction for middle-grade children, picture books for children, plays for young adults, biography. I'm like a cook trying to prepare several dishes at once. I go through a lot of literary mood swings to accommodate all the different audiences. So I don't have time or the desire to reflect. I move on.

My new book is called *Human Nature*. It's similar to *A Simple Plan* insofar as a lot of the poems in it look at the oddities of how we act as human beings. I'm thinking of my poem "True Story," and how when I was in a funk I took a walk and observed a rag-top VW chugging up the hill. When the VW slowed down—but didn't stop—I peeked in the passenger's side and saw a dog eating an apple—possibly an organic apple as I do live in Berkeley. A funny moment: out of the corners of his eyes the dog looked at me—he gave me three seconds of his life, which in human time is like twenty minutes. What wonderful therapy! The VW sped off and I went home to eat an apple on the couch.

"People in High Places" is a wonderful poem that straddles the serious and the comic. Can we talk briefly about this poem?

Sure. I used to work as a volunteer English teacher for Spanish-speaking immigrants. They are so powerless and have no one to turn to in moments of crisis. In that poem, a few young immigrants are doing trowel work on the walls of a building. They don't know anyone who could help them, except family. The only giving they know is from cousin to cousin, brother to brother, sister to brother, mother to son. Similarly, my wife and I one day realized we don't know anyone either. I can't call a senator or a congresswoman. I'm waiting for Oprah to give me a call! There are quite a few writers who know people in high places. But for this writer, the only one I know is my mail carrier. It's a funny poem, but there's a sadness there as well.

Do you see yourself as a spokesman for the Mexican-American community?

In the adult poetry arena I wouldn't say so. But for children in that demographic, I have a big readership; they're counting on me to write a really good story for them. Their teachers are counting on me, too. When I talk to kids anywhere I try to be very polite, kind, and open to them. We have a crisis in education, especially in Southwest California. Mexican-American kids are dropping out at very high percentages, and with an increase in immigration whole populations are uneducated. It's hard to claw your way back into an educational situation once you are married, have two children, are divorced, work spiritually deadening jobs. I'm not sure if I'm a spokesperson for the kids in these kinds of communities, but I am respected among them.

One of the most moving poems from A Simple Plan *is "Summer Work." In that poem you—or the poem's narrative voice—are working at a farm where you come across a migrant worker. You look at him and realize "he was my age, / Early fifties, and who was I facing/ But my immigrant self?" This could have been you? What kept you from becoming this man?*

My childhood, as I mentioned before, was bittersweet. I worked in the fields and knew poverty. I worked in car washes, collected cans, did everything to first keep alive and secondly to get myself educated. I was investing in myself.

In that poem, the man working in the fields is a man who is the mirror image of me physically. We're the same age, too. It's a matter of coincidence that I see myself in him.

But you made a decision early on to get yourself an education.

I found that the working life presented me with minimal options. I could be a fieldworker, a city laborer, a janitor, maybe a rec-center leader, a business owner, possibly a gardener. None of these options was attractive to me. I do not mean to denigrate those jobs, but knew *I* would not be satisfied doing them. Meanwhile, at an early age—16 or 17—I discovered this poetic side of me and knew I wanted to write, even though there was no evidence I possessed any skill. Part of my pursuit of an education was fear factor—I didn't want to do the labor-intensive jobs most Mexican-American males did; and part of it was satisfying my hunger for being an artist. It gave me a drive.

How did you discover that poetic side of yourself?

The music of the 60s. There was something exciting and magical in the music of the Beatles, the mystery of their lyrics, and my attempts to decipher them. The British invasion was exciting, and Bob Dylan and his odd lyrics that challenged us to decipher them. Of course, you can discover the power of the lyric in the Bible, classical literature, English folk ballads, proverbs, world literature for that matter, but for me it came about through my love of popular 1960s music. That ignited the fire in me. I took guitar lessons at 16 and *fortunately* discovered I did not possess musical rhythm or have good hand coordination. I suppose I could have become a mediocre guitarist. But I couldn't sing at all. My musical skills were somewhat embarrassing, so I shifted to writing poetry.

Do you see yourself as an American poet or as an international writer?

Some of my books have been translated into Spanish, Italian, French, Japanese, and next year Korean, so there is a sense that my work is being read beyond national borders. I also communicate with readers in Korea, Poland, England, and various countries in South America. Still, I see myself as a California writer, a regional writer.

The sense of place is very clear in your poems, but I don't get a sense that you are strictly a "California writer."

I'd love an international readership, but with my adult poetry I don't think that will happen. You might disagree with this, but I sense my poems are California-bound, reaching out perhaps to the Southwest. Maybe that's as far as they'll go. That's satisfactory to me. What I'm doing now in my later years is really addressing young people, tens of thousands of teens in the last few years alone. One can't go to a school in California in which there is not a whole set of my books on a shelf somewhere. But in the adult poetry world, my reputation has diminished.

That's unfortunate because I do not see a falling off in the quality of your work. A Simple Plan *is as strong and consistent as any of your earlier books. Do you know why your position in the world of adult poetry has changed?*

For many years, I published in strong literary magazines like *Poetry* and *The Nation, Iowa Review.* In 1994, my *New and Selected Poems* was a finalist for the National Book Award. These sorts of accolades ceased when I began addressing younger readers who were not in a position to honor me in any national sense. I do get T-shirts, sweatshirts, baseball caps from public schools throughout the southwest. These items, I guess, will be my Honorary Doctorate, my Pulitzer, my fellowships! Because of my young readers, I've cultivated the largest audience among contemporary American poets: I've sold close to 4 million books; I'm featured in 48 million textbooks nationwide. Then, finally, there is The Gary Soto Literary Museum at Fresno City College. I can't think of any other poet who has attracted such a large following. So although the other accolades that might go with the honor systems of our country are not going to come to my house, I've provided a strong body of stories, novels, and plays to the young people in California and the Southwest—and elsewhere.

Despite this, do you see yourself as a poet first?

Yes. But I realize that poetry has its limitations. A lot of people will not turn to poetry because they fear it—the complexities, you know. They'll turn to short stories and novels.

So, like Neruda, you are less interested in literary accolades and more interested in reaching people?

I would like to do that, yes. And I like that—Neruda and me in the same breath.

Soto, Gary. "Friends" and "Summer Work." *A Simple Plan*. San Francisco: Chronicle Books, 2007.

Poetry:

Sudden Loss of Dignity, Tupelo Press, 2013
Human Nature, Tupelo Press, 2010
Partly Cloudy: Poems of Love and Longing, Harcourt, 2009
A Simple Plan, Chronicle Books, 2007
One Kind of Faith, Chronicle Books, 2003
A Natural Man, Chronicle Books, 1999
Junior College, Chronicle Books, 1997
Canto Familiar/Familiar Song, Harcourt, 1995
New and Selected Poems, Chronicle Books, 1995
Neighborhood Odes, Chronicle Books, 1992
Who Will Know Us?, Chronicle Books, 1990
Black Hair, University of Pittsburgh Press, 1985
Where Sparrows Work Hard, University of Pittsburgh Press, 1981
Tale of Sunlight, University of Pittsburgh Press, 1978
The Elements of San Joaquin, University of Pittsburgh Press, 1977

Essays:

The Effects of Knut Hamsun on a Fresno Boy, Persea Books, 2000
Living Up the Street, Dell, 1992
A Summer Life, Dell, 1991

Selected Novels:

Amnesia in a Republican Country, University of New Mexico Press, 2003
Poetry Lover, University of New Mexico Press, 2001
Nickel and Dime, University of New Mexico Press, 2000

Speaking Through a Second Throat: An Interview with Patricia Smith

I first encountered Patricia Smith when watching a YouTube clip of her performing a hair-raising rendition of "Skinhead," an early, famous poem. Brazen yet controlled, she stalked the stage in full command of the effects she wanted to communicate to her audience—and the audience, as if under her spell, responded with a primal enthusiasm that was palpable even secondhand. What else might one expect from a four-time National Poetry Slam champion? It would be misleading, however, to categorize Smith solely as a slam poet, for her poems are far subtler than most works of the genre; and although she admits that all of her poems are composed for the stage, the best of them work well on the page and merit repeated attention. A playwright and teacher, as well as a journalist, Smith has received many awards for her poetry and was a 2008 National Book Award finalist.

In "Stop the Presses" you write: "There are no soft stanzas / in this city of curbed sleep and murdered children." Therefore, "We need soft words for hard things . . ." Are these words, in some sense, a statement of your poetics?

I've worked really hard to say hard things in soft ways so that people will listen. If I say them the way they come to me initially—hard and direct—it gives people a chance to turn away from the words. Sometimes I need to sneak up on people. I've made a commitment that there has to be one realm where I can talk about anything and say anything and that realm is my poetry. There's no other place like that in my life. So when I stand in front of an audience or when someone picks up one of my books, I'm visualizing that one person who says, "I have felt that way, I just didn't know there was a way to say it." If I have to pour an extra amount of lyricism on to get someone to see what's at the heart of the poem, then that's fine. We tend to underestimate the power in the softer elements of the language to get really hard points across. There's a skill in that and I don't think I'm totally there yet, but I spend a lot of time trying to strive for it. As a poet, I have a responsibility to talk about things that are not being talked about anywhere else. Sometimes the best poems talk about those things in a lyrical way.

It sounds as if you proceed with a vision: you have something to say; the ideas come first; then you choose ways to say them to reach your audience. This process is quite different than the one so many poets—particularly those schooled in the academy—have chosen, where one discovers what to say by experimenting with the language first.

Yes. I got introduced to poetry via the stage, where there isn't a place to crawl behind the language. You have to know what you want to say. Ironically, after writing four books of poetry, I am in an MFA program learning the bones and muscle of the language—the technical considerations. I'm learning to access what lurks in the language subconsciously. I'm exploring forms, too. But I established my signature as a poet first. I wasn't thinking, "I'm going to learn the technical matters to legitimize me as a poet." I already feel I've been legitimized. All the stuff I'm learning in the MFA program is just icing on the cake.

It's a testament to your commitment as a poet that you are willing to put yourself in the humble position of being a student after years and years of nationwide recognition.

Years ago I started going into high schools and middle schools and doing longer and longer residencies. This experience indicated to me that this was what I wanted to do with the second half of my writing career. Although some places were willing to hire me with my current qualifications, I didn't want any restrictions on where I could teach. So I decided to earn an MFA, and the low-residency option was doable. It's been an amazing experience!

In many ways, you're the ideal MFA student because you're not looking for the program to validate you as a poet.

Right. There are students going after grants and awards and looking to get published. I've already had that. Instead, I have this hunger to see what is going on in poetry beyond what I was doing. I want to see what I don't know. I'm not afraid to say, "I don't know this poet or how he fits into the canon." There's a woman who teaches in my program who is enamored with Emily Dickinson and I just didn't get it. I understood what Dickinson's poems were saying, but I needed to know why others thought they were great. I wasn't prepared to dismiss it. And I wasn't prepared to pretend to get it. So I let this teacher try to convince me that Dickinson's poems are great. These are the kinds of conversations I love having. I am learning so much from them. The whole experience is like being in an amusement park.

I was impressed—and a little surprised—to see how well you master a variety of styles and forms in Teahouse. *Your reputation as a "performance poet" is evident in the blustering rants of poems like "10 Ways to Get Ronald Reagan and Ray Charles into the Same Poem," as well as in the gutsy, blues-inflected poems like "To 3, No One in the Place" and "How to Be a Lecherous Little Old Black Man." However, there are many poems here that evince a quieter, more reflective style. Do you write all of your poems so that they may be performed? Put another way, is the dimension of performance always a factor when you write?*

Not any more. When I first started out I got involved in the Chicago slam poetry scene. There were three or four places every night to read poems. So I'd write poems and perform them. My process of revision was to go in front of all these different audiences and figure out interactively with the audience what the poem needed to be. At that point, I knew I'd be in the Green Mill Lounge every Sunday, and I knew I needed a new poem for each performance. This was also my social circle at the time. Poetry was a recreational exercise. It was lots of fun and there were always things to write about. It was amazing to me that of all the things one could be doing on a Sunday night in Chicago, the Green Mill Lounge would be packed with people wanting to read and listen to poems that were intensely personal, while others wanted to compete on that stage with one another.

Eventually, I wrote a few poems that some people in the audience reacted to not as performance pieces but as literature they could reflect upon. They'd come up to me afterward and say, "Thank you for the poem. I have felt that way and didn't know there was a way to express it." The performance was just incidental to their reactions. I started to think, "There's a responsibility here. When I write something, whether it's from my own life or not, it is going to parallel someone else's life. My poems may cause them to pick up a pen, may cause them to strip away the veneer and begin to truly think about something they paved over in their lives." That's when I started moving towards a commitment as a writer that went beyond the performances.

Now when I do readings it's important to me that even the quieter poems come across. I no longer write just to make something sound great on stage. I'm also going back to some of the quieter poems from my older books and rediscovering them. I didn't originally read them as part of my slam repertoire. But now I find myself returning to them. Of course, when you go back to an older poem you want to make changes; I've acquired more technical skill since then. I'll sometimes revise them for performance.

I'd like to talk about a line from "All His Distressing Disguises," where you write, "I believe that holy rests in the simple." Although this statement applies to a specific context within that poem, I see the ghost of the sentiment asserting itself as a universal throughout Teahouse.

I think we spend so much time looking for the huge answers instead of the answer right in front of us. We think there's an answer that comes from up high that will trickle down to us and solve everything. It doesn't exist. Sometimes there are very simple things we need to figure out. My husband and I, for example, have huge arguments about religion. My mother was a devout Baptist, so I had no choice growing up. I too was supposed to be a devout Baptist. It was a pretty demonstrative church: people jumping all over, passing out, fainting, God was with you all the time. My husband, on the other hand, doesn't believe in God. So we butt heads quite a bit. I'm not all that religious, but I told him, "I might in my gut know that I need that beacon to pray to; that's how I move my life forward." I think in the midst of those arguments, I realized I was looking for something that was too huge, meanwhile overlooking what was right in front of me. If you ignore the small problems in your search for the big answers, the small problems will get bigger.

I'm still struggling with my religious beliefs because poetry has become how I process my life. If I need to figure something out, I write about it. It may not even be a poem that ever reaches the open air. But I need to do this. It's become my own private religion. It moves my life forward; it takes me from one place in my head to a safer place; it helps me come to terms with how I feel about things, including huge catastrophic things I see in the news and small slights by family members.

The poem "Scribe" is about a son who writes his mother from prison to tell her he has become the resident bard, a kind of outlaw Orpheus capable of moving the fellow prisoners who read his work. Is it autobiographical?

Yes, it is. I'd been tiptoeing around writing about my son for a while. More precisely, I tiptoed around the *idea* of writing about him, but once I started to write I didn't tiptoe anymore. Nobody's life is without struggle. As a writer, I've made a commitment to myself that there's nothing I won't talk about. I can't tell you how many people are just trying to live their days holding in all sorts of things that need to come out. But for me there has to be a space in my life where I feel I can write without editing myself, without saying, "That's a topic I just can't touch, because some family member will be offended." I try really hard to knock down those barriers and be honest. Sometimes I find myself struggling with self-censorship and not getting entirely to that openness, but I just keep trying to move towards it.

My favorite poem in Teahouse *is a comparatively short but truly heartbreaking piece called "Listening at the Door." Could we discuss this poem for a bit?*

That was based on actual events. My mom and I lived in a tenement apartment that was basically two rooms—a big living room and a big all-purpose room. My parents were no longer together and she was desperate for companionship. She was a church-going woman from the South and not very savvy about romance. Her attempts were kind of stuttered. She had no idea how to go about getting a man. She'd have one over and bring him into the living room. I was not allowed in. I'd listen at the other side of the door, hear voices and the Murphy bed come down eventually. She would put on records, probably to drown out what was really going on in that room. But I didn't like her selections. I was a Motown baby and thought Smokey Robinson was the height of romance, so I wanted to yell to my mother on the other side of the door that she was playing the wrong songs!

Your first book is called Life According to Motown. *What does Motown mean to you?*

Motown is a whole mindset for me. The songs that came out of Motown were complete stories. Boy meets girl. Girl leaves boy. Boy gets girl back. Girl leaves again. The whole story was there, like a mini-movie each time. On a bigger scale it was glamour, it was people whose faces mirrored my own, people who looked like me but were sleek and polished and performing on big stages. Despite the heartbreaks one would find in the African-American community, there was always romance in those songs. There were men who begged for women. The Temptations were really good at that: "Please baby, come back; all I think about is you . . ." So, with no guidance from my mother about these things, I got my ideas about life, love and romance from whatever Motown songs were out at the time. In those songs, there was a man who'd ride up on a big white horse to whisk you away to a glorious life where he would dote on you. He wasn't going to skip out on you and your child. While it wasn't the healthiest fantasy, it was pretty good to have that dream to dream on for a while.

The fairy tale.

Yes. Even now I can put on a Miracles song and be brought right back to that time when I first heard it, which is a good feeling. It's not an "Oh, they lied to me feeling" anymore. Once you get through the stage where you realize that fairy tale isn't going to happen, you can listen to the songs and bask in what you were at the time you first heard them. One of my concerns right now is that many of those singers are very old, or didn't even manage to get old. The Temptations, for example. One died of lung cancer, one committed suicide, and one died in a crack house. There's just one original Temptation left. I'm so fixated on him. I don't know if I want to sit with him and talk or write a series of poems about him. Something's there and I keep coming back to him, working the idea of him in my head like a dog does a little bone.

"Women Are Taught" is a moving and important poem. Would you discuss the impetus for writing that?

That poem definitely began as a performance piece. It was written for the stage. I wrote it for a national poetry slam. I was on a team with another woman and two men. The woman and I did the female parts on stage and the men stood off stage speaking the male parts. Now I read that poem by myself and it's still powerful. There's a history in the African-American community of people quietly folding around things that happen. I remember a woman whose eye was black constantly and no one talked about it. I would say, "Mom, why is her eye—?" and she'd say "Shut up! That's not our business." The community's silence would translate into "My husband beats me, but he stays." That was the reality I grew up with. That was what love was. If you had a man who slept most of the time at your house, that was a good thing—no matter what else he was doing. But I didn't want to be silent.

If you were standing before a room filled with lost black girls and young women who have somehow absorbed the message that they are the receptacles for violence and abuse, what would you say to them?

When I go into a lot of schools or women's shelters and I have in my head a pretty clear idea of what I want to do, most of the time I have to put aside much of what I came to do because I need to spend time convincing the people there that their voices are legitimate. That's the first step in any discussion. There has to be a safe place where you can say anything. Sometimes it's a poem you write and you stuff it in a drawer and you take it out when you need it. It doesn't have to be a poem people will hear. Writing is our second throat. The only difference between someone who doesn't write and me is something in my life caused that throat to click open. Once you've discovered that second throat there's no way not to use it. It's what keeps me from shooting up post offices. Your reality may be that you are living with an abusive person, or holding onto someone else's secret. You have to reach a point that what you're doing for other people and allowing people to do to you is stunting the person you're supposed to be. When you write, you are writing towards your center. You write honestly and realize it's not always about audience. You reach that center and discover how important it is to stay as close to that core as possible.

Tell me a little about Blood Dazzler, *your new book forthcoming this fall.*

They're all poems about Hurricane Katrina. I write a lot of persona poems. Originally, I wanted to write one poem about the 34 nursing home residents who were left behind in the storm, so I wrote a poem in 34 stanzas, each section a voice. But what I realized in writing about this subject was that Katrina had become a recitation of tragedies. After a while, people became numb to those recitations. There weren't names or voices anymore. I wanted to slow down the story to give those people their voices back. Once the original poem was done, I felt there were other voices saying, "Wait a minute, this isn't done yet." So I kept writing for those voices. One poem is in the voice of a dog tied to a tree by his owners who never came back. The poems accumulated and I said, "This will be a segment of a book." But the poems kept coming and then I said, "It'll be half of a book." More came and I had an entire book. Then I wondered what I would do with the manuscript because most publishers would consider the subject too time specific, that after a while people would forget about Katrina. But it was the need to challenge that belief that made me want to write the book in the first place. In some ways, *Blood Dazzler* resembles my other books. There are a lot of persona poems. Even Katrina has her own persona. She makes comments on how she was born; she has brothers and sisters—the rest of the hurricanes of 2005. The main difference between *Blood Dazzler* and my other books is I feel a lot of the knowledge I've gained about form is in that book: there are ghazals, sonnets, tankas. I was able for the first time to say, "This topic calls for this form." I felt really competent this time.

Your persona poems remind me a good deal of Ai's work. I don't see imitation here, but I do sense a kindred spirit.

I discovered Ai after I had been writing for a while. At first I was amazed: she was writing totally in persona, and I loved it. But there is a difference between her work and mine. In many of her poems, Ai likes to chronicle the event. She puts in a lot of objective reporting I wouldn't put in. But one of the things I've tried to teach myself to do is enter the poem at a point of action. Ai sets up a lot, the character is often introspective and shares how he feels. I don't handle that well. I need for things to be jumping off the minute I enter the poem.

It's funny: I had this great experience with Ai while running a reading series. I had never met her before. When you pick up someone's book, you infuse it with your own voice. You visualize them as you want them to be. In reading Ai, I imagined her to be extroverted, full of energy. But she's a very quiet, superstitious, don't-ride-airplanes type person. She's also one of those people who, when she presents her work, picks up a book, reads, and after 45 minutes puts it down.

So she didn't measure up to your fantasy?

To be fair, not many people have put as much emphasis on reading as I have. I started out with that first and foremost in my mind. By contrast, most poets write, publish, and only later realize they have to go around and present their work to people.

Teahouse *is blurbed by, among others, Marvin Bell, Stephen Dobyns, and Thomas Lux. Given the book's focus on the lives of urban black Americans, how do you feel about endorsements from white male poets of the academic establishment?*

Here's the thing. Marvin Bell is there because I worked with him in Scores, a program that combines the teaching of soccer and writing in urban neighborhoods. I had no idea who he was when he called me to participate in the program. What I did for him was train teachers on how to bring poetry into the urban classroom.

Stephen Dobyns? When I first got into poetry, I had a habit of going into the poetry section of old, used bookstores and start at the beginning, just start pulling down books from the shelves. I didn't know who these people were. I only knew what I liked and if their poems spoke to me I'd buy them. One of the first titles I read where I loved every poem in the book was Stephen Dobyns's *Cemetery Nights*. I didn't know him from a hole in the wall. But he was an expert at resurrecting those tiny horrors, those things that happen in our lives that we say, "Thank God I don't have to think about that again." He pulls them up and writes about them. That's real risk taking. I loved his voice. His poems are like great cinema. People have asked me time and again who my favorite poet is, expecting to hear the name of a black poet. I always say Dobyns. Anyway, eventually someone invited me to read at

Syracuse where he was teaching. I was in awe that he would be there, since he was like a rock star to me. After my reading, he asked me about one of my poems and that was it. Later, he showed up for a reading in Boston where I was living at the time and I attended. Someone who knew him came up to me and asked if I was Patricia Smith. I said yes and was told that Stephen was really nervous about my being there because I was one of the best readers he'd heard. I was ecstatic. I got up the nerve to talk to him again and then we became friends. So much so that when Stephen was doing an endowed chair at Georgia Tech he recommended to Thomas Lux (who was also there) that I take the endowment when he vacated. In the midst of all this, I interacted with both of them as friends. I never thought, "Here's another white male poet." For a long time there was a supposed rift between performance and academic poetry, but those men knew what I was doing and respected it. They were listening and understood. I feel privileged to have come upon them the way I did. I'll be teaching with Lux and Dobyns this summer at a program at Sarah Lawrence College.

In "Related to the Buttercup, Blooms in Spring" you write, "You must / own one word completely before you can claim another." In the poem, that word is "anemone" a word the young, aspiring poet wraps her mouth and mind around in order to proceed as a writer who eventually "wrote myself hero, wrote myself white / Cherokee, cheerleader, distressed damsel . . ." Could you discuss the importance of words in your transformation from "girl" to "writer"?

I was an only child. I don't quite know where my fascination with words came from. My father was a great storyteller, so I learned to think in terms of stories I could tell. But my mother was very staunch and religious and didn't care about such things. I transferred a lot of what I needed from my home to my teachers, who were perky little white women from the suburbs who came to the inner city to teach. I was one of those crazy kids who thought, "I'm just going to start with 'A' in the dictionary and learn all these words." When I heard a word that felt good in my mouth and that sounded sweet on the air, I held onto it for a long time. "Anemone" was the first word like that. I kept it. I collected these words like little gems and thought, "One day I'm going to write something with all these words in it."

In terms of making the transformation from girl to woman, I don't know if I *am* fully woman yet. What keeps me striving is *not* wanting to entirely grow up. A lot of my wonder and fascination for life is related to the fact that everyday I feel like the canvas is blank again—and I don't know how to fill it. I don't build a cage for myself. I don't define myself as one kind of writer. Everything is on the horizon for me. I'm very much a little girl. When I talk about the choices I make in writing my poems, it sounds like I'm a crusader, but I'm frightened a lot. Sometimes I don't want to put myself out there. Each day, as a writer, however, I wake up and start at point "A." I have to have my eyes open as wide as a child's or I'm going to miss a lot.

Smith, Patricia. "Stop the Presses," "All His Distressing Disguises," and "Related to the Buttercup, Blooms in Spring." *Teahouse of the Almighty.* St. Paul: Coffee House Press, 2006.

Poetry:
Shoulda Been Jimi Savanah, Coffee House Press, 2012
Blood Dazzler, Coffee House Press, 2008
Teahouse of the Almighty, Coffee House Press, 2006
Close To Death, Zoland Books, 1993
Big Towns, Big Talk, Zoland Books, 1992
Life According To Motown, Tia Chucha Press, 1991

Children's Fiction:
Janna and the Kings, Lee & Low, 2003

Nonfiction:
Africans in America, Harcourt Brace, 1988

A Glimpse of the Beautiful: An Interview with Scott Cairns

Scott Cairns is one of the most salient examples of a unique subgenre in contemporary American letters: literary Christian poetry. There is nothing new about poets writing of God, as some of the best premodern English-language poetry embraces matters of faith; but by the middle of the twentieth-century—in part due to the cataclysmic cultural shifts brought about by two world wars, the public's awareness of mass genocide, and the dismantling of many social hierarchies that were often associated with traditional (Christian) religious expression—poetries of faith and praise became increasingly passé, pushed to the margins as irrelevant and reactionary. For years, most people knew religious poetry only as aesthetically-wanting inspirational verse. However, as discussed below, the 1970s saw a gradual emergence of real poets writing about their faith. In the wake of this trend, Cairns's own verse experienced radical transformation, "from a primarily open-form, anecdotal, expressive undertaking . . . to a more meditative, linguistically engaged process." This process is informed by Cairns's reading of Eastern Orthodox theologians whose "terms are provisional" insofar as they "admit that we can't know anything conclusively . . . a theology that finds great pleasure and joy and beauty in pressing language for a taste of immensity." But the quality that marks this poet's verse more than any other is its sensual beauty, for it never loses sight of the splendid physicality of the created world. A Professor of English and Catherine Paine Middlebush Chair at the University of Missouri, he was awarded a Guggenheim Fellowship in 2006.

Religious themes, in particular meditations on the "fullness of faith," are important in your poetry. Do you see yourself as a religious poet?

Yes, I suppose I do. Still, folks who hear me say that might therefore assume that my poems are written to express my faith—in a way similar to how a poor *political* poet or a not-so-accomplished but nonetheless zealous *vegetarian* poet might be satisfied to write little verse tracts advocating for an ideology or a lifestyle. If I shared the commonplace *mis*understanding that poetry is an expressive undertaking, I might become guilty of writing religious tracts in verse; the heart of the matter is that I don't suffer this misunderstanding, and that I don't approach poetry as an expository genre. My sense that poetry is a way of knowing—rather than a way of sharing what you think you know—pretty much spares me, and spares the reader as well. So, yes, I've been working for a while now to become a religious person, and I've been working for a while to appreciate how the poetic operation of language is primarily a way of seeing—a matter of pressing language for glimpses of revelation.

You have written six books of poetry since 1985, starting with The Theology of Doubt *up to your most recent collection,* Compass of Affection: Poems New and Selected, *in 2006. How has your work evolved thematically and formally during this time?*

The most apparent development occurred between books one and two, when my entire approach shifted from a primarily open-form, anecdotal, expressive undertaking (the same sort as I enjoy disparaging today) to a more meditative, linguistically engaged process. Still, it's all a matter of degree, but each successive book has been—in terms of form and procedure—increasingly attentive to suggestive ambiguities in language and the fruits of those energies. Simply put, the poems have evolved from the glibly denotative toward the more suggestively connotative. As for themes, well, that's also a matter of degree; I've been a self-diagnosed God-obsessive most of my life, and the poems have simply become increasingly a greater part of the contemplative practice that assists my finally growing up.

Your poems are certainly nourished by your passion for reading. Can you discuss how your reading in theology, philosophy, poetry, and the classics has guided you in specific directions?

There may have been a time when what I read or how I read was somehow separate from my writing process; if so, it was too long ago to remember much about it. For as long as I *can* remember, however, these practices have seemed like two sides of the same coin, or two activities feeding a common project. Reading leads to writing, and writing leads to further reading. One writes to fan some spark or other, ignited by reading; one returns to reading to feed a continuing hunger. Also, these various disciplines—theology, philosophy, poetry, etc.—seem less discrete to me than our academic structures might suggest. I suppose that if one were primarily interested in making a career in one of these fields, he would do well to stick to one of them, becoming master of its jargon, its hermetic monologue, its arcane premises. On the other hand, if one were primarily interested in making a dent in his own ignorance, in becoming a more coherent human person, he might find that all of these areas tend to overlap a good bit, and he might find that in engaging these areas of overlap—and in pressing their vocabularies for further information—there may be some provocative matter worth working over.

In my own case, my God-obsession had been complicated early on by what turned out to have been an untenable, if nonetheless popular, version of Christian faith. Rather than abandoning Christ, I dug in to discover an earlier version of the faith, which turned out to be full of beauty as well. I've always been a sucker for beauty. That earlier version of the story also appeared less cranky, less fearful, more generous than its popular counterpart, privileging a therapeutic model of recovery over a juridical model of retribution. I suppose that the recurrent themes in my poems—those concerns I can't stop yammering about—have been the direct result of my having embraced the model of recovery, healing, endless development.

When did you realize you wanted to write poems? Was this realization brought about by a need to communicate matters of faith in verse? Or was the impulse to write poetry deeper than any conscious effort to write?

While I would take care to distinguish between earlier and later motives, I should admit that my father was an English teacher who loved poetry. We therefore always had poetry in our house, and my father was also an inveterate versifier, often called upon to produce occasional verse for friends and family. As a teacher in the public schools, my dad also hosted a number of "poets-in-the-schools" visitors, and would invite them to dinner. That's how I first met William Stafford, who struck me as the real deal. He came to our house maybe three times during my junior high and high school years; and he manifested quiet wisdom, and genuine interest in the goofy kids at the table. When I heard him read, I remember I started noticing how meaning was made, how it was collaborative, the result of considered speech being offered to another, who was then obliged to make something of it.

My father also had a penchant for reciting Robert Frost, whose language and lines further insisted upon an uncommon attention to language. Giving language this kind of keen attention proved addictive, compelling, pleasurable. So the impulse was, fairly early on, an impulse to make chunks of language that might please me and please others in this way. In graduate school—at Hollins and Bowling Green—I got a little off-track for a while, writing the same sort of anecdotal, denotative lyrics as my peers. At Utah, however—working with Richard Howard, Mark Strand, and Larry Levis—I recovered this first love, and have stuck with it.

As for how my motives have evolved, I'm not sure I want to say, mostly because my motives for making poems have become increasingly personal, interior, part and parcel of somewhat grander motives, essentially spiritual motives. Still, since you've asked, my chief motive these days most often is to employ the poems as a meditative means of apprehending the holy presence of God, and to lean into that presence, and to partake of it. I want to become holy. It's not so much that I've stopped caring about the reader, only that I've come to suppose that both the reader and I are better served with poems that move some distance beyond performance.

So, back to your question. No, I've never felt a need to communicate matters of faith in verse. There are many reasons for this, not the least of which is the futility of that approach. Mostly, as I've already said, I have never understood poetry to be an expressive art. It is not a vehicle for passing along what is already known; rather, it offers a scene in which meaning is made. When that scene is sufficiently well made, it is capable of offering a glimpse of the endless, roiling, inexhaustible, and vertiginous overlay that I'm pleased to call Truth. This can happen, of course, in fiction or nonfiction as well, but when it does—that is, when you're reading along in a novel and find yourself suddenly noticing the words themselves, suddenly unable to, as it were, see *through* the words to some idea or fictive scene they're pointing to, then you are witnessing what I would call *the poetic*. When you see the words *as such*, the imagination kicks into another, collaborative register, and constructs further matter, duly provoked by the words on the page. This sort of experience can happen in one's own writing as well as in one's reading; the effects are so similar as to render the distinction moot. When I'm attending in this way to the words I'm writing, I see more than I'd meant to say. This is my motive; this is why I continue to write.

You are often seen as a religious poet but in truth my first exposure to your work was through poems that were not overtly religious in theme. I'm thinking of an early poem like "Mud Trail," which I have often taught to poetry classes as a fine example of free-verse lineation. In fact, one of the most impressive features of your verse poems is your deft handling of lineation. Can you discuss how you developed your strong sense of craft, particularly with regards to lineation and the shaping of poems, but also in other respects?

Early on, I noticed that the pleasure of poetry lies in flights of the mind, flights that an odd, suggestive word choice can occasion, and similar flights occasioned by a line that *works* as a line, that *does* work as a line, a line that may even momentarily misdirect, but misdirect to additional, suggestive richness. That is to say, I learned to savor those lines that serve to trouble, to complicate the sense supplied by syntax. I learned this by closely reading Frost and Stevens, attending to how many possible readings they can pack into a line.

In Compass of Affection *you demonstrate a stunning breadth of stanza forms, so much so that it would be hard to pinpoint what a typical Scott Cairns poem looks like. Nonetheless, despite the variety in their shapes, your poems are marked by a humble dignity that seems almost like your undersong. Would you agree with this?*

Well, I like that a lot. Hope it's true. Let's say it is. I do know that I have a fairly constant voice in my head, the same voice that—less humbly—constructs unspoken rebuttals to daily offences. Some of those responses have been cast as poems, though these are not the poems I'm most interested in. To me, poems like "Narration" and "Late Apocalypse"—while they have some pleasing moments—don't continue to satisfy; they feel, finally, overly determined by what I'd meant to say, and to me they feel a little thin. On the other hand, when that voice is more honestly employed in shaping the considered speech of a poem, it's genuinely interrogative, speculative. Given that my overall project has become something of an interrogation of language, it seems likely that this voice might remain the one constant throughout my books.

Translation seems to have nourished your imagination as of late. Some of the newest poems in Compass, *for example, are translations of twentieth-century Greek poets Seferis, Elytis, and Cavafy. What do these Greek poets mean to you and how has your intimate knowledge of each of them informed your work?*

Here again, I would draw upon the notion of pressing language for information. The more Greek, or Hebrew, or Latin one acquires, the more able he is to detect the ghosts of those languages haunting his English. One's tapping into those registers of connotation offers huge benefits in terms of packing multiple meanings into a discrete line. And the act of translation—of poring with such strenuous attention over a text—is itself exhilarating. The one Greek poet who has had the longest attraction to me is Cavafy, whom I have been reading for over 30 years. Something in the way he manifests a fiery subterranean heat beneath the patina of the cool surface is really compelling to me. I hope my own poems can do that someday!

I'm also a fan of Yannis Ritsos and Kostis Palamas, and a huge fan of the fiction writer Alexandros Papadiamandis—they have become my teachers, my colleagues, my circle of friends. I've long had a circle of poets with whom I've maintained an ongoing conversation; that circle includes, as I've said, Frost and Stevens, but also Coleridge, Auden, Bishop, Dickinson, and others. More recently, having more or less adopted Greece as my second homeland, I've adopted these poets as well, and as I develop my Greek, I've also taken great pleasure in fiddling with these poets' Greek poems. I'm not so much concerned with making translations for others as I am pleased to pore over these Greek words, hoping to see something that can further invest my English with additional textures.

English is really a museum of many other languages. An English sentence is haunted by a wealth of etymological and connotative value derived from the languages that have fed into English. Before Greek, I muddled a bit through Spanish and German and noticed how the translation process really lit up certain English words that had been somewhat dimmed in my thinking, that had not seemed so laden or loaded with suggestiveness as they then did during my efforts at translation. It's that habit that I continue to play with. I'm really fascinated with languages and their effects on English.

The image of travel, of a journey, be it internal or external, seems central to so many of your poems. Could you talk about this?

I'm guessing that anything I will say about that will surely sound like a cliché, but let me point out the recurrent trope of pilgrimage (sometimes overtly stated and sometimes merely implied) that informs both my poems and my memoir. I've tried—without editorial support or marketing department willingness—to title a couple of my recent books *Slow Pilgrim.* In any case, that figure of a pilgrim—and a slow one at that!—continues to inform my disposition towards both my life and my work. Over the past five or six years, I've become a pilgrim in fact, a literal pilgrim, traveling to monasteries in the U.S. and, mostly, in Greece. I've made ten pilgrimages to Mount Athos in northern Greece, and hope to continue visiting those monastic enclaves with some regularity for the rest of my life. The journeys themselves, of course, become an outward expression of an interior pursuit; when all goes well, progress along the interior pursuit generally accompanies the physical journey.

Suffice to say that the interior drive informing what you've called my undersong has to do with progress, has to do with getting somewhere.

You are such a master of lineation that I was initially surprised to see more than a handful of prose poems in your selected work. What considerations determine whether you will write a poem in verse or in prose?

Degree of yammering. Some poems obtain a density and relative directness that seems better served by verse, and that seems to call for the further complications afforded by lining; other poems depend more upon a desultory, meandering syntax of qualification, which I suppose nudges me into prose. I'm never quite sure how much fussing a reader will put up with; so if the syntax is already complex and loaded with modifiers, I feel less inclined to further complicate matters with the trouble of a troubling lineation.

"Three Descents" is a compelling poem. Each section of this three-part poem could stand on its own. Why did you choose to group them together?

In order to answer you, I would have to have *had* a reason and would have to be able to remember it! But maybe I can come up with something here, even if it's largely fictive. I wrote them pretty much in the order you see them—"Aeneas," "Orpheus," and "Jesus." Richard Howard published "Aeneas" in *The Paris Review* a thousand years ago. I was midway through "Orpheus" when he asked me what I had on hand, so I sent him that first one and he liked it. That's the only time it has occurred to me that those sections stood separately. I had conceived the sequence as a whole—I had even flirted with the idea of including a couple other descents in there, but the three I chose seemed like the most famous. I always felt a little funny about that poem because it seems like Christian apologia in that it certainly privileges the third of three. I've always been slightly embarrassed by that, because it seems to be meddling in a way that I usually try to avoid. At least I like to imagine I don't normally meddle like that.

How do you see the third poem as privileged?

"Jesus" is the one that turns out well! Whereas "Aeneas" ends haunted by the vision of the underworld and "Orpheus" ends with his vital presence having an adverse effect upon those he meets along the way, in "Jesus" Christ brings a vivifying agency to Hades itself. So, thematically, I've clearly privileged Christ's descent over the others.

And yet, in terms of theme and your handling of theme, it can be argued that "Aeneas" is the most compelling poem of the three. Its premier position in the sequence may also privilege it in terms of an initial reader response.

I'm glad you read it that way. As I think back on the poem, I'm at a loss as to remember what other descents were vying for inclusion. I'd have to go through my piles of papers and look through the revisions.

Do you usually keep your drafts and revisions?

Well, I used to a lot more than I do now. I keep fewer drafts now. I use to save all my drafts, had been doing that for many years, and it's resulted in a lot of boxes of crap in the basement.

What's the composition process like for you?

It essentially involves my coming up with a line or two, or reading somebody else's work and being caught by some figure or some line and poring over that. So, I basically start writing long hand on a yellow pad and then write until I get stuck, and then rewrite all of it again. Pretty much long hand, yellow pad, No. 2 pencil. That's been my habit for a long time. At some point, when a draft seems viable, I move to the word processor these days. I guess I'm happiest when I've pretty much gone through a whole legal pad before I get to the end of a poem.

One particular poem can take you a long time?

Yes. There are exceptions, but in general I'm a pretty slow, methodical, language-focused poet. I write that way because that's the only way I'm able see those words hiding in the words, those connotative ghosts. If I were just typing it all out from the beginning, I'd be less likely to glimpse the etymological suggestiveness, the provocations of meaning that I discover in writing longhand, etching the word slowly enough to attend to the whole word as it's being written. So, these are my goofy, elementary habits that result in my more textured poems. The less textured poems are probably less textured because I've spent less time on them and was therefore less concerned with how the words echoed one another, etc.

Do you find that your less textured poems are the ones some readers enjoy because of their comparative immediacy?

Yes. I still have friends, good friends—I should probably mention my wife among them—who actually, of all my books, prefer the first.

How does that make you feel?

No more isolated than I normally feel anyway. What passes for poetry in my mind is pretty much an acquired taste. I appreciate the fact that most people have better things to do than pore over a poem in this way; still, I like to make poems that someone *might* pore over, someone who was so inclined—and perhaps inclined to return to the poem another day. The more chewy a poem is, the more likely one is to return to it to some advantage.

There has been an evolution in my process. Early on, like most poets around me at that time, I was writing anecdotal bits that were referential to experience. And if pathos was evoked in any of those poems, that pathos was due to some emotion buried in the prior experience. Put another way, my early poems allude to some human emotional effect of an experience that was recovered or referred to in the poem, which in turn was worked up into some emotional experience for someone else—the reader I suppose. I have steadily moved away from this approach in my thinking and in my practice. Now, instead of seeing the poem as an expression of what I think I've already detected, I am pouring over language to actually discover something I didn't anticipate.

So Philokalia*—which refers to a collection of spiritual texts written in the Middle Ages by spiritual masters of the Eastern Orthodox tradition—is an apt name for the first of your two New and Selected books of poetry.*

Yes. The word itself means "the love of the good, the beautiful." One tends to give full attention to that which is good and beautiful before him, and one tends to savor it.

Is one of your goals as a poet to create beauty?

I would say the goal of poetry is primarily to observe the beautiful, to glimpse the beautiful. That's why *I'm* doing it, anyway—to serve my own desire to glimpse the beautiful. It's gravy if anyone else bothers with them.

"City Under Construction" is a fine poem.

Thank you! That's one of my prose pieces. On the one hand, the city's builders in that poem long for a conclusion, an outcome that is at least as good as was expected. On the other hand, such conclusion or completion is not possible, and even if it were, it wouldn't be desirable. The whole point of human life is to move into—to become acclimated to—an enormity that isn't conclusive. The penultimate paragraph of the poem, if I can recall, is nostalgic for the plan or purpose, a childish longing to obtain what the builders set out to make. But then the poem moves closer to the real issue—that what we most deeply desire is figured beyond what we see.

Yes, and the word "desire" is key to understanding this poem. It's an allegory of our desires in general. Michael Waters once told me that poets dream of writing the perfect poem, and if they're lucky they will never write it.

I think that's exactly right. You long for something better, but you don't want it to be conclusively better, so that it's done. That feels meager.

To reach perfection would be a kind of death.

Yes. The beauty of the whole project of one's life is that it progresses, and that this progress is continual, and ever.

I also admire "The Beginning of the World."

It was around the time that I wrote that poem that I really became committed to the idea that one writes to speculate, that one performs the speculation through the writing. That's about when I realized that the job was *not* to go through a speculation, form an epiphany, and then write notes about it. It was around the time that I was writing that poem that I was really embracing a commitment to writing as a way of knowing. That said, I think that poem needs to be edited. It's a little long. Three quarters of the way through, the poem seems repetitive—and not in a pleasing way. I love redundancy and repetition, as you probably have figured out, and the slight tweakings of those repetitions. I'll probably have another go at "The Beginning of the World" someday, make it shorter.

In a 2006 feature in Christianity and Literature, *you discuss the importance of stillness, how the "scattered person" must "still white noise" and other distractions in order to be able to, through discipline, "collect and become quiet. And then the beginning of prayer." This kind of discipline is also required of the poet—or any serious artist. Do you feel your work as a poet has enabled you to achieve stillness spiritually as well? Or is this all connected to the same thing?*

I agree that this is the essential discipline required of any artist—this uncommon degree of attention focused on the matter at hand—whether that matter is language, pigment, clay, or stone. Whatever. And, without question, the habits I've acquired as a poet pretty much led me into—assisted—my acquiring similar habits in prayer; I daresay, as well, that my practice of the Jesus prayer has also enhanced my practice as a poet. So yes, at this point in my life, the two undertakings seem to be mutually efficacious, collaborative means by which the central chore, the primary art—constructing a better self—is pursued.

In that same feature you discuss the importance of the liturgy as a consolation for those who keep falling and failing, that its presence in one's spiritual life works on one over the years. How has the language of the liturgy influenced your poetic style—if at all?

Yes, pretty much all of this suggests to me that progress, healing, recovery, etc., is cumulative.

One doesn't suddenly become a poet, nor any kind of artist, nor any kind of saint. One develops. One improves. One falls and gets up again. And one learns to be watchful, avoiding the continuing distractions and derailments that would keep one languishing in adolescence. Adolescent poetry *or* adolescent prayer. One hopes, at some point, to move ahead. And yes, the Divine Liturgy itself—the central, Eucharistic service of the Orthodox Church—is a practice that continues to open up, continues to open *us*, into increasingly greater apprehension of the immensity in whom—as Saint Paul has it, quoting the Greek poet Epimenides—we live and move and have our being.

You have a poem called "Bad Theology." What would you call a bad theology?

I guess any theology that presumes to have God in its pocket. Can I explain this without sinning further? We'll find out. The community in which I was raised did what they would call theology, but it was always a kind of cranky, brutal reduction of lush and beautiful complexities into the lowest common denominator, the dullest version. But when I went away to school and started reading more, I became increasingly dissatisfied with any theology that replaces the enormous, immeasurable real with very measurable and very calculated replacements. I'm not saying this very eloquently, but I guess bad theology articulates as definitive and conclusive that which is unknowable and without end.

Not to paint with too broad a brush—because there are a few wonderful exceptions to this observation—but, in general, Western Christian theology sits on one hand and Jewish theology and Eastern Christian theology sits on the other. I'd say that other hand holds a mystical theology—that is, a theology that acknowledges its terms to be provisional, a theology admitting that we can't know anything conclusively, a theology finding great pleasure and joy and beauty in pressing language for a taste of immensity. The Western tradition has settled for more brutal, more scholastic theologies that have pretty carefully, pretty deliberately sought to diminish the mystery to what is a pocket-sized, utilitarian, and—I'd say—a meager and very often embarrassing replacement.

Given what you have to say about bad theologies, I would surmise that they not only reduce the mystery but also discourage people from asking further questions.

Exactly. A bad theology doesn't recognize—or refuses to acknowledge—its own inherent limitations. A good theology presupposes its limitations, yet nonetheless takes pleasure in pursuing the object of desire, which is truth and beauty, and the pursuit of what is real—God, I suppose.

How have poems, like "Bad Theology," been received by the members of the religious community in which you were raised?

Well, my father always walked pretty casually through that community, so he was always slightly estranged to it anyway. He passed away in 1988, but if he were alive I don't think there would be any estrangement between us. There'd have been some good conversations. Safe to say, though, that I'm utterly estranged from the community in which I was raised. To be honest, any of the friends I touch base with when

I return to my childhood home are no longer part of that community either. They've all gone elsewhere, some of them deliberately away from any kind of religious life or religious community. Others, like me, have embraced other traditions that are more satisfying. The puny is no longer satisfying, and the large is desired. Most of them have moved towards things that are larger.

You are pulled towards the enormity of the world.

Right, nor are Holy Scriptures themselves to be reduced to signs pointing to something that they're hiding. They are to be savored and interpreted, made over. I love how the rabbis do that in various rabbinic genres—Midrashim being the most obvious, but any Talmudic commentaries that savor the unknowable and offer their interpretations with accustomed modesty—that's compelling to me. Another interpretation. Exactly that—another possible way to speak of what cannot be named. This disposition acknowledges a humility that honors the mystery itself, prefers the truth to whatever reductions we can make of it.

This approach to savoring the unknowable, ongoing interpretation also keeps that mystery alive. You see a good deal of this in the Eastern Orthodox tradition.

Yes, though there are exceptions, of course. You no doubt could find plenty of practicing Orthodox Christians who are as brutal in their interpretations as any fundamentalist. But in terms of the theological tradition, the writings are more like the writings of Jewish theologians, in that they are more speculative and modest, and very much aware that the whole genre is limited by the human points of view and language.

There was a point in my life where I was so fed up with Evangelical Christendom—its untenable textual idolatry—that I actually began studying to become Jewish. In the process of doing that, I came upon a Syrian Saint named St. Isaak, sometimes called St. Isaak of Nineveh, who opened up for me this Christian community in Syria, the earliest Christian communities around Antioch. These communities had a very Semitic approach to language because they were also Semitic, bringing a very Jewish approach to Christian texts. It was their own Semitic awareness that language is a live thing and not just a sign pointing to a dead thing. It was in reading first St. Isaak and then other theologians from that tradition, such as St. Ephraim—who was actually a poet who wrote his theology in verse—that I discovered a middle ground where I could hang onto my Christian faith and also adopt what I would characterize as a very Jewish habit of reading. It seemed as close as I was going to get to a satisfying religious life.

Despite the earnestness of their themes, many of your poems display a refreshing humor. Can you talk about the importance of humor and, by extension, laughter in the life a poet, and—more specifically to you—a poet who has turned to religion for spiritual guidance and illumination?

Well, I have a pretty good sense of humor, and enjoy a good joke. And I've been blessed with an inexplicable joy, an inveterate giddiness, even. But in terms of how these things are employed in my poems, you should remember that when I began writing in the early 70s, religious discourse was, in most intellectual and academic circles, wholly disregarded, disparaged even. Given the quality of much of that discourse, you really can't blame folks for discounting it. Since then, the "postmodern turn" has granted equal (if equally arbitrary) footing to pretty much anything that passes for an idea; with that turn, spirituality in general and religious discourse in particular recovered a patina of legitimacy. Still, when I was starting out, one could not write about such things without a strongly ironic disposition. So, what probably began as a defense against embarrassment—and perhaps also as a preemptive disarming of those who might be predisposed to discounting any poetry that wasn't blithely materialistic or profane—became a continuing rhetorical strategy. While things have changed a bit, they haven't changed all that much. So it's never a bad idea to lead with a joke; and irony is always most useful when, somewhere near the poem's final turn, it falls away.

Cairns, Scott, and Kathleen Norris. "Looking Backward, Looking Inward: Scott Cairns and Kathleen Norris in Conversation." *Christianity and Literature*: Summer 2009.

Poetry:

Compass of Affection: Poems New and Selected, Paraclete Press, 2006
Philokalia, Zoo Press, 2002
Recovered Body Poems, George Braziller Inc., 1998
Figures for the Ghost, University of Georgia Press, 1994
Disciplinary Treatises, Trilobite Press, 1993
Sermons for the Wary, Franciscan University Press, 1993
The Translation of Babel, University of Georgia Press, 1990
The Theology of Doubt, Cleveland State University Press, 1985
Finding the Broken Man, Window Press, 1982

Nonfiction:

The End of Suffering: Finding Purpose in Pain, Paraclete Press, 2009
Love's Immensity: Mystics on the Endless Life, Paraclete Press, 2007
Short Trip to the Edge: Where Earth Meets Heaven—A Pilgrimage, Paraclete Press, 2006

Open Secrets: An Interview with Jane Hirshfield

In her essay, "Thoreau's Hound: Poetry and Hiddenness," Jane Hirshfield writes, "Hiddenness is the ballast in the ship's keel, the great underwater portion of a life that steadies the rest." Like many of Hirshfield's prose statements, this concise, quotable utterance offers valuable insight into her poems, which, among other things, explore the paradoxical terrain of hiddenness, that place where revelation and concealment co-exist. Often aphoristic and elliptical in approach, Hirshfield adheres to a less-is-more aesthetic, an economy and restraint one associates with the world's best poetry. Although she has been hailed as one of America's leading "Zen" poets, Hirshfield's intelligence is more eclectic and inclusive than a single label suggests. Sensitive to the rhythms of history and how art and ideas have developed over long periods of time, she is also drawn to the discourses of science and philosophy. She has received many honors, including the Poetry Center Book Award, the California Book Award, and Columbia University's Translation Center Award; and many fellowships, including ones from the National Endowment for the Arts and the Guggenheim and Rockefeller Foundations. *Given Sugar, Given Salt* was a finalist for the National Book Critics Circle Award in 2001. While never a full-time academic, she has taught writing at a number of universities, including the University of California at Berkeley, Bennington College, the University of San Francisco, and the University of Cincinnati. She was elected a Chancellor of the Academy of American Poets in 2012.

You are clearly a private person. Your poems do not reveal much of your autobiography—at least in the way most people understand autobiography. There is a persistent tension in your poems between what is revealed and what is hidden. Yet, there is an almost unbearable intimacy in some of your poems that makes them universal and immensely personal at the same time. Are you aware of this tension? If so, can you talk a bit about it?

An interesting conundrum: how does a private person talk about being a private person?

Poetry began for me as a field of solitude. It gave me a way, from childhood, to query and provision a self, to find out for myself who I was, what I felt, what I thought. But once a piece of writing is put forward for others to read, the field expands: where once there were trees, making windbreak and shelter, now there are bleachers. The privacy-crafted self is *seen*. While writing, a poet is predator: you hunt word, world, feeling, music, responsiveness, attitude, resilience; hunt grief, joy, your deep question and that question's momentarily-sufficient answer. With publication, though, a poet is suddenly prey, subject to judgment—which, whatever the judgment, is an entirely changed relationship to the poem and the world. The leap into public life as a writer was for me awkward, both painful and strange. And yet, I also knew that we are ultimately communal beings, whose life does not end at the skin. Art is never a matter of just the single self, made as it is with the shared materials of language and craft-history, a set of cups to hold the intoxicating spirits.

Yes, it's always a matter of the communal holding the personal and the personal holding the communal, isn't it?

Intimacy, immediacy, and a plumb line between the personally pressing and the more broadly human, all do matter to me a great deal as a writer. That's true even though I've never much written the directly autobiographical narrative poem—though I can read such poems with the happiness of a horse with his nose in the oat bag. But even in the poetry of personal narrative, art is never only the simple, direct story. The simplest anecdote is selected out of the day, out of the life, as a trout is selected out of the river. We reach into experience for something that can sustain us, and also delight. If you're thirsty, it's the river water you want; if you're hungry, it's the fish. My particular hunger in writing poetry seems to be for the sudden flash of comprehension, for feeling and seeing something new of world or self. For the epiphany made possible by the lyric.

I should add that all my poems do emerge from what are essentially personal dilemmas and questions. The newest book, *Come, Thief,* holds meditations on late love, the puzzle of eros, desire, time, and aging, and various losses, as well as poems whose subjects are equally out of the life, but in ways perhaps more under the surface. One poem, for instance, arrived after I'd cooked an accidentally frozen egg—this happened, and I was rather fascinated by how it worked out. Still, the poem wasn't a poem until something both larger and more intimate walked into it. But the pressure of the personal is equally present in poems I've written over the years that might seem to be outwardly seated. The Rwandan genocide, the first Gulf War and then the Iraq and Afghanistan wars, the Chilean dictator Pinochet's death in his own bed, the invasion of Grenada, the crises of environment and climate, the Indonesian tsunami, the events of September 11, 2001, Indira Gandhi's assassination, the Robert Bork Supreme Court nomination, the Velvet Revolutions of 1989—all have precipitated poems. I wrote those poems because these events raised in me some intimate, immediate question I found myself unable to enter or answer any other way. Questions of fate and fairness, for instance, have haunted me all my life. I can't help but feel uneasy before my own relatively good fortune, in a world where others suffer in ways far more blunt.

Perhaps I've ducked your initial question by answering it as I have here. Yet the answer is the truest I can muster. I write poems the way a mouse thrown into a bucket swims: to stay alive. This is true for the "public" poems, and true for the private ones. I've come to think of it this way: my poems are x-rays, not nude portraits. A reader may not be able to see the outer story or events of my life, or follow its factual narrative, but the inner consequence is there quite clearly, and I myself feel the poems entirely revealing. My exposure—any poet's exposure, if a poem's any good—is complete. And that is what intimacy means, to me: being willing to see and be seen, being willing to know and be known, being willing to feel without swerve or camouflage, and to let that feeling be felt and witnessed by others. If the poem-harness is not attached to such a wagon, what would be the point of all our beautiful high-stepping horses? Beauty matters, liveliness matters, inventiveness and music matter—but so does it matter that something that matters is being pulled.

Following rather directly from this first question, I have another. In your poem, "Three Foxes by the Edge of the Field at Twilight," from The Lives of the Heart, *there's a startling admission: "There is more and more I tell no one, / strangers nor loves." Could you say something about that statement, and the tensions it carries, in specific?*

I've wondered from time to time how much anyone notices that line, and how a reader feels about it if he or she does. Shut out? Curious? Insulted? For me, it felt a strangely transgressive confession: even to say that there's something you aren't saying is saying too much. It's also a very odd statement to place in a poem. Aren't poems supposed to tell, or at least show, not withhold? Yet the line is not meant to wink. It is—how ironic, to say this—simple, autobiographical fact.

It's perhaps a good example also of the intersection of the personal and the shared, which you mentioned earlier. The unsaid plays an enormous role in anyone's life. What is kept hidden, that there *are* things that are hidden, carries huge charge. For those whose childhood included forced suppression of family truths, secrecy can be intolerable. But for me, to keep something rightly unsaid, or to hold something unsaid on behalf of another, is mysteriously strengthening. One dying friend entrusted me with a secret that would have caused pain, if ever spoken elsewhere. I never have.

We live in an age of chosen revelation and also of enforced sharing. Often, that can be good; people are wildly various, and the range of what's human clamors for acknowledgment and inclusion, if we're to live up to the most straightforward ideals of human rights and democratic co-existence. But a functioning ecosystem of the psyche needs also its burrows and nests, its attics and cupboards. Gestation requires protected space, ripening requires both permeability to the outer and non-disturbance. Whatever the culture leans toward, art will lean toward the other side. In cultures of totalitarian censorship, surrealism will leap through the keyhole. In a culture of almost ubiquitous display, perhaps some quiet advocacy of privacy is the most shocking thing you can offer.

Poems are open secrets, in any case. I mean that in both directions.

Donald Hall titled one of his essays "The Unsayable Said," and speaks of a hidden, secret room at the center of any great poem. I have found this more and more to be so—poems are desks with false-bottomed drawers, whose contents confound easy understanding. For me there is also some deep connection between the hidden and a sense of amplitude. A line in "French Horn," the first poem in *Come, Thief*, asks, "What in this unpleated world isn't someone's seduction?" But the seduction is first of all in the pleats' existence, in the folds of our lives, the places where more exists than can ever be seen.

You say, "Whatever the culture leans toward, art will lean toward the other side." That's an interesting proposition. How have you come to understand this?

I came to the idea after looking into the transition between oral and literate poetic cultures, for what became the eighth chapter in *Nine Gates*. Briefly, the story goes something like this: In preliterate times, poems served both as ritual—as vessels for enacting some transformation of being, whether lullaby, work song, marriage, or funeral—and as mnemonic. Rhyme and meter can hold in place with accuracy what would not otherwise be precisely remembered. Think of the kinds of entropy that happen in the children's game of "telephone," then think of "Thirty days hath September"; information that would fall apart as a regular sentence or list stays intact when put into the memory-form of art. But once you have written words to hold information precisely in place, poetry begins to function differently. It becomes less a culture's oral encyclopedia and more a way of capturing what only poems are good for sieving and holding. Poems begin to look at the unobvious, the subtle, the peripheral, the repressed, disregarded, ignored. They're written from the condition of exile, not from the capitol. This is often true quite literally—instead of Homer or the *Beowulf* bard reciting epics by heart in the royal banquet hall, we find Ovid, Dante, and Po Chü-i writing from banishment. The same is true in more metaphorical ways—poets write from the edge. Exile is loss of certainty, but it's also a liberation: when poetry no longer has to tell the official story, it's freed to tell others.

What I see in poetry's development over the millennia is an ever-widening range of subjects being investigated in ever-widening ways. Once memory can be placed into cuneiform, hieroglyphic, and ink, poetry can be magnetized by the task of finding new subjects. The thrill is in finding not only beautiful and memorable speech, but beautiful and memorable speech that makes a discovery. This is certainly how I feel it in my own life: I need poems to think about what I *don't* understand, or can't understand, by ordinary thought. Poems hold what's incomprehensible by other means.

The same is true of other art forms as well. Another way I came to think about art as cultural counterweight is by noticing something about gardens. When the world was a wilderness, gardens were structured—places people found restful because they were orderly. Paths and beds were geometric, trees were tamed into topiary, you had strict borders and manicured hedges. Now that the world is, for most of us, a rather regimented place, we want cottage gardens, mazes, hidden benches, drifts of wildflowers, and some restful disorder: a place where everything is *not* so controlled. We seek in a garden an experience the opposite of our everyday life on subways and city grids.

By implication, then, what you're saying is that the growth of art through the ages moves from a way of adhering to ritual and record keeping, and—through both these functions—a means of reinforcing the dominant values of the culture, to a representation of the more subversive and marginalized elements of the culture.

Yes. But also of the more subtle. These things intertwine and blur. Ritual can either enforce the status quo or offer a way to change it, and to call art's job purely subversion risks an aesthetic of dramatic dead ends. So I agree, so long as the statement's taken with some subtlety and nuance. What I want of art is expansion, not destruction—"creative" shares a root with "increase." I want a renovation beyond refusal. I want art to make me wilder, weirder and smarter, more compassionate and capacious, more vulnerable to the accuracies and idiosyncracies of our human joys, griefs, passions, ideas, connections.

Subversion and subtlety are both, you know, aspects of Trickster, and in many cultures, the Trickster figure is also the inventor of writing.

Trickster challenges, queries, and changes the existing order; his eros, invention, irreverence, and humor are lubricant: they allow things to move. What art, and Trickster, want, I think, is to *escape* the dominant, to slip its edges and leave familiar ground for somewhere new. Trickster is also the figure at the crossroads, the god who faces more than one direction at once. That multiplicity too is, for me, almost the hallmark of any art I find good.

You said earlier that you don't have any inclination toward the directly autobiographical poem. Do you often feel the need to escape from an age of enforced sharing?

I feel the need to escape from many things in our age! But so many people take up arms against confessional poetry so vehemently, you have to wonder why. So let me make clear again that I'm for it. I read, and teach, Robert Lowell and Sharon Olds and Dorianne Laux, even as I also admire Marianne Moore's saying that she was "as clear as my natural reticence allows." Perhaps it's my own natural reticence that makes me admire the less reticent more, not less—they offer the kinds of poetry that I cannot myself make. I have a strong impulse to protect the poem of personal feeling from attack for being what it is, and an equally strong impulse to protect other poems from being interpreted as if they were personal. I want to read poetry without any preexisting program in my mind, and for me it doesn't add anything to Wallace Stevens's "The Snow Man" if I find it described as a response to his bad marriage. Yet it does for me expand Eliot's "The Waste Land," somehow, to hold the same hypothesis in mind. I can't justify why I feel these contradictory responses so strongly, except to say simply that I am for the poem itself, always. In any case, confessional poetry is unfairly trivialized by people who attack it for its basic project. No poem is a matter of subject matter alone. Good poems of personal story do what all good poems do. They expand the penumbra of multiple understanding, the penumbra of beauty, the penumbra of compassion. They open us to more of our shared human condition than we were able to know before.

I think a lot of hostility towards confessional poetry is disguised misogyny. Although Lowell was trashed for it first, the more frequent practitioners of it have been women.

I agree. Just look at the way the phrase "domestic poetry" is used, as a kind of unarguable term of dismissal. What is domestic cannot be important, it seems. As I've looked at my own recent work, and noticed how many images are taken from housecleaning, I've begun to think that may be the next label I'll be given to carry. Perhaps I can drop the mantle of Zen poet and become the poet of housecleaning—which would be, of course, a far better description of Zen than the word "Zen" is. One famous koan asks, "What is Buddha?" and the answer is, "Have you eaten your breakfast? Then wash your bowl." That's actual Zen: doing the dishes because they need doing. And feeling that any work of caretaking and attention is equal to any other. Anyhow, it seems I am awfully often in my recent poems washing doorknobs or cooking or mopping a floor. Now, if the particular poem "Washing Doorknobs," which ran in *The New Yorker*, happens to be also about empire-grief, and if it happens to hold, immediately under the surface, some bitter contemplation of our country's extended state of war, well . . . a house roof keeps nothing in or out, does it? As the old sixties motto says, the personal is political. We are permeable to everything, and so are our poems. I think of Wisława Szymborska's note-perfect poem about the intersection of history and domesticity, "The End and the Beginning": "After every war / someone has to tidy up." It is her continual remembrance of and faithfulness to the unchampioned "someone" that makes Szymborska one of the most necessary political poets of our time. She, and her fellow Polish poets Czesław Miłosz, Zbigniew Herbert, Anna Swir, Tadeusz Różewicz, saw what happens when the individual is forgotten in the face of History or Theory.

You said earlier that poems are open secrets. That is interesting to me. It reminds me of something Stanley Kunitz once said: "I don't want poems that reveal secrets but are filled with them." He also said, "A poem without secrets lies dead on the page."

What a gorgeous bit of wisdom. There are so many kinds of secrets you can think of in response. Any metaphor is an unopenable cupboard of secrets. There's tremendous mystery at the heart of lyric comprehension, image comprehension, musical comprehension, how they actually function within us. If a poem weren't filled with secrets it wouldn't be poetry.

I said that I meant the phrase "open secret" to face in both directions. Should I expand that? If the secrets of poems were not open, we could not find such pleasure in them, such meaning in them, as we do. An apple can be eaten without knowing its molecules' fragrance by name. And yet an open secret is still a secret; there's always a further corner to go around. One of my "assay" poems describes the famous Japanese rock garden at Ryoanji: no matter where you stand in it, you can never see all the rocks at once. Poems are like that. You can never see every part of their meaning at once, and that very unseeability is no small part of how the whole functions.

I suppose your question wants a more personal answer but I don't want to give one. (laughs)

Good—since part of the point in asking it was in recognizing that you wouldn't give a personal answer! I had the good fortune of attending one of your lectures more than a decade ago. During your presentation, you spoke of wanting to make more memorable statements (i.e., pithy, aphoristic assertions) in your poems. Judging from the work of your last three books, I'd say that goal has been achieved. I'd like to cite a few of these statements-in-verse from your most recent book, Come, Thief, *and give you an opportunity to talk about these kinds of statements, and how writing them relates to your vision of poetry as a whole, and to your own path as a poet:*

"A story travels in one direction only, / no matter how often / it tries to turn north, south, east, west, back." (from "Tolstoy and the Spider")

"It is the work of feeling / to undo expectation." (from "Sheep")

"The heart's actions / are neither the sentence nor its reprieve." (from "All Day the Difficult Waiting")

"I don't know what time is. // You can't ever find it. / But you can lose it." (from "A Day Is Vast")

"Some thoughts / throw off / a backward heat / as walls might, / at night, in summer." (from "A Thought")

"Think assailable thoughts, or be lonely." (from "Sentencings")

An odd experience first raised in me that awareness of the excerptable poetic statement or line. When my second book, *Of Gravity & Angels*, was coming out from Wesleyan University Press, they asked for a brief quote from a poem to put in the catalogue, and I had a terrible time finding anything to suggest. That showed me something I hadn't realized: that my poems and their language worked only on the level of the full poem. There's nothing wrong with that, of course, and it's true of many poems by others I love. But I realized that one thing I myself turn to poetry for is a phrase, a line, a sentence that in itself sifts something worth carrying, something needed. Shakespeare was of course the great master of this. Seeing how little I had exercised that particular poetic function raised in me the desire to do it.

Perhaps strangely, for me this was a matter of courage. Naked statement exposes. A person can hide behind ornate language, even behind lyricism and image, in ways that can be terrifically fertile and useful. It's clear how much I love the implicit and its powers. But I do think as well that poems not only feel things, they know things, they make discoveries, and some of the time, those moments of knowledge are sayable, and if not the discovery itself, then a catalyst towards one. Clarity, simplicity, directness can be tremendously refreshing, done well, and are very often the lines you find carried in people's daily pockets. "We must love one another or die." Auden cut that line from his poem, and it still couldn't be throttled.

From my own work, take the final line from "Sentencings": *Think assailable thoughts, or be lonely.* On its own, it's just prose; but it was arrived at by poetry, and when I've read that poem to audiences of scientists, there's a surge of surprised recognition. Any new idea, in science, will be assailed, will have to be defended by argument—yet that very argument is the conversation by which discovery goes forward. The poem's statement both acknowledges that and brings into foreground the emotional dilemma of that process. If you think only the obvious thought, no one has any reason to talk with you, really. But if you think something new, you will be attacked. And for all you know, the new idea may well be wrong—most are—but if you can't risk being found a fool, you'll never find anything worth finding, and you will also discover yourself off to the side of the room, alone with your wine and cheese plate. The same is true in poems. Safe poems—those that only repeat what's been done before or else are incomprehensible, beautiful language outside evaluation—may feel comfortable, but in the end they bring solitude and boredom.

On this question of statement-making in poems, I've begun noticing the almost inexplicable power of certain ways of saying the obvious. Here's a tiny example I fell quite in love with, two lines from the poem "Table" by the Turkish modernist poet Edip Cansever: "Three times three make nine. / The man puts nine on the table." The first sentence, dull as dirt on its own, is electrified by the second—or at least it is for me in the context of the full poem.

There are many keys on poetry's piano, and perception ranges up and down the scale: notes so low they are almost inaudible in their chord; high clear ones; major, minor. Of the lines from *Come, Thief* quoted above, some use image, some are abstract. Each I hope is at once both clear and definite and carries as well some uncapturable perfume—the merely definite is journalism, the wholly uncapturable, well, that's a vagueness that risks failure.

You spoke above about poetic statements and memorability. Can you say a little more about that?

One test of a poem for me is memorability—is there something in it you'd ever need or want to turn to again. Poetic statement is clear, that's why we feel it a statement. But what makes it *poetry* is that it also holds meaning not entirely contained, or containable, in the words—you have to think or feel further, beyond the words, to know fully what is there. The recognition of emotional repercussion, ethical repercussion, intellectual and philosophical repercussions, the ability to be made to pause or shiver, are part of the permeability to wideness poems ask of us. That extra is what poems exist to give. It's what makes them something we want to remember, and need to revisit.

Finding that entrance to *extra* is not only one of the great joys of writing, but also one of the great reasons to write—to not only live but live more extravagantly, deeply, broadly, vividly, subtly, wildly. To find in the obvious day not only the obvious day, but its complications and amazements. As evening opens the pupils wider, poems open us to our own faculty for amazement.

Distance is another powerful motif running through the poems in Come, Thief; *it manifests itself in many ways. Sometimes it is conceptual, as in the poem "Critique of Pure Reason," where you write, "Perimeter is not meaning, but it changes meaning, / as wit increases distance and compassion erodes it." Other times, the distance is physical, as it is in "The Present," where you write, "I stood on one side of the present, you stood on the other." Sometimes distance is willed: "To go great distance, / exactitudes matter" ("China"); other times it exists in us as limitation: "the feelings: / how one cannot know another completely" ("Narrowness"). Can you talk about the ways in which your awareness of distance has shaped and is shaped by your poems?*

I think you've captured something very true about the work in this new book. Distance and its inevitable companions, closeness and intimacy have, indeed, been much in my thoughts and my pen. One of the seeds may be that in these past years, there've been so many deaths, and death is surely the most uncrossable distance of all. That's the experience at the center of "The Present," a poem in which the word "present" moves from meaning "gift" to meaning "this moment in time." Everything else is just here, by comparison to the dead, who are so profoundly, impossibly, abruptly, not. Another seed for the distance references in the poems may be something quite literal: I have been "going great distances." This seems to be the stage of my life when poetry takes me traveling—I've been to Xi'an, Shanghai, Kyoto, Damascus, Ramallah, Nazareth, Athens, Istanbul, Cracow, Vilnius, Lindisfarne . . .

Here's one example of how that traveling has come into a poem, given that I'm not a poet for whom the immediately seen goes directly into the writing. When the Silk Road appeared at the end of the poem "The Decision," it was, first of all, the metaphor needed for that moment in that poem. But it was there to come to hand because the Silk Road became for me real in a different way after I recognized that I'd stood at both its ends. In 2007, I watched a shadow puppet master perform in Istanbul; in 2009, I saw the same puppets in the Islamic Night Market in Xi'an, China. In between, there surely are places where that millennia-old trade route must now be only a few deep ruts in the ground—like the wagon train routes still visible in the desert in the American West. But the evidence of profound connection was in front of my eyes. I saw in those profiled figures, often painted on donkey skin leather, immense distance, immense time, and also the intimacy of connection. Any original perception like that is thrilling. Book knowledge of a thing suddenly breathes, takes wing. It becomes a charged electron in the mind, that excitement, one that looks for something it can attach to.

Like many important but steadily present things, the experience of distance is so fundamental it's almost invisible, most of the time. How often do we stop to notice gravity or a ceiling, for instance, unless they suddenly vanish? Where else could experience, knowledge, feelings, exist, if not within our three-dimensional lives and bodies? A transformative book about this is George Lakoff and Mark Johnson's *Metaphors We Live By*. It altered my understanding both of language and of what it is to be human. Perhaps I found these ideas riveting because I was already interested in questions of near and far, up and down, in the meanings of northness and southness. But it seems impossible to me that anyone might not be. Robert Hass once said that the beginning of poetry is a baby crying when the mother and her breast are not near: "Whaaaaaaa!" first; then a sonnet.

Poetry itself is a paradoxical intertwining of intimacy and distance. What begins in the body, in the life, in the heart/mind, leaves that interior existence when it sets forth into language. Yet the language of poetry and art is an attempt to awaken inside the body and life of another what was in yours. Our tongue, our pulse, our breath, our heart, our mind, are inhabiting the gestures and patterns the poet's tongue, pulse, breath, heart, mind placed there. To say, or read, your own poem, is to return yourself to a condition that stepped into being in its making. Poems implode time and space, in their ability to summon and resummon a particular shape and constellation of presence. They are perfume bottles momentarily unstoppered—what they release is volatile and will vanish, and yet it can be released again.

Another powerful theme in Come, Thief *is the importance you place on searching. In "Perishable, It Said," you write, "I found myself looking"; in "The Question" you seek the dead and the living for answers to an unspecified question. In both cases, it seems the quest for clarity is as crucial as the mo-*

ment of clarity itself. Can you speak to the ways in which searching is central to you as a poet and to your poetry?

I cannot think of any better description for the experience of writing a poem than that it's a search for something that only that poem, and nothing else, can find. This is true even if the poem's discovery vanishes almost at once. We are a species for whom awakeness is hunger. Satiety is an instant's happiness, and then—how strangely sleepy and unsatisfying it becomes.

I don't want to dismiss the joy of rootedness, of familiarity, of finding oneself in one's own bed with one's own love. Yet what poem do we murmur there, to preserve that joy? "O Western Wind, when wilt thou blow / That the small rain down can rain? / Christ, that my love were in my arms, / And I in my bed again!"

There's a neurochemical explanation for the power of longing—but how reductionist, to speak of dopamine, when instead we can read Yeats's "The Lake Isle of Innisfree" and realize that no small part of the poem's power is that it's about an imagined place, an imagined future—Yeats stands amid the bee-loud glade with his feet on a Dublin roadway. The art forms that take place in time are bound to change and discovery, and the discovery must be a restless, evaporative one. Anything simpler could be contained by a vessel less protean than art. Poems oppose binary simplicities of understanding. They are built to do work more multiarmed, multiminded, and necessarily choral, to hold things unable to be held any other way.

The perfection of things as they are is also true, and a very few poems can hold that trembling balance. But most of the time, the goad is longing and search, not having, and my own poems reflect that. It may be that each poem is the record of its own making: an archeologist's notebook, dig, and findings all at once.

Over the years your poems have become increasingly concise, as if all unnecessary language has been stripped away. And yet they are quite sensual. That must be a difficult balance to strike. The best Japanese poetry achieves this balance, too. You have translated two collections of Japanese poetry. How have those endeavors shaped your own aesthetic?

The first book I bought, at age eight, was a Peter Pauper Press book of Japanese haiku. I was growing up in New York City, a child far from the natural world—what drew me so strongly I cannot now reassemble. All I can say is that these brief poems of compressive image and large worldview were irresistible. Another influence in my love of the small that can hold the large may have been a set of worn, tiny leather-bound books my mother had acquired somewhere along the line. The books were an inch, perhaps an inch and half tall—I remember Shakespeare, a Bible, a dictionary perhaps. Some had snaps holding them closed, one was green leather embossed with a gold diamond design. Back then my eyes could deal with that size type. I would read in them, and the experience was thrilling: universes releasable from something so small by my own awareness, as the tea inside tea bags is released by hot water. Yet another wonder of early childhood was Chinese paper flowers—you would drop some nondescript bit of weightlessness into a cup of water, and they would blossom. Something in me has remained thrilled by such mysterious transformations, entirely akin to how meaning and feeling unfold from the small words of poems. The more work done by the least words, the more mysterious and explosive. A brief poem that succeeds in moving a person is very high-octane fuel.

By the time I came to co-translate, with Mariko Aratani, the poems of Ono no Komachi and Izumi Shikibu in *The Ink Dark Moon*, reading Japanese poetry in translation had already shaped my own sense of poetry and its workings. The second book, *The Heart of Haiku*, with its co-translations of Basho, is even more recent; it began as a lecture I was asked to give early in 2007. So the influence of Japanese poetics is surely there—but predates the translating, per se. Translation taught me other things. It released in me a more capacious spirit of revision, and confirmed me as a close-reader. It did reimmerse me in a kind of poem I'd already been long drawn to—but if anything it also inoculated me against any direct imitation of that particular form. It's difficult to say exactly why—too easy a temptation? Or perhaps it felt something more like an incest taboo. *Come, Thief* does include one *haibun* (a form in which a prose preface accompanies a haiku), but that's the only one I've written, in all these years.

My models for brevity and cleanness of language also haven't been entirely drawn from Asian poetics. Sappho's fragmentary lyrics, the poems from the Greek Anthology, the shorter lyrics of Catullus and Horace, the English sonnet, some of the briefer works of Auden and Yeats and Pound and William Carlos Williams—these were also early influences toward a poetics of compression. These kinds of poems are not simple. The language may be spare, but complexities are present, they're just found in a different realm—the conceptual, the associative, the worldview. A later set of influences along these lines were the poems of Cavafy, of Anna Swir, of Tranströmer, Gustafsson, and Wisława Szymborska. Each of these poets is a poet of great feeling and of multifaceted responsiveness to human experiences of the subtler kind, and also a poet of spare-leaning language.

I'm in any case the kind of poet who writes in more than one mode. I do write poems that work more by ornamentation and some of the other more baroque pleasures. The poems I've called "pebbles" are an exploration of brevity, hybrids perhaps of the Japanese brief-poem forms with more Western modes. The ones I've called "assays" are usually far more meandering explorations. There's a set of poems in *Come, Thief* whose axle of drive is what I think of as "wandering rhyme." The book contains also the one villanelle I've ever attempted (again, it wanders slightly, each time for a reason); there's a blues poem in waltz-rhythm and one I hear as a kind of Irish ballad crossed with Emily Dickinson. Some poets write very consistently one kind of poem, I've rather consistently written many. New and different modes of writing magnetize new and different meanings.

Despite the spare and concise shape of many of your poems, they remind me a bit of those skeletal trees on the cover of Come, Thief*: their standing naked displays the surprising ways in which they have branched. Take the opening lines of "French Horn," the first poem from that collection. Those eight lines could easily stand on their own as a wonderful poem, one that evokes all of the pregnant imagery of a classic Japanese tanka or haiku. However, rather than ending the poem with that arresting question ("What in this unpleated world isn't someone's seduction?"), you chose to extend it for 15 more lines, moving from the gazer-at-the-window motif to the recital hall, where one of the performers locks eyes with another,* *which the poem's speaker observes. What are some considerations that inform the unexpected branches of your poems?*

I wrote "French Horn" a few days after returning from performing on stage myself at Carnegie Hall, reading a poem that is spoken as part of an extraordinary symphonic song cycle, *The Old Burying Ground*, by the composer Evan Chambers. The Mahler piece described in the poem's second half was the second one on the program that day—when a new piece of music is performed, it's often coupled with something well-known, I assume to reassure and draw in the audience.

When I began writing, I had no idea the poem would go where it did. That's not unusual, and it's related to what you asked about earlier—my sense of a poem as a search. While I sometimes do know what I'm investigating, most often I start writing without any knowledge of subject or destination; I simply have a kinesthetic feeling that something is there, and my task in that moment is to become an open gathering place for some congregation of self, language, knowledge, voice, and music. That gathering makes the poem. We sometimes then call this the "muse," a word needed because it's so clear that it is not solely the conducting self that makes poems. I began, then, to write that morning because of the plum tree—it was in wild blossom, as it is just now, as I answer this question, in wild blossom outside the same window. The tree was, as Rilke put it in *Sonnets to Orpheus*, inside my ear. But once the poem brailled its way to "seduction," the young man from the concert hall leapt up to meet it, as a fish comes to some brightly-tied fly. How this happens is a mystery to me. That it happens is for me the *sine qua non* of writing at all. If some discovery and shift of being into new comprehension doesn't occur, whatever has found its way into words is not, for me, a poem—it's notes and jottings.

The question "What in this unpleated world isn't someone's seduction" felt like a discovery—and many people, after reading it in *The New Yorker* asked me about that one word, "unpleated." But for me that line was the opening of a gate, not the poem's destination. The poem then needed to travel somewhere further and unexpected, to find something I did not yet know I was seeking. It wasn't complete until it reached the bee, and the idea of "sumptuous disturbance" linking its separate emplacements. The poem's ponderings have something to do with beginnings (a plum tree in blossom), youth (the two performing musicians), eros, the power of beauty to overwhelm and also its transience, and something to do also with what is kept, what can be kept, from an experience of having been shaken. The largeness and beauty of Evan Chambers's music shook me as much as the Mahler, and left me permeable to Mahler's constellations of gorgeousness and vanishment in a way that required of me some response. This poem.

I have given you, necessarily, a specific answer to a general question. But your question includes its own answer, for me, in a single one of its words: "unexpected." Poetry for me will always build a chamber of the paradoxical and unexpected. For those things to enter, what's knowable must branch into what could not have been known, until the poem itself makes a path by its own explorations.

Earlier, you mentioned one of your assays. I wanted to talk with you about them. You're one of the few contemporary poets who have been writing them with any frequency. They qualitatively differ from most of your other poems insofar as they insist upon more development—even though this is still a very selective development. They're great contributions to a neglected subgenre.

Thank you. I think of these poems as related to the centuries-old *meditatio*, the meditation poem, but in a current-day diction and strategy. They are a way to look at something and think around and through it in a concentrated way. I stumbled into the form, though; it wasn't something I set out to explore. The first-written of my assay poems was the one about Edgar Allan Poe. I had been writing about Poe in the essay-lecture on hiddenness in poetry we spoke about earlier—isn't it interesting how that theme keeps coming back into this interview?—and I'd spent a long time rereading his stories and critical writing. I finished the essay and thought I was done. Then, a couple years later, I was working for a month at Yaddo, where tradition says Poe wrote "The Raven"—though long before it was Yaddo, back when it was a trout-fishing farm. The story goes that a child of the family that lived there heard a man marching around in the woods shouting "Nevermore!," and I'm sure that is why Poe came back to me when I was there—now in the form of a poem. But because all the thinking I'd been doing about him was in prose, the poem (which is in the book *After)* carried that essaylike quality of speech. The voice still had in it much mind, the flavor of thinking and speaking that comes when you're working in prose.

The language was more discursive.

Exactly. And yet it wasn't prose either. It was poetry that carried some rhythm and music of thought that is thinking, not singing, and when it was done, I looked for some title that might better prepare a reader for what it was, and came up with the idea of "assay." At least one person has assumed I came to this word through Kenneth Rexroth's book of essays titled *Assays,* but it wasn't through that lineage, nor through Montaigne or through the French. That linguistic rootstock must of course be part of it, but consciously, the word arrived by way of scientific journals: I live with a molecular biophysicist, and his magazines sometimes have ads for $500,000 assaying machines on the back cover. I've also spent a great deal of time in recent years talking with scientists. So, in my own sense of it, my assays are hybrid, connected to both the French *essayer* ("try") and to the assaying of science, in which you take a substance and put it through some evaluative process to see what it's made of, in a molecular way. It's that kind of assaying—the California forty-niner gold miners would take their nuggets to the assaying office to find out how much gold was in it, and of what grade. That sense of a disassembling into parts—done not through chemistry but through imagination—is what underlies the tone of my poem-assays. When I finished the Poe, I assumed it was one-of-a-kind. But the voice and strategy somehow caught me, and kept coming back.

Your assays are fascinating because they walk that fine edge between discursive prose and poetic utterance. Kenneth Koch worked in a similar vein, but he was more verbose. Not a lot of people have explored this subgenre.

Yes. That's another perceptive connection on your part—Koch's *New Addresses* is a book I love. Something may have been in the air; W. S. Merwin's *Present Company* is another book along similar lines. My assays, like the work in both those books, are often variations on ode—they're written in the grammar of second person—though a little more over towards *meditatio* and prose and a little less celebratory than odes classically are. I don't think art is ever made wholly from scratch; as in nature, the new is made mostly by recombination. Occasionally, there's some accident of happy mutation, and you find you've done something perhaps slightly different than what's been seen before. I don't think of my assays, or my pebbles, as offering some new form—but for you to say you see something new in them, that not many others are doing, makes me happy. I've always found enormous pleasure in R. P. Blackmur's statement that a good poem expands the available stock of reality.

I like the assays because they have information. It's great to read a poem and think, "This has some great information in it, and I couldn't get it any other way than in this poem."

Yes—when information turns into an experience of lyric epiphany, whether small or large, the mystery of how that has happened makes the poem even better. Galway Kinnell is a master of this, I think, in certain of his poems. And one of the poems by Czesław Miłosz I love most is "Winter." It begins lyrically and then goes through an intensely sand-papery, rough-talking passage, full of opinion and history and judgment, then returns to lyricism at the end. For me, the experience of going through a different kind of language, a different condition of mind, makes that second turn into beauty, image, and lyricism even more overpowering. A fact, set into a poem, can have the same effect. We rebound into more powerful feeling for having traveled into the realm of intellectual knowledge as well.

More than the poetry of most of your peers, your poems have an incredibly rich relationship to philosophy. While Zen Buddhism informs many of the poems in Given Sugar, Given Salt, *your essays in* Nine Gates *demonstrate a broader understanding of other philosophers and philosophical systems. Do you see yourself as a poet-philosopher?*

If by poet-philosopher you mean a person interested in inquiry, yes, certainly. But I also feel some discomfort at such a label—it's rather too grand, and poetry is a verb, not a noun. I am still uncomfortable with even the sentence, "I'm a poet," though I've come to say it more often than I'd prefer. In any moment you can possibly think, "I'm a poet," you're necessarily not one. For the person who is actively being a poet, the poem is all that is there, making itself somehow through you, the way quartz makes itself by some intersection of pressure and molecules and time. How can we say then what happens? The language makes the poem, my life makes the poem, the culture makes the poem, the precipitating event or question or blow of beauty makes the poem. In the end, poems make poems. Yet the person holding the pen cannot be dispensed with.

Still I was, not long ago, a guest on the public radio program *Philosophy Talk*, hosted by two Stanford philosophers. Usually their "literary" guests have been writers who've had as well some formal philosophical training—Troy Jollimore, Rebecca Goldstein. I'm not sure how they came to invite me. I am a person who does sometimes read philosophy, and I refer to various philosophers in my poems—Kant, Empedocles, Novalis, Simone Weil come to mind—but I tend to read philosophy for the poetry, rather than in any systematic way. Still, when they asked me to suggest a theme for our conversation, I found I did have one, "Poetry As a Way of Knowing," and we went on to have quite a good conversation on the subject.

Might you say a little more about what systems of thought (or, more specifically, which philosophers) have influenced your poetry—and in what ways?

Poets are magpies, lifting whatever glints brightly into the nest. As a young writer, I carried Wittgenstein's notebooks with me, as I described it, "for the poetry"; that is, not because I understood his ideas in any systematic way, but so that a phrase, a sentence, a proposition, a way of looking and knowing, might have its way with me, might set its hook. Metaphor-making itself asks of its writer a kind of pantheism, of idea and of self. Parallel structure, meanwhile, and the sonnet's turn, are magnetized by the structures and reassurances of logic. Mythological and Jungian comprehensions have informed me over my lifetime—not taken literally, but as fields of expanded understanding, association, companionship. Rhetoric has been an abiding lighthouse.

Each of these things is a vocabulary of both feeling and thinking, a way of understanding the world that is part of the spectrum by which I see and by which my poems speak. I would not put Zen first, or even as given influence in any poem, though many people have come to write about me in that way. My poems are, I promise, not illustrations of any particular Buddhist teachings or of "awakened" mind. They are just my poems. Whatever of Zen is in me will be in them, is all. But I don't comb through my work or anyone else's and gauge poems as systems of thought. Poetry stands most happily under Whitman's supple banner: "Do I contradict myself? Very well, then I contradict myself."

And now I will contradict myself, just a little, to say that I do think that poems embody moral and ethical ground, and that that dimension matters. By this I mean very simply that I think poems are consequential: they affect how we come to lead and feel our lives. The way this works itself out in art can't ever be programmatic, if the art's any good—it needs on the contrary to be complicating, subtle, questioning, doubtful and doubting. And yet, I would say that somewhere in the revision process one of the questions worth asking a poem is if its words are offering something you would be willing to stand behind with your life. Osip Mandelstam was sent to the gulag for a few lines in which he set loose his opinion of Stalin. The phrase "dulce et decorum est" altered two cultures, two millennia apart, in opposite directions. So I suppose I'll say this: good poems can be, must be, heterodox, but not frivolous, in the stances they take in the face of our shared human sufferings. They enact investigations in which every possible path needs to be open, but they also wear the consequences of action and speech. This is, I believe, not a very postmodern thing to say. Yet I believe it.

Anonymous. "Westron Wynde." *Oxford Book of English Verse*. Ed. Christopher Ricks. Oxford: Oxford University Press, 1999.

Cansever, Edip. "Table." *Dirty August: Poems by Edip Cansever.* Trans. Julia Clare Tillinghast and Richard Tillinghast. Jersey City: Talisman House, 2009. (See Permissions Page.)

Hirshfield, Jane. "Three Foxes by the Edge of the Field at Twilight." *The Lives of the Heart*. New York: Harper Perennial, 1997.

______. "Thoreau's Hound: On Hiddenness." *Brick: A Literary Journal:* Fall 2001.

______. "Critique of Pure Reason," "The Present," "China," "Narrowness," "Perishable, It Said," "The Question," and "French Horn." *Come, Thief.* New York: Alfred A. Knopf, 2011.

Szymborksa, Wisława. "The End and the Beginning." *Poems New and Collected.* Trans. Stanislaw Baranczak and Clare Cavanagh. New York: Harcourt Brace and Company, 1998. (See Permissions Page.)

Poetry:

Come, Thief, Alfred A. Knopf, 2011
After, HarperCollins, 2006
Pebbles & Assays, letterpress chapbook, Brooding Heron Press, 2004
Given Sugar, Given Salt, HarperCollins, 2001
The Lives of the Heart, HarperCollins, 1997
The October Palace, HarperCollins, 1994
Of Gravity & Angels, HarperCollins, 1988
Alaya, Quarterly Review of Literature Poetry Series, 1982

Nonfiction:

Nine Gates: Entering the Mind of Poetry, HarperCollins, 1997
The Heart of Haiku, Kindle Single, 2011

As Editor and Translator:

The Ink Dark Moon: Love Poems by Ono no Komachi and Izumi Shikibu, Women of the Ancient Court of Japan (with Mariko Aratani), Vintage Classics, 1990
Women in Praise of the Sacred: Forty-Three Centuries of Spiritual Poetry by Women, HarperCollins, 1994
Mirabai: Ecstatic Poems, with Robert Bly; Beacon Press, 2004

Putting Blood Back into Words: An Interview with Martín Espada

Perhaps more than any of his peers, Martín Espada embodies the political tradition in American poetry. A poetic descendent of Walt Whitman, via Pablo Neruda, Espada sees poetry as a means towards understanding and change. A pervasive theme in his work is justice: how we struggle to achieve it; how others are denied it; and how we must recognize that the plights of the disenfranchised are relevant to our lives. But no matter how persistently he pursues his themes, Espada's poems are never tiresome or strident; rather, they are like windows through which we begin to see what was once invisible. A former tenant lawyer, Espada is a persuasive orator who can move an audience from indifference to empathy. He is the recipient of many awards, including the Paterson Poetry prize, several NEA fellowships, a United States Artists Fellow Award, and the Paterson Award for Sustained Literary Achievement.

You have managed time and again to do something rare in American letters—write an effective, enduring political poem. Can you speak to this?

I have various ideas when it comes to writing a political poem. Obviously this is something with which I'm closely associated. Others have raised this issue with me before, often couched—for lack of a better term—in certain kinds of *objections*. Readers and critics in this country often begin with negative assumptions about political poetry.

We spend a great deal of time in this field looking for traditions, antecedents and influences so that we can link them together, point to them and say "Aha!" We don't do that when it comes to the tradition of political poetry in this country. I think this is a shame, a great loss, because there are poets we are not reading that we ought to be reading. Poets like me belong to a tradition that is largely unacknowledged and unrecognized. As readers, we need to search for political poetry. It's almost a random process. Because we don't recognize a tradition of such poetry in our country, we often do not look to the best political poets and political poems. If we do encounter a political poem, we don't *define* it as such.

For me, the tradition of political poetry in this country starts with Walt Whitman. Whitman—whatever one thinks of his politics—is clearly a political poet, a poet not just of democracy but *radical* democracy. There are places in *Leaves of Grass* where he declares his intentions explicitly. If you look, for example, at section 24 from "Song of Myself" Whitman proclaims he is the poet of democracy, and that he is, more importantly, the poet of the downtrodden, an advocate who speaks on behalf of those without an opportunity to be heard. In that section he speaks of "the pass-word primeval" and "the sign of democracy." He says, "Through me many long dumb voices." He says, ". . . voices veil'd and I remove the veil." A motif runs through "Song of Myself": advocacy in relation to people like prisoners, slaves, prostitutes—the most despised people in society. Whitman consciously chooses to identify with them. Obviously, there are places where he identifies with *everybody*, but he keeps returning advocacy for those who have no voice.

From Whitman springs a whole tradition of political poetry that runs North and South. It's not just a matter of looking at the North American lineage, but the Latin American lineage, too, because Whitman really sparked a fire in Latin America.

You address this point directly in The Republic of Poetry, *specifically in how Neruda was influenced by Whitman.*

José Martí introduced Whitman into the Spanish-speaking world. Eventually, Neruda became Whitman's greatest disciple. He kept a portrait of Whitman in his writing desk.

From Whitman, we see the tradition of political poetry build and build. At some point along the way, the tradition got buried in this country. It was dismissed entirely, as if it never happened. Poets writing political poems, if they were acknowledged at all, were sanitized. The political voice was disregarded or trivialized. That the tradition of political poetry was buried is not an accident.

In the 1930s, the tradition of political poetry in this country was quite strong. One could trace a line from Whitman to Langston Hughes and other African-American poets writing very good political poetry: Sterling Brown, Claude McKay, and so on. Whether they were part of the Harlem Renaissance or not, African-American poets in the 1930s were writing political poems like mad. There were also urban, working-class poets who called themselves the Proletarian Poets, or the Anvil Poets, because they were associated with that small press. The best among them was a guy named Edwin Rolfe. Rolfe published a collection of poems in the 30s called *To My Contemporaries*. He then went off to fight in the Spanish Civil War. Because of this, he became ultimately known as the poet of the Abraham Lincoln Brigade, the brigade of volunteers from the United States who fought against fascism in Spain. Rolfe returned to the Unites States and was blacklisted for being a communist and a Lincoln veteran. He couldn't publish anywhere. He wrote a beautiful poem called "Elegía" about the Spanish Civil War. Ernest Hemingway read it and cried, but Rolfe couldn't publish it anywhere in this country. He ended up having it translated into Spanish and published in Mexico. Years later, he published his collection of Spanish Civil War poems, called *First Love*. It was, for all intents and purposes, self-published. Nobody cared. No one read it. He finally dropped dead of a heart attack at an early age.

Rolfe's fate was typical of the Proletarian Poets, the radical poets and the revolutionary poets of the 1930s and 40s in this country. What killed them? It wasn't their political excesses, although they were there. It was McCarthyism. We tend to forget McCarthyism wasn't only a political reaction, but a cultural one as well. Quite aside from what McCarthyism did in the political realm, there was a terrific impact on the culture, on poets and their poetry. Blacklisted poets could no longer teach in certain places, could no longer publish, could no longer speak in public, could no longer get even menial jobs. Some of them disappeared. Others, like Rolfe, dropped dead. Rolfe had the good fortune of being rediscovered years later by Cary Nelson, a terrific critic and historian based in the University of Illinois, Champaign-Urbana.

If one reads these poets, it's much more difficult to talk about political poetry as something that doesn't work. It works for *them*. Yet, many have come to accept the conventional wisdom of the New Critics and the judgment of the Agrarians. Allen Tate and Harold Bloom told us what political poetry can and cannot do, what it is and what it isn't. We rarely challenge their assumptions or look at the tradition of political poetry in historical terms. If we did we would realize there are all these buried treasures. If we unearthed them we might begin to see some exciting alternatives.

Another thing to keep in mind is that there are plenty of great works that aren't explicitly political, or have been separated from their political context, or sanitized, and therefore are not defined as political. Some might argue Milton's *Paradise Lost* is political. *Leaves of Grass* is political. *Spoon River Anthology* is political. People don't think of Edgar Lee Masters as a radical, but he was. He was a lawyer, Clarence Darrow's law partner in Chicago. That tells you a great deal about him as an advocate. You can see his political sensibility clearly in the persona poems that comprise *Spoon River Anthology*. In those poems, he often speaks in the voice of the damned and despised. Spoon River's cemetery is peopled by more than just the town banker and town judge. Through Masters's eyes, you see the marginalized that were spat upon. One of the most moving poems in *Spoon River Anthology* is called "Yee Bow," named after the one Chinese resident in town. He was a child who felt dislocated in Spoon River, and ended up murdered in the schoolyard. What's that poem doing there? It's there because Masters is a political poet and *Spoon River Anthology* is a work of political art.

Although they began as populist poets, Edgar Lee Masters and Carl Sandburg have been widely avoided in college literature classrooms.

Yes. It's all about "the bubble reputation." In Shakespeare's *As You Like It* Jaques makes a famous speech about the "Seven Ages of Man." In that speech he refers to "the bubble reputation." It's the perfect metaphor: that which rises suddenly pops. Sandburg won a couple of Pulitzer Prizes, but contemporary critics and poets treat him as if he had a bad skin rash. It's no coincidence that Masters's book was the most popular volume of poetry of its time: now almost no one cares. Even Langston Hughes, who is read everywhere, is simultaneously trivialized, regarded as a minor poet by certain critics.

Hughes's contributions are largely ghettoized, too. He's a black American poet first, not an American poet.

Definitely. The common denominator for all of these poets is a radical humanism that is reflected in the political poems they wrote. Their voices have been silenced over time. In order to appreciate them, we have to reject the received wisdom that such things can't be done. In the last few years, however, I have seen more and more poets returning to political poetry. Why? Because the times demanded it, because even those poets who ordinarily feel uncomfortable expressing themselves in political terms and taking on political subjects simply could not stand it anymore. They looked around and saw George W. Bush waging terrible wars. They also saw the emerging Age of the Know-Nothing. They saw hostility, coming from Bush's administration and filtering out into the culture, to ideas themselves, to literacy itself! In the recent campaign we saw Barack Obama attacked because he was "eloquent"—as if his very eloquence was indicative *per se* of some deceptive practice.

Moreover, many believed his eloquence and intellect were somehow anti-American, whereas George W. Bush was celebrated for his folksy, down-to-earth persona.

There was such a pride in ignorance, not only in this campaign but also over the last eight years, in the Bush White House, that it alarmed even poets who don't normally speak in a political vocabulary. I began to see more of these poems. I felt like saying, "Welcome aboard! What kept you?" This sudden resurgence in political poetry is indicative of an awakening in the culture as a whole. People are becoming more alert to the real threats that surround them. There is, too, this whole battle over what language does politically—and poets have some say in that. One legacy from the Bush years is that we have seen language divorced from meaning. Violently so. In place of meaning there are these euphemisms that evolve. The classic "WMD" for Weapons of Mass Destruction. "Enhanced interrogation" for torture.

The language has also enabled us to turn human lives into abstractions.

Yes. And what the poets can do, given our sensitivity to language, is to respond by reconciling language with meaning, putting the blood back into words.

Your poems do this quite a bit, in part through the precision of the metaphors in your lines.

I have my own rules. When it comes to writing a political poem, I begin with the language itself: metaphor, simile, the image. My work is grounded in image, as it relates to all five senses. I also need to have a substantial connection to the subject.

Your poems almost invariably begin with a particular instead of a generalization.

Yeah, I don't open a newspaper, point to a headline and say, "That's my poem today." I don't think anybody can pull that off, with a handful of exceptions.

You're not making political poems ready-to-order.

No. I don't begin with a political statement and work back to the poem. Just the opposite. The poem begins with something concrete, organic. If that ends up working towards a political statement, so be it. But that is secondary to the process, secondary to the language. It's also secondary to the tale being told. A lot of my poems are obviously narrative poems, and for me a good story is a good story. I was always taught that conflict lies at the heart of a good narrative; therefore a political subject suggests itself naturally to me. But this subject must begin with the particular and the individual. These individuals are people who have walked through my life and had no opportunity to gain access to the culture as a whole. They are invisible. One of my obligations as a poet is to make them visible.

Obviously your experience as a tenant lawyer has fueled many of these particulars. One word I found repeated over and over again in Alabanza *was "landlord." What does that word mean to you?*

Think of the language itself: *land lord*. This is language from the feudal days. This is language that suggests power exercised with impunity. Landlord: there's no recourse from that. "Landlord" does not come from a democratic vocabulary. It comes from the days when aristocracy and monarchy ruled the land. Now, the fact that we still use this phrase *tells* us something about the political and economic relationships between those who own the land and those who live on it. There is still a feudal aftertaste to these relationships, a lingering legacy of that bygone age. Most poor people rent, and that puts them at the mercy of those who own the space. I think it's hilarious that, in the midst of this economic crisis, poor people were blamed for all those bad mortgages when, in fact, the vast majority of poor people rent. Most of these people do not have leases. They are usually living in housing without documentation, on a month-to-month basis. The landlord in those circumstances can get rid of you for a good reason, a bad reason, or no reason. Enter the tenant lawyer.

I graduated from Northeastern University Law School in 1982 and worked in the Boston Latino community for a number of years. I was supervisor of a program called Su Clínica Legal in Chelsea, which is a gateway city, a city of immigrants outside of Boston. In the last generation, these immigrants have come largely from the Spanish-speaking Caribbean and Southeast Asia. Chelsea is not only one of the poorest cities in Massachusetts, it also has some of the poorest housing conditions. We dealt with eviction defense, no-heat cases, rats and roaches, and crazy landlords. That was an experience that affected me profoundly, and reflects itself in my poetry. You can't see the naked exercise of power and greed every Thursday morning in District Court—on what they call Eviction Day—and not be changed by that somehow, whether you're a lawyer or a poet.

Some of your poems, like many of Neruda's, boast a rhetorical fullness, an almost oratorical quality. However, many of them are stunningly terse. The depth of your range is quite deceptive, insofar as many of your poems, though linked by similar subject matter, are quite different in form, tone, and scope. I think of a poem like "DSS Dream" which has the kind of surreal terseness I sometimes see in Gregory Orr and contrast it to the title poem from Imagine the Angels of Bread, *which has a high rhetorical power. Considering their significant differences, I'm amazed both poems come from the same pen.*

I do try to write and speak in different voices. There are times for me when a poem is complete after a single image is sketched on the page. There's something about that image hanging in the air that feels complete to me, whether it's the influence of haiku or other poets who write with great conciseness and focus. I'm not sure. I think of that William Carlos Williams poem ["The Great Figure"] about the fire engine—an image captured perfectly, not only the object itself but the way that object feels to us.

The "thing" communicates.

Yes, and if you can write a poem in a single sentence and that sentence hangs on the page, says everything you have to say, I consider it to be a feat.

A few of your most notable poems are each one sentence arranged across several lines. I'm thinking of "St. Vincent de Paul Food Pantry Stomp" and "Revolutionary Spanish Lesson." These poems are remarkable for their construction.

It's a balancing act to try and keep that one sentence going across the lines. It's a test of skill to see whether or not I can keep it together grammatically and still make it rhythmically interesting. Such things concern me. As you point out, the "rhetorical" poems are also a challenge to write, but in a different way. I don't see a contradiction in speaking through either the terse or oratorical modes. Incidentally, "Imagine the Angels of Bread" has cropped up recently in the wake of the Obama campaign and all his talk about hope and change. It's a result of what I refer to as the political imagination.

It's interesting that you just referred to the political imagination here because you reference the Holocaust in that poem, which many scholars now assert was, among other things, a failure of the human imagination.

There's an argument in that poem, which is not surprising, given that I am a lawyer. The poem is taking a position, and asking the reader or listener to imagine a world where certain radical changes for the good are not only possible but inevitable. At first this seems like an argument for utopianism, a crazy pipe dream, but at the turn two thirds of the way through I reason that if we could imagine a world without slavery and abolish that institution, then we can face the troubles we have now.

That is an effective turn, not least in part because of the reversal of the syntax. In the first portion of the poem, you begin each discreet grouping of images with "This is the year," whereas in the latter half you invert this by beginning with "If" and leading to "then, this is the year." The "if-then" construction is almost syllogistic.

The Holocaust reference occurs in that stanza. What I'm saying there is that if the world could overcome the fascism that led to and perpetrated the Holocaust, then the world today can face and deal with anything. Who was it that imagined a world where the Nazis could be defeated? There were those who looked upon that war machine and said: this can and must be destroyed. That resistance, no matter where you find it, even in places where it was defeated, such as in the Warsaw Ghetto, began with an act of imagination. Resistance begins with the imagination, even when the situation appears worse than hopeless.

And we must cultivate a world in which one has the permission to imagine, which brings us back to Whitman.

Right. Some people, Whitman among them, imagined a nation without slaves, without slave manacles, and over centuries that nation came to be.

When I read through the first few poems in The Republic of Poetry, *I thought you might be moving away from the concrete, particular world you so movingly record in your previous books. Very soon, however, I realized this was not the case. In one of this book's best poems, "The Soldiers in the Garden," you not only render the local details about a specific experience Neruda had squaring off with soldiers from Pinochet's regime, but you conclude the poem in such a way that elevates those local concerns to world-wide relevance.*

We have something to learn from Chile. Part of the problem with American exceptionalism is that it does not look beyond its own borders. We say: "We are the best country in the world, so why bother to look at examples of other nations and cultures?" Yet, one of the things I learned when I visited there in 2004, and when I returned later, was that we had forgotten the lessons of Chile. In 1973, when the U.S. backed the military coup that overthrew its socialist government, Chile was very much in the news. But over the decades, Chile disappeared from our awareness. In Chile, centuries of history were telescoped into just a few decades. If the people of Chile could take their democracy back after seventeen years of Pinochet's dictatorship, then we could take ours back after eight years with Bush. And look what happened two days ago! [Barack Obama was elected President.] We need concrete illustrations of this principle in order to digest that principle thoroughly. Looking at Chile helps us with this process. The anti-communist Pinochet came to power with the support of the U.S., but at what cost? More than three thousand people were killed. Many thousands more were tortured and imprisoned—for what? To protect Chile from communism? For something called "security"? The isms change over time. Terrorism is a new ism.

How many times have we supported mass murder in the name of an abstraction, in the name of an ism?

And by doing so, we engage in deals with the devil. You can't chip off the Bill of Rights one right at a time and get a little more security back every time you give away a right. You can't say, "I wasn't using the First Amendment anyway!" It doesn't work that way. All we have to do is look at the example of Chile. You want to engage in the torture of suspects to keep us safe? Take a look at what torture did to Chile, not only to the individuals who suffered directly from it, but to the psyche of the country as a whole.

Your assertion that we could learn from Chile is a fairly radical one insofar as Americans so rarely look to other nations as models, especially Latin American ones, which we presume are backward and chaotic. But you dipped down geographically into that forbidden landscape and came back wiser. The poem "Not Here" illustrates this perfectly.

Yes. When the Chilean coup happened on September 11, 1973, I was a teenager who was wrapped up in my own petty problems. I didn't think things so far away could affect me. But I have learned to take my sources of inspiration where I find them. Even though my poetry is often associated with very particular circumstances and very particular identities, I'm also a citizen of the world. I may be a Puerto Rican from the East New York section of Brooklyn, but I claim my right as a citizen of the world in poems like the ones I wrote about Chile. I'm not going to let any expectations or labels stop me from doing it.

I was moved by the poem "Black Islands" where so much is communicated through the imagery. Could you talk a little about that poem?

That particular poem was the first of the twelve Chile poems I wrote for *The Republic of Poetry,* and like all the rest of them, it was based on an actual experience. On July 11, 2004, one day before Neruda's birthday, I visited Isla Negra, the poet's famous home on the Pacific coast. I was doing an interview for Chilean television in front of this huge anchor that sits in Neruda's garden. Everywhere I went during this celebration I was the object of curiosity. I was wearing a black hat and raincoat and had a full beard: I looked like Hagrid from the Harry Potter movies. People didn't know who I was or what was going on, but they could see the cameras filming me, and cameras create interest. After I was done talking to the cameras, a man came out of the crowd with his small boy. Without a word, he walked right up to me, lifted the boy up to my eye level, and spoke not to me but the boy. "Son, this is a poet," he said. "He is like Pablo Neruda." I was, as you might imagine, stunned. Aside from the attention directed at me, I was trying to digest the fact of a culture in which something like that could happen. I understood that for most Chileans July 2004 was a highpoint for poetry and Neruda, that this excitement couldn't happen everyday in the streets. But it still happened! And I was amazed that this man would point me out to his son, the way fathers in this country might point to pro football players.

The father was socializing his son to the culture, and for him poetry was a large part of that process.

"Son," he was saying, "this is a moment you will want to remember, and it has something to do with your value system and your priorities." I thought, "What if the world looked like this, if this acceptance of poets as a major part of cultural life was a rule instead of an exception? Readers and writers of poetry in this country spend so much time putting themselves down. We constantly bemoan the fact that our audiences are small, and we blame ourselves for this. We constantly internalize our own marginalization. We minimize our impact on the world. We have to stop doing this.

Poets marginalize one another, too. Our insecurities have lead to a great deal of backbiting and jealousy amongst ourselves.

We have to stop doing that. We have to stop assuming that we have no impact on the culture and society. Why don't we see ourselves as people with the capacity to affect the world and change it for the better? Poets have done this demonstrably in other cultures and at other times in the history of the world. Why not us?

I wonder if you could talk a little about the poem "My Father as a Guitar." It's quite delicate and moving, quite intimate.

"My Father as a Guitar" is one of several poems I've written in the last decade or so about illness. It's a natural process: as you age, people around you get sick and die. Eventually, you join them. Intimacy is a good word to describe that poem, which tracks the relationship one develops with the dying. That poem was about my father, but my wife, who is disabled, who suffered a stroke and a brain hemorrhage in 2001, is also the subject of poems with this theme. Not only did her illness change our family life, it changed my poetry. I necessarily became more focused on thoughts of illness, mortality, and how one survives with some dignity in the dehumanizing world of our medical and economic system, that quickly deprives you of dignity if you happen to be sick. Given my age—I'm 51—more poems will come about this. The losses are starting to add up. In moments such as these I've discovered that people call upon poets to say something, whether at a wake or a funeral or elsewhere. I found myself writing elegies because I was moved by the loss, but also because by presenting this elegy to those who have lost a loved one, I might participate in the process of consolation. In the last few years I have lost a lot of people. There are more coming. In *The Republic of Poetry* there's an elegy for Robert Creeley. More recently, I wrote one for Sandy Taylor of Curbstone Press, who was not only one of my closest friends but a surrogate father and mentor for me.

Your poems to your father and wife deal with loss and suffering, but the language is paradoxically energized by these emotions. When I finish reading one of them I'm not drained or depressed, but enlivened, aware.

When I write a poem about my wife, it is informed by the fact that her battle is not over. Her toughness and resilience are remarkable; indeed, they are the stuff of poetry. It is one thing to recognize that you're in the grasp of a terrible disease or that the brain has suffered a terrible injury; it is another to see how the body fights back. The spirit resists. *That* is the story. *That* is where the poem is.

Not only her resistance, but yours, too.

To some degree, we are talking about the poem itself as an act of resistance. There is a battle for human dignity going on. When you are dealing with catastrophic illness and catastrophic injury, you are subjected to one humiliation after another. You are stripped of everything. Poetry can respond to this humiliation by claiming dignity as a human right. The closer you are to that, whether it be your own situation, or your father, or your wife's, the more intimately and authoritatively you can speak to that particular struggle.

What infuriates me is when I watch people who are sick or injured or dying being humiliated *because* they are sick or injured or dying. Recently, in Liverpool, I did a reading and had a heart problem—nothing serious, but I needed to go to one of their national health clinics. My experience there was incredible. I was seen in less than five minutes. Nobody asked me how I would pay for it. Nobody asked me about my immigration status, yet they knew I wasn't British. Nobody at any time in that process humiliated or dehumanized me, and after years of watching my wife being humiliated and dehumanized in the medical system of this country, I was flabbergasted. Through poetry, I attempt to reclaim her dignity.

Poetry:
The Trouble Ball: Poems, W. W. Norton, 2011
The Republic of Poetry, W. W. Norton, 2006
Alabanza: New and Selected Poems, W. W. Norton, 2004

A Mayan Astronomer in Hell's Kitchen, W. W. Norton, 2000
Imagine the Angels of Bread, W. W. Norton, 1996
City of Coughing and Dead Radiators, W. W. Norton, 1993
Rebellion in the Circle of a Lover's Hands, Curbstone, 1990

The Embrace of Everything: An Interview with Gerald Stern

Gerald Stern is one of America's most celebrated and accomplished contemporary poets, and he's a force of nature. Passionate, ebullient, comical, serious, Stern is a generous conversationalist who enlivens and is enlivened by all manner of human interaction, as this interview, conducted at his home in Lambertville, New Jersey, reveals. Stern—aka "Jerry" to all of his friends—is fascinated by all things at once, which leads not to fragmentation or distraction, but to a wild synthesis of innocence and experience. The breadth of his intellect is astonishing, almost as much as the consistent warmth, passion, and humanity of his poems. As he admits below, he has taught poetry to just about every audience imaginable. He has also won several important awards for his work, including the 1998 National Book Award, the 1996 Ruth Lilly Poetry Prize, and the 2005 Wallace Stevens Award.

In "Someone to Watch Over Me," from Last Blue, *you say, "In this decade I am taking care of the things I love. I'm / sorting everything out starting, if I have to, with the / smallest blossom . . ." Is it possible that these words might serve as a statement of your poetics for the last ten years?*

Yes, I think so. I'm remembering everything. There are two things that move me, besides the technical issues, in poetry: one is an extreme anger, *à la* the Jewish prophets, about injustice and stupidity—maybe more stupidity than injustice, although the two are deeply tied together; and the other is forgiveness, or "lovingkindness," if you will. It's a part of realizing that life is limited, how short it is, and you can't make the radical changes you wanted to make when you were 18 years old. You have to forgive a little bit—but not too much! This lovingkindness that I speak of is also paying close attention to the dear things, such as the hollyhocks, the irises, the weeds, and the flowers, to people you've neglected. Not that I've become in any way saintly; if anything, less so. I'm still myself a mean bastard. I call a spade a spade. I've been doing that all my life. I've been fired from one job after another for fighting with idiots. I'm not sure where this fight comes from—I've never gone through psychoanalysis. I suppose it comes from a certain sense of needing to right things.

In my book of essays, *What I Can't Bear Losing,* there's an essay called "Mother's Day," which is a series of numbered events of crazy political and outrageous things I've done, starting with a poem I wrote when I was 14, on Mother's Day, as a gift to my mother. She and my father were sleeping in our tiny apartment. I woke up and went to the rickety secretary and wrote my poem down. When she woke, I gave it to her in a sealed envelope. She started to cry, not out of sympathy—I'd have been glad about that. My father said, "Hey, couldn't you have gotten her a gift, kid?" And my poem was such a great gift! I remember the first three lines of that poem, which I quoted in that essay: "On Mother's Day and Father's Day / it is the custom now / to harbor deeds of reverence that rival the kowtow." There was a kind of sprung rhythm there, as in Gerard Manley Hopkins.

Many poets write their best work in their midperiod, often when they're in their forties or fifties. You are 85 years old and not only still writing, but writing voluminously, and writing arguably the best poems of your career.

It's true. I write so much I don't even have enough time to appreciate my own poems! It's as if I'm on a crazy journey and I have to visit every place possible, every poem that comes my way. Now I'm doing this in prose too, with a vengeance. So I think it's a good comment you make.

In the seventh line I say, "I would have picked the berries up one berry at a time." I was realizing their glorious individuality, and this amazing gift, their taste, their smell, their beauty, and such. So I think it is so. There's a lot about my life in this poem. Later, for example, I write about "a disgrace involving my seventh grade music teacher," Miss Steiner. I was a beautiful, high tenor whose voice broke over the January break and I became an ordinary baritone. She never forgave me. She hated boys. And then later in the poem: ". . . If it weren't for my large lips / I could have played the French horn." My lips were too big so I switched to the trombone. ". . . If I didn't like mulberries— / one among a million, I know . . ." refers to that fact that nobody eats mulberries; they're kind of disgusting, but I liked them! ". . . and eat them—without sugar— / the way a grackle does his from the downtrodden branches . . ." Now those are branches pushed down by the fruit, which brings in a political image. ". . . I wouldn't be standing on a broken chair, and I wouldn't be shaking; / and if I didn't slide from place to place and walk / with a toothbrush in my pocket and touch one bush / for belief and one for just beauty I wouldn't be singing." All of this is by way of an explanation, I suppose, namely my devotion to and embracing of the deprived, the hopeless, the lost, whatever it is, economically, politically, physically. This is a common theme—identity with the outsider, the unacknowledged—and it could be called sentimental. But I mean what I say. So there is the mulberry, which is unacknowledged and often cut down. I just made this connection now; I identify with this poor fucking little piece of shit fruit.

And this is one of the ways in which you are connected to Whitman.

Yes, I think so, the embrace of everything, the connection with everything, or at least the attempt to do that.

You have often been compared to Whitman. Could you talk about your relationship to Whitman? In what ways do you see yourself as his descendant? In what ways do you see yourself as different?

Charlie [C. K.] Williams just wrote an incredible book about Whitman called *On Whitman*, which has been published by Princeton. At first, I thought, "God, *another* book about Whitman? I've got about ten upstairs in my office. What is Charlie going to say that has not been said?" But he managed to say something new. He talked about what Whitman meant to him, and about the music of the poetry. A little while after the book was published, he got an e-mail from a woman in Tel Aviv who asked him why so many American Jewish poets identify strongly with Whitman. Charlie sent the e-mail to me and I wrote a response to this woman, and explained what I saw as the Jewish connection with Whitman.

I think Jewish poets easily identify with Whitman because he doesn't really come out of the Protestant—the Christian—tradition. There is such a tradition in English poetry whether the poet is an observant Christian or not. Obviously Donne and Herbert are Christian poets; and Byron—even Keats—can be seen as non-Christian, even though the two of them come out of that tradition. I don't think we've entirely resolved *where* Whitman comes from; maybe the *The Bhagavad Gita*, maybe Transcendentalism. When I talk about the Christian tradition, I am talking about terms of reference, origin, and mythology.

I love Whitman, but I came to resent people saying I was "a reincarnation" of him. It's just not true. There are some surface similarities. I, like Whitman, use anaphora a lot. I taught Whitman for years, of course, and read him, but I may have also gotten this syntactical device from Blake or the Jewish Bible. Parallelisms, too: the prophets as well as Whitman use them. So I came to resent people identifying me with Whitman, and I began to resent Whitman because of it, which is illogical of course, but then what's new? Why all the focus on Whitman when I also loved Smart, Blake, Milton, Roethke, late Shakespeare, and Chaucer. Rimbaud as well. Still, in spite of resentments, I love Whitman. I think he was a great poet. And I'm more and more beginning to see that he's a mystic, really, particularly in his middle work, the poems he wrote in his late 30s—a kind of real mystic without realizing it. He thought he was deriving information from the influence of opera, Transcendentalism, Emerson, Thoreau, and such; he thought he was a kind of New England poet, that his journalism stood him in good stead, as well as his sympathy with African Americans at the time (though he didn't take an extreme position), but finally there's something else that maybe even he wasn't totally aware of and didn't pay much attention to; even in his last years, when his powers declined, when he was pushing his fame endlessly, writing letters, living in Camden, New Jersey, the grand old man, revising his work. In any case, if you write in the Protestant tradition, which is the dominant one, it excludes most Jewish poets.

Images of burning occur frequently in your work. You reference burning and fire quite a bit. I imagine the reasons for this are complex and many-layered. Could you discuss some of these?

Yes; there's *Everything Is Burning,* the title of one of my recent books. It just came out in a dual-language, German-English edition in Germany. I toured Germany, went to five cities and gave readings, read even a few in German. My book there is called *Alles Brent.*

I'm not altogether sure why burning is so important to me. You know that the poet is the last to know. *Everything is Burning*—everything is being consumed on a literal level, everything is dying, the Milky Way is dying. We all know that's the case. But another name for burning is living. Everything is alive, everything is turning. I suspect on both of those levels—it's not just that everything is being destroyed, but all of life is occurring. Is living a form of burning? I suppose it is: you start dying when you're born, and I suspect both of those levels are involved in the concept of the title of that book.

Also, I'm older. It's kind of weird being older. When you're in your 80s you look at the life you lived in your 20s and 30s differently than you did when you were in your 70s looking at that, or 60s. You realize the course things take. Now, traditionally, the writers of Europe begin to be more conservative in their old age, those who survived and didn't die before they were 30. Wordsworth is a prime example; he was radical when he was young and became almost reactionary when he was older. I don't find this the case with me, and I don't know why, because I am more radical now than I've ever been. Not necessarily radical politically, but that too. Radical in all kinds of ways, a kind of freedom approach. This reminds me. The other day Anne Marie and I were coming down from Boston to Lambertville. We stopped and had coffee and salads at some horrible diner. I went into the men's room to wash my hands. There was a guy there, I guess my age, at the paper towel dispenser—you know, a movement-directed machine where you have to move your hands to get some paper towels. He handed me one and said: "There's not many of us left." It was so mystical! I don't know what he meant literally; he may have meant World War II veterans—though how would he know if I were a WWII veteran?—or more simply old people, or poets! So what? I loved it. I'll never forget it. There aren't many of us left. You get this sense when you're in your 80s. I just got a copy of the new issue of *The New England Review,* a magazine I respect and have published in from time to time. I looked through it and didn't recognize anyone in the magazine. Some wonderful young poets. Some not so wonderful. I'll leave them alone. They'll go through their own thing: they'll either learn to write or they won't. The world is still going to disappear anyhow. I'm more tolerant now. But there's almost no barrier between me and the other thing—whoever I'm engaged with.

Anne Marie and I were in Rome in January sitting at a restaurant. We were having this really incredible meal. A woman owned this restaurant. She was going out so I said, "You're leaving so early?" She said, "No, I'm coming back." And then she asked, "May I kiss you?" I said sure and I wiped my mouth first with a napkin. (Anne Marie was pissed off that I wiped my mouth first!) So then this woman put her arms around me and kissed me. Her kiss lingered there for ten seconds. But this incident seemed like a normal thing for me. Was it sexual? Did she have a father my age? Was it an Italian-European respect for older people? All of these factors may have been involved.

But whatever it was, there was an opportunity for a connection with her and you weren't going to set a boundary on it.

Exactly. Nor would I be shocked, nor take advantage of it or make an inappropriate comment. It was extremely sweet.

There's a kind of Buddhist element to your outlook there: you accepted the situation and didn't impose your will upon it. Or in more familiar terms, what will be you let be.

Que Sera, Sera! I loved it. This kind of thing happens to you when you're older. I take liberties in my new poems even. I don't care if they're understood or not. I'd like to talk to you about a couple of recent poems that you probably have not heard or seen. The first one is a short poem called "Goat." In Czechoslovakia they had what was called defenestration: they threw their political enemies out of windows. That idea sparked this poem about an argument between two Jews. In The Jewish Bible, the sacrifice of an animal—in this poem a goat—is called *korban*. It's that idea that I'm referring to when, in the final lines of the poem, the rabbis are debating what to do with the broken-necked animal. Can you eat a sick animal? They could argue for hours. "Well you can eat a sick animal if the upper part of the neck was broken and you cut away that dark layer." "No you can't do that, because it says in

Numbers!" "No, you don't consult Numbers . . ."

The second poem is called "Journey." It's a personal memory of being sucker-punched outside a drugstore. This poem is about me. I was I guess 19. There was a drugstore called the Beacon Pharmacy and there was a plaza outside. I was with a friend of mine, a big guy, but he had a bad back from playing basketball. We were sitting eating ice cream and talking philosophy. (I used to have thick glasses but I had surgery ten years ago so now I don't need glasses.) And there were two guys standing in the door as we were leaving. I said, "Excuse me." One of them said, "Fuck you, you kike! Take your glasses off." I said, "Happy to oblige." I took my glasses off and he sucker-punched me. The blood came pouring out of my eye. I came staggering out of the store. There was a bunch of people there. There were two, no three of them, sneering. I could hardly see, there was so much blood pouring down. I walked over to the guy who hit me, picked him up like a rag and started to kill him. They had car bumpers back then that had sharp points extruding from the car. Nine people had to pull me off of him. I was incredibly strong when I was 18 or 19. Nobody could beat me at arm wrestling. I was a piece of muscle. And I was killing him. He would have been dead in 20 seconds but they pulled me off him, took him onto a streetcar and rode off. I discovered that he was a professional boxer. The guy I was with, Billy Kahn, was the son of Ziggy Kahn, a famous athlete who directed the Irene Kaufman Settlement House. He made the discovery and the guy I beat up was disqualified from boxing. I was a sophomore in college at the time. I remember that my eye was swollen for weeks.

Well, those are two examples of what I'm doing now. There's also some political stuff here, a lot of political stuff. I'm reading (at my poetry readings) poems that are more or less available on all levels, ones about Eleanor Roosevelt, for example. I've read one poem about her on so many occasions, I've started to believe that I actually knew Eleanor Roosevelt! Anne Marie said, "You didn't know Eleanor Roosevelt!" "Yes, I did!"

Another poem I recently wrote is called "Died in the Mills." I knew James Laughlin whose father owned J & L Steel Company in Pittsburgh. They had a system of how much they would pay somebody depending on his ethnic origin, how many years he had left to work, and what he did. They were making millions. This poem is about that: it's very political.

I am particularly fond of your recent poems. Most of them, though no more than one page, are marked by an urgency that remains with me long after I have put the book aside. Overall, the poems seem improvised like great jazz: sentences flow forward with exuberance and, because of the absence of punctuation, fuse into unexpected directions. No matter how much you edit and rework your poems—and I'm assuming that you do—they still seem like unpremeditated bursts of feeling when they appear in book form. How do you strike this difficult balance between spontaneity and polish?

God knows! A lot of the newer poems are short, like one statement, like one scream, or one note. Some of them do not have punctuation. And as you wisely observe they seem to be of a moment, without thinking, just bang, wrote it out. Some of them are exactly this. Some of them I spend weeks on to make it *seem* as if they've just been pounded out! I don't care where the narrative—I'll call it a narrative—where the line takes me anymore. I'm interested in communication very much, not interested in obfuscation or evasion, or obscurity, unless obscurity is applicable to a poem, unless it works for a particular aesthetic or philosophical-intellectual reason. But even though I try to be communicative, I know many times I am not because my mind moves from one place to another. I'm very well aware of this. And I know a lot of things. I've been to a lot of places and don't have any shame in mentioning them. There's some solipsism there. I can't help it. So I write about the things I know, about my experience, about things that other people might not.

You know what I did the other day when I was in Boston? My son David has two children. One of them is five-and-a-half years old. His name is Dillon. David asked me, "Dad, you don't have to do this, but how would you like to come to Dillon's kindergarten class and talk to them for ten minutes about poetry?" I said, "I'll do it!" So, I grabbed my *Early Collected Poems*, which is about to come out, because the early poems, I think, are much simpler. They have animals in them, and narratives and such. So, they all sat there, about nine or ten five-year-olds, and I read three poems. I made them repeat certain lines, I told stories, I told them lies they knew were lies, and they delighted in it. I made them sing. Even in those early poems, which I thought were simple, there are complexities. One of them is about a mole. It's called "Underground Dancing." It starts with a black birch tree that used to be in front of my former house. My wife would put a bag of suet in the trees for the birds to consume during the winter. In the last stanza, I say:

> There's a mole singing hallelujah.
> Close the rotten doors!
> Let everyone go blind!
> Let everyone be buried in his own litter.

They loved it! I made them say, "There's a mole singing hallelujah." They didn't know what "hallelujah" meant, but they loved singing it. Then we talked about animals that lived underground. And they went wild! Rabbits, ants, all kinds. They made up animals. I said, "Elephants live underground, that's why they have long trunks, so they could breathe through their trunks." Oh, they loved that, even though they knew it was a lie! The teachers were a little astonished and were worried the kids would tell their mothers and fathers, "This guy told us elephants sleep underground."

As you said earlier, you're not closing down experiences, and you went in there and related to those kids on their level.

That's right. It's the first kindergarten class I've ever taught. I loved it!

In "The Picasso Poem," gathered in Early Collected Poems: 1965–1992, *you write, "I waver between / that world and this. I travel back and forth / between the two. I lose myself / and crawl off singing or come back crying . . ." Do you feel this wavering between two worlds is common for poets? Are poets modern-day shamans in this regard?*

I was on one level confusing my life with Picasso, who was 55 years old in 1936. I wrote the poem when I was 55, in the midseventies. I was thinking of Picasso driving to New York across the Pulaski Skyway, which is something I did, not Picasso. On one level those were the two worlds I was collating, compounding.

I'm always going between two worlds. I see it as a natural thing. In one of my poems I wrote about the year I love: 1910, how important 1910 was. Another time, I can't remember what the poem was, I regret not being born twenty years earlier, when my heroes were alive, like Lewis Mumford and some of those musicians. So, I'm hustling, living in these two worlds, and living in two worlds I'm aware of both of them at once. I'm doing this, but I'm also aware of it. And I try to explain. Maybe it's a religious experience, an encounter with the "other," the word has a power, or an existence, or a reality outside of me, which most people are not aware of. Maybe a lot of poets have that feeling. I think Larry Levis had that, a poet I very much admire.

In "The Picasso Poem" I say:

> . . . I waver between
> that world and this. I travel back and forth
> between the two. I lose myself
> and crawl off singing or come back crying,
> my face wet with misery, my eyes deep holes
> where the dream was lost . . .

There I'm talking about the world I could have had, full of regret that I didn't do that thing and did those 40 other things, like become a painter, for example. In one of the chapters of the book I'm writing now, I talk, ironically, about regret. Why didn't I become a painter, since I was doing a lot of things with crayons and pencils? Why didn't I become a musician?

When I say, ". . . my hands up in their favorite / position, the two unbroken fingers," I'm referring to a time when I had all these broken fingers from playing baseball. Then I say, "cutting the air / thirty feet above the river." This takes me back to my house on the Delaware River, "beside the hostas and the mugo pine, / the dirty bottles and the stones / fixing the boundary for another summer." The boundary of what? Am I doing it literally with a garden, because I used to grow tomatoes and strawberries and such; or am I thinking of what I am going to do that summer, restricting myself, giving myself certain obligations and duties.

Or is that boundary the threshold between two worlds?

Yes, that's there, too. I'm grateful to you for that observation. I was probably doing all of this in a kind of innocence. There's no question that it's not just Picasso's world in 1936 and my world in 1975 that I'm comparing. I'm comparing two other things: a visible world and an invisible world. So that sounds religious, or metaphysical, or transcendental, shamanistic. So many things! That kind of observation gives me a certain quiver.

What are your thoughts about Stanley Kunitz? On the surface, his poetry does not really share much affinity with yours: your poems tend to be more formally and thematically expansive, and seem—for lack of a better word—extroverted. You are also far more prolific than he ever was. Despite these differences, both of you are Jewish-born Americans who, being blessed with longevity and intellectual curiosity, have written some of your best poems in your later years. As Kunitz was, you remain a mentor to a whole generation of younger poets. Could you talk about him and your relationship with him?

I could talk for hours about my connection to Stanley! Let me preface my answer with a story about another poet. I've led an odd life for a poet of my generation. I chose, for whatever reason, not to take workshops, but to write on my own. The only poet I was in touch with from the older generation was W. H. Auden: I took courses with Auden, met with him, and was subject to rejection from him. Back in the fifties, I wrote a horrible long poem called "Ishmael's Dream." In those days we wrote letters. I wrote a letter to Mr. Auden with the poem enclosed and got a note back from him asking if I could come and see him. He was living on Cornelia Street in the Village. My two friends—Jack Gilbert and Dick Hazley—were jealous because we all thought this was going to be the laying on of hands. We discussed what I should wear: should I arrive in a leather jacket like a Pittsburgh tough or wear a suit and tie like a fifties academic? I don't remember what I wore, but when I went to his place, there were three or four other people there talking about theatre and cheese. All I knew about cheese was American, Pimento, and Velveeta! They were New York intellectuals and I was totally uncomfortable. Finally it was getting dark so I asked Auden if he was going to say anything to me about my poem. He said, "Oh, I do like the last ten lines." There were hundreds of lines! I was pissed off at him for years. But I eventually realized those *were* the only good lines of the poem! I don't know why he invited me. Anyway, I eventually found an opportunity to mix with people who were more sympathetic to what I was doing—and Stanley Kunitz was one of them. Theodore Roethke was another. You know they were friends. Roethke was teaching at Lafayette College and Stanley was living down the river in New Hope, Pennsylvania, on Bowman's Hill. Later he taught in Seattle, taking Roethke's place when Roethke was in the hospital. I could have easily gone out there. Jack Gilbert was there. A lot of people from my generation studied with Stanley, but I was too shy, too proud, too ignorant, too lacking in self-confidence, so I didn't meet Stanley until much, much later.

I met him at a couple of readings he gave in New Jersey. Later, I went up to the Fine Arts Workshop in Provincetown. He invited me to read there when *Lucky Life* came out in the late seventies. I went, read, and spent the rest of the evening with him. We stayed up until five in the morning. It was light already when I left. He was an incredible drinker. He drank martini after martini. We became very good friends. I would see him all the time in New York City. I knew his daughters, loved his work. In the last ten years of his life, when he was going through a big revival, we even shared the same editor, Carol Houck Smith, at W. W. Norton. I would also visit him a lot in the Cape. One time he hurt his back. I had a girlfriend at the time and we climbed into my station wagon and got some bundles of sea grass for his garden up in the Cape, for fertilizer. He was so happy! "Put it over there! Put it over there!" We brought it up to him.

Our poems are quite different, but we had a mutual respect for one another's work. Once, after I gave a reading, he walked up to me, put his hands on my cheeks and said to me, "You are the wilderness in American poetry!" He was very supportive of me. Of course I love him and his poetry, too.

There are some similarities in our lives. We both lasted a long time. We were both intent on teaching. I didn't realize until recently how important teaching was and still is to me. I have always helped people out. I wasn't doing it aesthetically, pushing my own stuff on them: whatever they wrote they wrote. Li-

Young Lee was my student, Deborah Digges, Larry Levis . . . I could go on and on. I was at Columbia and NYU; I did the YMHA in New York, I did Iowa for fifteen years; I ran the Poetry-in-the-Schools program in Pennsylvania in the mid seventies. I hired 40 poets and trained them at a summer institute at Bucknell University. You know Edward Hirsch, the president of the Guggenheim Foundation? There's a picture on the wall in the other room of Eddie and me—he was one of the poets I hired in Pennsylvania. I did a lot of this sort of thing. So did Stanley. He was very involved.

But he wasn't as political as I was—on the literal level. I led marches and strikes. I was a labor organizer, too. I was the enemy of the Governor of New Jersey, who tried to fire me for my union activities. Students walked out when he tried to do that. At several colleges this sort of thing happened to me. Stanley was a little more aesthetically motivated. He loved Gerard Manley Hopkins. I love Hopkins, too, but acted on it in a different way. He was more accepting of Eliot than I was. I had total fury at Eliot as a poet, and not just because of his anti-Semitism. Hart Crane was right in saying Eliot set American poetry back 50 years. Of course Pound, I loved Pound. He was a big influence on me when I was a young poet. In "Sam and Morris," a poem I wrote about Pound, I say:

> . . . so young I was, and I was reading my
> Ezra Pound already and I was ashamed of
> what he said about Jews . . .

I end that poem with "Pound, you bastard!" Stanley didn't write poems like this. He didn't hate Pound because of his anti-Semitism. But this is what happened to him. He went to Harvard young, at age 16; he wasn't motivated as a Jew, but as an aesthete. At Harvard they had a system where if you had the highest grades in English, they gave you a three-year scholarship, a Ph.D., and a teaching post there. But they said to him, "You've got the highest grades, and you deserve this, but you know we can't do this for you because you're Jewish." They assumed he would swallow this, but he didn't. For the first time he realized he was a Jew. Much, much later, around 1985, there was a wonderful week-long meeting at a place outside Philadelphia—Cheltenham—a group of six Jewish poets and six Jewish scholars from the Reconstructionist Rabbinical College. Stanley was there, C. K. Williams, Louise Glück, Allen Ginsberg. We had an incredible time arguing back and forth. By this time, Kunitz was very Jewish.

He wrote the most beautiful lyrics. If I was Stanley and I wrote like him, I would be afraid that the poem wouldn't come back to me, that I had lost it. Stanley didn't seem to have this fear because months and months, even years would pass before another extraordinary lyric would occur. Maybe he wrote other poems that he didn't publish. I never talked to him about this. I don't think he did. But he was very, very happy. I loved him and we were very close.

I remember when he had a "false" death, which reminds me of a poem I wrote about him called "Two Daws" about the false dawn before the real one. When he was 99 or 98, he decided it was time to go. Everyone came to visit him: Phil Levine, Galway Kinnell, Sharon Olds, Louise Glück. We each spent fifteen minutes with him, said goodbye, kissed him a hundred times. Then he was taken to a hospice to die. But by then he decided he didn't want to die anymore! He wanted to see his garden in Provincetown, so he came back home. He lived another two years or so. When he did die he passed very peacefully. We all came back again knowing this was the real thing.

I can't explain our closeness because it wasn't a shared lifestyle, it wasn't a shared aesthetic—though, as I've said, I loved his work: he was in a way more literal than me and yet out of the literal came the incisive lyric moment. And he loved my work: I'm grateful for that. A brilliant man. He had an odd life. He was a farmer, and raised his own food. He was in the army, but he wouldn't kill anybody, so they gave him other work to do, like cutting trees down and digging ditches. He was a friend of Auden's. He loved to gossip. He loved to talk to me late into the night about something that happened 30 years before, why they gave the Pulitzer to this one instead of that.

As I said before, Stanley was a great teacher. He taught at Columbia for many years, taught people like Louise Glück, that generation. And then he picked poems for the Yale Younger Poets series. He was incredibly intelligent, Stanley. Someone would ask him a question and he would answer in fully developed, beautiful sentences. You'd have thought he had written his answer out before. He would go on and on, without any interruption, without hemming or hawing.

Maybe that's why he didn't write so voluminously. A lot of his creative energy was spent in conversations.

Possibly. I don't know. Finally, he came from a different place than I did—we all came from different places. His father disappeared and he was the youngest in his family, kind of orphaned. I felt very close to him.

He loved his wife a lot. I used to call him up and she'd answer, and put me on hold and yell "STANLEY, it's Jerry on the phone!" She died before he did. His oldest daughter is a doctor who lives on the West Coast. She's writing poetry, too. He was very close to painters. In his house, at the Cape, there was about three to four million dollars worth of work lying around. Some were on the walls, others on the floor. He knew all the best painters and they'd give him work. I don't know who has them now, or if there's a foundation.

He also founded the Provincetown Fine Arts Center. And Poets House in New York, which was originally located in an old high school in Chelsea. That's the kind of sociopolitical behavior he'd engage in. He wasn't a rebel, but he wasn't an anti-rebel either.

A lot of your new poems are brief bursts of feeling, but occasionally, as in "The Preacher," you give sustained utterance to a long poem.

Exactly. I also have another long poem, called "I," about Isaiah. A 40-page poem. I say, in the introduction:

> All poems start by accident, and every poem worth its salt was unpredicted and, as often as not, has its genesis at a low point in the poet's journey—which turns out to be a good metaphor: Once, I was on a bus going south on Second Avenue in New York, an especially low point, when I saw from my window an odd-looking one-story building made of smooth stone, sort of shining there, at the southeast corner of Twenty-third, with a phrase from Isaiah carved in its side: "This house shall be called a House of Prayer for all People." I pressed the magic strip and jumped out. I had been given a gift—the material for a long poem in the very middle of a busy neighborhood on an as-yet untransformed, unredeemed corner.

> The building was a synagogue, or to be more accurate an ex-synagogue, called the East End Temple. The windows were boarded up, there were building permits pasted and nailed to the plywood, and it was waiting to be rebuilt, remade, or torn down. The building next door—all this I indicate in the poem—was a standard three-story red-brick with a fire escape on the outside. It probably housed the rabbi's study, meeting rooms, classrooms, and the like. It was also empty. My guess is the whole corner will give way to an apartment building for the nouveau-greedy and the House of God will be just a memory, since the whole neighborhood is rousing itself. Across the street, to the west, is the Cosmos Diner, an old local greasy, and to the east, a few blocks distant, is the East River, and Greenpoint, across the way, in Brooklyn. All this is in the poem . . .

I published "I" online in *Blackbird Review.* There's so much in this poem. It's about New York, that building, my mother, full of generalities, madnesses, details, horror, so much. I conclude the introduction with a musing on Isaiah's death:

> Somewhere I read that Isaiah—Proto-Isaiah?—was finally sawn in half for being too insistent, too uncompromising, naming names and the like. I hope he died on the straw instead, or the wool, whatever they used. I don't know where "I" will die.

"Soap" [also gathered in Early Collected Poems: 1965–1992*] is an iconic poem in the way Plath's "Daddy" is iconic. Both poems make allusions to the Holocaust and, though historians have long since concluded that soaps were not made from Jewish bodies, this doesn't make the story—which was widely believed to be true—any less powerful. What were your concerns when you were writing this poem?*

I had a small book, *Underground Dancing,* translated into Polish. When this book came out, I gave a reading from it—with my translator, in Cracow. We loved Cracow! I read to the literary society from that book in English and then my translator and a couple of others who spoke English translated the poems into Polish. I read "Soap" there. A woman in the audience insisted that it was Poles who were turned into soap and not Jews. Poles are great martyrs.

Anyway, "Soap" is an interesting poem. It came about as an accident. As the poem indicates, I was in a place buying some unguents and soaps, and then I started to think about the mythology of burned Jews being turned into soap. I guess I never truly believed that myself, but I did for the sake of the poem: it became representative or symbolic; it became the act of metaphor. Phil Levine and I used to send each other poems, so I sent him "Soap." "I like the poem," he said, "but I don't like the beginning." I kept the beginning, but he may have been right. I suppose, technically, it can be confusing.

I have written four or five Holocaust poems. My favorite one to read is "Adler." Jacob Adler was, as you probably know, a great actor. He was so famous that John Barrymore used to come to watch him perform. He was one of the greatest actors of history, at a time when the Jewish theatre was thriving. There were 23 Jewish theatres in a three-block area on Second Avenue on the Lower East Side of Manhattan. One of them is left. Adler wrote a play called *The Jewish King Lear.* I talk about that in the poem, where everybody goes outside afterwards to discuss it, and I'm happy that they are not put on cattle cars and murdered. I knew Adler's daughter. There is the Stella Adler Acting School in New York, which is extremely powerful and important. I wrote a play, *Father Guzman,* about a crazy Jewish priest that was put on there several times. It is set in Venezuela, and it takes place in a giant cardboard box. The priest turns out to be a Jewish intellectual from New York. But that's another story . . . "Soap" is an interesting, bitter, angry poem.

It begins with this terse phrasing, the givens are strange—"Here is a green Jew"—and moves from there.

Yes. Let me read you the first few lines:

> Here is a green Jew
> with thin black lips.
> I stole him from the men's room
> of the Amelia Earhart and wrapped him in toilet paper.
> Up the street in *Parfumes*
> are Austrian Jews and Hungarian,
> without memories really,
> holding their noses in the midst of that
> paradise of theirs.
> There is a woman outside
> who hesitates because it's almost Christmas.

"I think I'll go in and buy a Jew," she says.
"I mean some soap, some nice new lilac or lily
to soothe me over the hard parts . . ."

What's interesting here is that the Jew has been contained and marketed for consumption by Christians.

Yes. And there's the bitter hatred of the myth itself. Towards the end of the poem, I "move between worlds"—as I do in "The Picasso Poem"—and imagine myself as a European Jew:

My counterpart was born in 1925
in a city in Poland—I don't like to see him born
in a little village fifty miles from Kiev
and have to fight so wildly just for access
to books, I don't want to see him struggle
half his life just to see a painting or just to
sit in one of the plush chairs listening to music.
He was dragged away in 1940
and turned to some use in 1941 . . .

There is anger there, but I keep a distance. There isn't any self-pity.

It's a hard poem that deals directly with some hard truths.

Exactly. Here in America we claimed that we didn't know what was happening in Europe, that we weren't informed. The truth is we were so close to fascism ourselves. That's why F. D. R. didn't intervene on behalf of the European Jews until we conquered Germany. Many Jews today are angry with F. D. R. for his inaction, but there was so much anti-Semitism in America that it would have been difficult for him to make any move. There was the America First Party, there was Lindbergh, Ford, and Father Coughlin. There were the rednecks; there was the Old South, and he needed to get reelected. The American Jew hid his head in the sand. The rabbis gave sermons in the synagogues about how terrible Hitler was, like Haman who persecuted the Jews in the book of Esther. But the American Jews never suffered themselves as the European Jews. The feeling here is guilt.

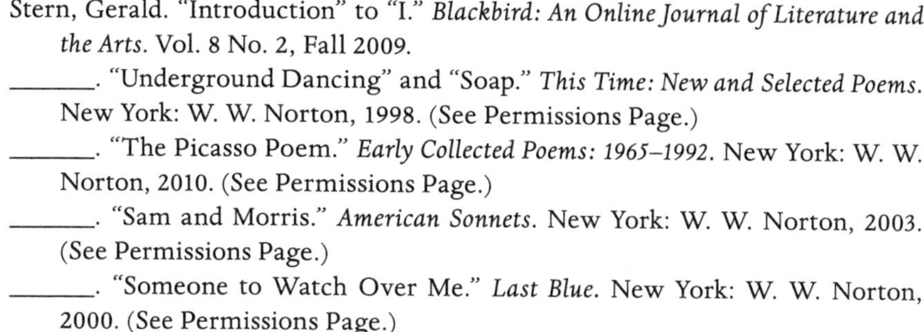

Stern, Gerald. "Introduction" to "I." *Blackbird: An Online Journal of Literature and the Arts*. Vol. 8 No. 2, Fall 2009.

______. "Underground Dancing" and "Soap." *This Time: New and Selected Poems*. New York: W. W. Norton, 1998. (See Permissions Page.)

______. "The Picasso Poem." *Early Collected Poems: 1965–1992*. New York: W. W. Norton, 2010. (See Permissions Page.)

______. "Sam and Morris." *American Sonnets*. New York: W. W. Norton, 2003. (See Permissions Page.)

______. "Someone to Watch Over Me." *Last Blue*. New York: W. W. Norton, 2000. (See Permissions Page.)

Poetry:

In Beauty Bright, W. W. Norton, 2012
Early Collected Poems, 1965–1992, W. W. Norton, 2010
Save the Last Dance: Poems, W. W. Norton, 2008
Everything Is Burning, W. W. Norton, 2005
Not God After All, Autumn House Press, 2004
American Sonnets, W. W. Norton, 2002
Last Blue, W. W. Norton, 2000
This Time: New and Selected Poems, W. W. Norton, 1998
Odd Mercy, W. W. Norton, 1994
Bread Without Sugar, W. W. Norton, 1992
Two Long Poems, Carnegie Mellon University Press, 1990
Leaving Another Kingdom: Selected Poems, Harper & Row, 1990
Two Long Poems, Carnegie Mellon University Press, 1990
Lovesick, Perennial Library, 1986
Paradise Poems, Random House, 1984
The Red Coal, Houghton Mifflin, 1981
Lucky Life, Houghton Mifflin, 1977
Rejoicings: Selected Poems, 1966–72, Fiddlehead Poetry Books, 1973
The Naming of Beasts, Cummington Press, 1972
Pineys, Rutgers University Press, 1971

Nonfiction:

Stealing History, Trinity University Press, 2012
What I Can't Bear Losing, Trinity University Press, 2009
What I Can't Bear Losing: Notes from a Life, W. W. Norton, 2004
Selected Essays, Harper & Row, 1988

Poems Woven from a Sacred Thread: An Interview with Nathalie Handal

More than most English-language poets living in the United States, Nathalie Handal's poetry possesses a global consciousness. Informed by her rich and varied ethnic heritage (French-American of Palestinian parents from Bethlehem, born in Haiti, and whose family now resides in Latin America), and by her identification with the Palestinian Diaspora, this consciousness is made manifest by a sustained lyric intensity, which, though often passionate, is masterfully controlled. A frequent world traveler ("It's only when I am moving and can catch my *longings* that I feel whole"), the discussion below demonstrates Handal's ability to center herself and find "home" in the moment, wherever she may be. She has earned many honors and fellowships, including a 2011 Gold Medal for the Independent Publisher Book Award, a 2011–12 Lannan Foundation Fellowship, the 2011 Alejo Zuloaga Order in Literature Award, the 2006 Mendana Literary Award, and the 2002 Pen Oakland/Josephine Miles National Book Award. Currently a professor at Columbia University and part of the MFA Faculty at Sierra Nevada College, she also lectures internationally, recently in Africa and as Picador Guest Professor, Leipzig University, Germany.

In his blurb for Love and Strange Horses, *Yusef Komunyakaa writes that your "cosmopolitan voice belongs to the human family." In reading the book, I would agree that there are a number of ways in which your poems transcend a national consciousnesses and in so doing cross both geographical and ideological borders. Could you discuss some of the ways in which you see your poems doing this?*

The simple act of writing a poem transcends boundaries. That is what art does: it places the specifics of our experience into a wider context. Our story, then, is not limited to a geographical or historical context but becomes a global one, a human one. My experience has been one of borders—Palestine/Israel; Haiti/Dominican Republic; France/United States. Today these borders don't exist in my mind in that they are no longer fragments but part of one thread, weaving together what might seem unweavable. All the different images I have grown up with strangely and beautifully coexist inside of me. And of course, multiple languages inhabit my pages, and as grammatically and rhythmically varied as they are, they find their way together to create a different type of movement and music.

You seem determined to place your work in the context of world literature. One of the more obvious ways you do this is through the numerous citations to world poets throughout your work. In Love and Strange Horses *alone, you refer to Anna Akhmatova, St. Augustine, Jorge Luis Borges, Constantine Cavafy, Mahmoud Darwish, François Jacmin, Ingrid Jonker, Federico García Lorca, Louis MacNeice, Amado Nervo, Octavio Paz, Fernando Pessoa, Yannis Ritsos, and Voltaire. And there are probably others I've missed. Not only is this a long list, but these writers are quite different from one another for a number of reasons. How do they come together through you?*

These poets are cited in the book because I felt connected to their work at one point or another. I did not think, "this one is South American," or "this one is Greek." Poetry converses and is inclusive—eliminating whatever marginalizes us or defines us rigidly. In terms of their aesthetic differences, although there are writers I constantly return to, I read widely. If a line by one of these poets comes to mind or finds itself on my pages while I am writing, I allow it. Why not?

Do you see yourself as someone in search of a home or as a citizen of the world?

I'm a citizen of the world. But mainly, I'm a poet and on the page "nation" does not exist in a geographical sense. Home is where I am at the moment. It is wherever my parents are. And it is also where I return to—Bethlehem, Paris, New York. Home always comes back to me, even when I think I've lost it.

In your poem "In January, Amor y Lluvia,*" you write, "I would never abandon Darwish." Although you cite and allude to a range of poets from varying geographies and historical periods, you seem especially connected to Mahmoud Darwish. Could you take some time to reflect upon the many ways he influences your work?*

I met Mahmoud Darwish in my early twenties while he was in exile in Paris. Until then, his was the only work I could go back to in order to help me understand the empty mountain inside of me, help me understand my contradictions and my experience as a Palestinian—of being between here and there, of knowing a place so deeply yet not knowing how to belong to it as I am told I should. Soon after we met, I started writing for his journal, *Al-Karmel*, one of the most important in the Arab world. He gave me my first interview assignment: none other than Allen Ginsberg—who admired Darwish. It was a monumental moment for me. The night before I interviewed Ginsberg, he wrote "Fame & Death," and he died a month or so afterwards. It took me a while to understand the experience. I don't even remember what I wrote as an introduction because I don't think Ginsberg can be properly introduced and I wasn't mature enough to understand his complexities. My encounter with him took me to uncomfortable places and heightened my curiosity about everything. My questions became deeper, more layered. When Darwish died, I started writing about this crossing. It took more than a decade for me to understand the encounter the three of us had.

I don't remember ever not reading Darwish. I asked him endless questions about writing and Palestine along the years. His answers almost always surprised me. He had a way of answering in metaphors. In fact, his answers could have been poems. Our discussions on literature were also important to me, his thoughts on the works of Walcott, Tranströmer, Lorca, Paz. But mostly, he helped me see that there are pieces of the emptiness that can become worlds, and those worlds can become books, and those books can become monuments, and those monuments can represent hope. And if not hope, they can at least be the start of a conversation.

In the epigraph to Love and Strange Horses, *you "return" to Darwish by citing one of his poems. Images of abandonment and return are central to your work. Can you comment on this?*

Returning is a way of staying. Which also means a way of leaving. It is a way of accepting. Which also means a way of questioning. It is a way of existing. Which also means a way of resisting.

For me, there is only a symbolic return. You can never really return to anything, whether it's a lover or a homeland. Inevitably, where you return has changed. However, the act of returning is important even if disillusioning, because you don't find the exactness you imagined.

On a recent trip to Haiti, a woman who knew my mother screamed my name when she saw me. She greeted me warmly and was delighted to see me. I, on the other hand, didn't remember her. I was too young when I saw her last. She spoke to me as if we had crossed yesterday. As if she knew me. For her, 25 years had not passed. For me, it had. It isn't that she hadn't changed during that time, it's that she continued to exist in the same social and cultural context, in the same ambience, so the fundamentals had not moved. I, on the other hand, exist in many other spaces. She didn't know all the colors on my canvas. She assumed the colors she knew were the only ones that defined me. This is not uncommon when one belongs to many different cultural spaces.

People only refer to you from their point of reference. You can never fully satisfy everyone because each person has his or her version of you. Hopefully, one day, if they really want to know the *whole you*, they will go beyond their definitions and will discover.

The incident in Haiti was an extreme situation because I constantly navigate all the places I belong to—France, Latin America, and the Middle East. In the case of Palestine, I never cease returning or perhaps I should say cease *trying to return to* that Palestine, and in particular that Bethlehem, that my soul is so deeply anchored in. Though it is not there. The land is there. It hasn't moved. But my Bethlehem is not there. The land has been cut into pieces, the wall imprisons even shadows. This experience of presence and absence is incredibly disturbing. So returning is freedom and imprisonment. In other words, returning is in many ways unattainable but we never stop trying. In most of my poems, *return* lingers somewhere on the page, between or underneath the words.

You are the editor of The Poetry of Arab Women: A Contemporary Anthology *and coeditor of* Language for a New Century: Contemporary Poetry from the Middle East, Asia, and Beyond. *What were your reasons for embarking on both of these equally important and ambitious projects? What are some of the lessons you learned in compiling both of the anthologies?*

I believe in the transformative power of the word. It informs and, in so doing, helps us understand different worlds, cultures, realities, and what we might fear in others. With less than three percent of literature in translation and having an international background, I feel an immense duty to participate in translation projects and the dissipation of global literature. Literature is dialogue. I want to be part of that conversation not only as a writer but also as a literary activist.

When I started the *Poetry of Arab Women*, I did not know what I was doing. I certainly did not know the massive amount of work it required, and thankfully so—I might have been discouraged. It was an education at so many levels. When I left the United States for Paris in 1992, I started to work more with the Arab world, and I soon realized that Arab women writers were marginalized in Arabic literature and the Arab literary scene. I also knew that in the United States, Arab-American women authors were one of the most invisible groups in the American literary circle. At the same time, Arab women writers were virtually unknown to Arab-Americans and Americans in general, and vice versa. So it became vital for me to give birth to this project in order to eradicate invisibility, introduce Arab women poets and show the diversity of Arab women's poetry. It was equally essential to unite these Arab women poets regardless of what language they wrote in and whether they were born in the Arab world or not. It was also important to write a substantial introduction on Arab women's literature and to highlight the particularities of every Arab country. So my "Introduction" presents the feminist movement, the women's literary scene, the poetic commonalities and differences between these poets as well as the political and social contexts that surround them.

So much has changed now. I am currently editing the ten-year anniversary edition of this book, and I do everything via e-mail, for example.

People are connected via the web, and other social networks. It is a completely different landscape. When I was working on the first edition, I was like a detective, a hunter, trying to gather books, permission slips. It was a real adventure. I remember asking a friend in Tunis via letter or phone to kindly help me make sure one of the poets signs and mails her permission slip. I found out afterwards that she drove two hours to the countryside to get that signature. I would have never asked if I knew it was going to be such an imposition. To her, it was normal. This is an example of Arab generosity.

Language for a New Century was conceived following the events of September 11, 2001. Taiwanese-American poet Tina Chang, Indian-American poet Ravi Shankar, and I felt a deep solidarity between ourselves and others of Eastern descent. We felt troubled by the negative views showcased in the media about the East. We did not have solutions for what was going on nor could we explain or define the East so rigidly, but we felt a deep need to respond in any way we could. So we went to what we knew best, our natural prayer: poetry. We went to the human voices that have enchanted us and changed our lives and spirits, in hopes of adding to the ongoing dialogue between East and West.

I am currently working on an ambitious project of Dominican poetry in translation and started the blog-column *The City and the Writer* for *Words without Borders*, which I enjoy immensely, as it allows me to connect more deeply with the cities I am traveling to.

I was rather surprised when reading Love and Strange Horses *how involved your understanding is of the breadth of locales and cultures. In the poems (and I'm assuming this is, rightly or wrongly, a mirror of your life) you move rather fluently between borders: the opening poem, "Pasaje," centers on a town in Ecuador; "In the Ruins" cites Lorca and Darwish; "Pendule" and "Scènes dans une Chambre Mauve" indicate a French sensibility; "Lubhyati: Love Letters" an intimacy with the Arabic world. Could you talk about this fluidity of movement in terms of the physical and intellectual?*

This is the reality I know. What might seem unusual to others is natural to me. I grew up eating at a table where everyone spoke the language they were most comfortable in and we all understood one another. The conversation moved along coherently and smoothly even if the back and forth was in various languages. As a writer, I hope I have created my own English, one that comes from many cultures but despite its vast differences—culturally, musically, rhythmically, grammatically—coexists and creates its own music on the page. I am also used to family members being from different parts of the world but what unifies us is our Palestinian background, and that sacred thread is powerful, and perhaps unbreakable.

What is this sacred thread?

It is that force that is impenetrable, whose root is family, tradition, and homeland. When I think of my family history, it is deeply inspiring because it tells me that love can endure anything—history and war, death and time. When I say love, I mean that greater power which encompasses all associated to family, such as language, culture, place. My Bethlehemite family is spread all over the world, from Asia to Australia, Latin America to the Caribbean, Europe to the Middle East. Yet, we have found a way to stay connected and profoundly entrenched to where we are originally from. Maybe that's why I believe, if you have lost your home along the way, it will find you again.

*Many of your new poems concentrate on erotic themes and the politics of the bedroom. In the wonderful serial poem, "Love and Strange Horses—*Intima*'," you claim, "I suppose we need evidence of desire— / to have a heart broken in this dangerous world; / evidence that we belonged somewhere once." If we're lucky, desire strips away differences and brings us closer together: "He came toward me . . . And we listened to the untitled music / circling the earth like an anthem / free of its nation."*

It is less about the politics of the bedroom and more about what is revealed to us in intimacy. Everything vanishes when we are intimate—our politics, society, morals and ideologies. That should make us question the things we allow to restrain and confine us.

I think the heart is purer than we are. It breaks down our walls. It denudes us, takes us to a sort of birth and there we are free, even of ourselves.

What do you mean, "free of ourselves"?

We constantly have to negotiate our social boundaries. And we might be a victim of a political situation, a certain circumstance or person, but nothing or no one can imprison our spirit. Only we can do that to ourselves. When I say, "free of ourselves," I mean free of the limitations we have imposed on ourselves, the walls we have built around us, visible or invisible. Free of what's within us that halts us, and prevents us from being all that we can be.

In "History by Candlelight," you restate and extend the same theme: "we held each other / and turned the small humming / of furious beats deep in the heart / into who we are meant to be." Such coming together may even be powerful enough, as it is in "Intermisión," to dismantle previous ways of knowing the world: "a feeling shivering electric / on the flesh, the fever of what / I no longer know." Are such lessons and revelations fairly radical for a woman with cultural ties to parts of the Arab world, where expressing the liberating powers of desire could be fatal?

Every society and culture has its limitations and restrictions. There are also extremists in every part of the world. I feel free to write whatever I want. That does not mean I will read some of my more erotic poems to a conservative Arab audience just like I wouldn't read them to a conservative Catholic audience in Texas. That seems logical to me. Otherwise, it's nothing but provocation. This act is not self-censoring; it's simply a more constructive way to open a conversation.

I particularly admired "Javier," the seven-part prose poem that centers the collection. The poem begins by establishing a passionate connection between two lovers that not-so-slowly devolves into desperate attempts to keep that passion alive. It's such an honest, unsentimental poem. I was wondering if you might discuss some of your reasons for writing it.

I am interested in what keeps us apart while we are together. Those details are so telling, they are worlds yet we often dismiss them. How do we stay together, continue to trust, to love, and most of all, see each other. How do we eliminate the noise, reconcile with ourselves, our truths, what disconnects us, what myths do we create? It is an intimate and a collective rumination.

Is "Javier," then, emblematic of intimate relationships or more a rumination on a particular relationship? Is the trajectory of the couple's story a personal reflection or a metaphor for all such relationships?

It's not only a metaphor of such relationships but of life; of not paying attention to the details, the life-beats around us. Of forgetting that in each breath, there is a universe. We are often so preoccupied with wanting more, that we never actually take the time to see, listen, sing.

*In "Love and Strange Horses—*Intima'*," you write, "to confess something sacred / to name something lustful . . ." The parallel structure of these lines suggests a yoking of the sacred and secular passions. Can our carnal desires bring us salvation?*

When we are free to live and manifest, that saves us. I once met someone from Bethlehem who fell in love with someone from Jerusalem. It grew increasingly difficult for them to see each other despite the fact that the two places have always been sister-cities. A Bethlehemite cannot live in Jerusalem and if a Jerusalemite (Palestinian) moves to Bethlehem he or she will lose his or her ID card. Over there, even love is occupied. On the day before her wedding to another man, he decided in spite of everything, he couldn't lose her, so he headed to Bethlehem. En route, Israeli soldiers detained him. They detected that he was nervous and unsettled, therefore suspicious. He never made it to Bethlehem. He told me, "If I said, 'I was trying to reach my love.' Who would have believed me?"

Throughout Love and Strange Horses, *I see repeated images that exploit tensions between proximity and distance, as well as presence and absence. Can you talk about such tensions as you see them at work in your poems?*

The closer we get, the farther away we are because we realize at that moment that the return is different than we imagined it to be. Yet, we continue to pursue the closeness because we want something of what's passed. Perhaps there is no closeness nor is there distance, they merge somehow. Often we are closer in the distance. The same with absence and presence—we are often more present in absence, more absent in our presence. The poems flirt with these notions in an attempt to be close to closeness, to absence, to distance, to *this* present.

I loved the poem "Akhmatova and I: Boleros." What prompted this poem? It seems like there's a great story behind it.

I have always been drawn to her. And I have always felt connected to Russia's melancholic side. My mother is an avid reader and all of her children have names from Russian novels. Once while in St. Petersburg, Phillip Lopate was giving a reading at The Literary and Memorial Museum of Anna Akhmatova. During his reading, I heard her voice in the distance. She was singing. Of course, I don't know her voice nor do I know if she sang. But by the end of the evening I felt very strongly that she was telling me, *don't stay in the past*. The last line of the poem, when she asks me, "have you ever danced a bolero?" is intended to be a surprise question; you are not prepared to think about it, question it or try to understand it, you just trust it and go with it. That's what I felt that evening. I trusted the encounter. That night, Lopate suggested I leave Europe and come to New York. A year later, I did. I think that changed the course of my writing life. Akhmatova's *Selected Poems* is placed on my bookshelf where I can see her.

Formally, the poems in Love and Strange Horses *are shaped by your knowledge of various rhetorical strategies common to Arab literature, as well as aesthetics shaped by American, Hispanic, and French literatures. Moreover, the book is structured in musical movements, a fact that is further reinforced by references to instruments throughout.*

Music has always been important to me. It is not bound to nationality while being rooted in the tradition of a place. When an instrument stands alone, it's quiet. When a hand is in contact with it, they create music together. The image of the hand on wood, brass, ivory creating sound is powerful to me. But I also began to listen to the quietness, and slowly started hearing it. When I listen to music, I see people, places, phantoms. I wanted to see what those images in my mind, inspired by music, looked like on the page.

Many of the poems in The Lives of Rain *involve dramatically poignant moments of arrival and departure. Such moments are often heightened by a speaker's complicated sense of identification with the place he or she arrives at or leaves. Could you talk about themes of arrival and departure in this book?*

I am always arriving somewhere, and while arriving, I am already departing; always departing and while departing, arriving—to that place which is not arrival or departure. It is unnamed but it belongs to me. It's undefined and the most defined inside of me. In that place there is no exit because neither arrival nor departure exists. It's my version of infinity. The perfect symphony. It transcends everything that binds.

You speak of that place the way one might speak of the power of a poem? Is it through poetry that you find such places?

Yes, poetry has that transcendental quality. It is everywhere at once. Everything is alive and immortal in a poem even when the speaker or the character in the poem is dying. In poetry, death finds a way to live.

Another motif in The Lives of Rain *is the frequent recurrence of the word "between," which is used in several contexts—some literal, others metaphorical. Even in poems where the word does not appear, the notion of the self as being between two worlds or two states of mind is prevalent in these poems. Could you talk about this?*

In between is a country. A place not everyone finds or feels comfortable in but in that discomfort there are illuminations. My life has been filled with longings. It's consoling to be in between, on my way to another place I miss. It's too painful to accept that although I can unite all of my worlds in my work, I cannot in my reality.

You conclude the poem "Bethlehem" by saying an old man "has left me secrets between his footsteps." Not only is this a powerful way of circling back to the opening line about the persona's grandfather, it seems an apt metaphor for the function of the poems in The Lives of Rain. *Each poem is, in a sense, a secret between the complex, outer realities on a global and personal scale. Do you see your poems functioning in this way?*

I see the poems as bridges gathering *messages*. Asking readers to listen to what is unsaid.

Most likely if I wrote this poem today, I would not have used the word *secret*. This was the title poem of a book edited by Naomi Shihab Nye and published by Simon & Schuster. It was in the early to mid-90s and the word Palestine wasn't as frequently used in the United States as it is today. During my undergraduate studies in Boston, saying I am Palestinian was problematic to many, and at times, I was made to feel afraid. It was very unsettling. After 9/11 people in the United States were forced to become aware of who Arabs and Muslims are as well as the history of the Palestinian-Israeli conflict. I try to understand what lies beyond what I hear and what I am told, what I see and what I am taught. I've learned the more I know, the less afraid I am. We constantly focus on difference yet there are so many more commonalities.

In "Strangers Inside Me" you write "a tiny echo is calling me / as I travel and move / from one continent to the next, / move, to be whole."

It's only when I am moving and can catch my *longings* that I feel whole. It's unbearable to think about all the places and people I miss, all scattered around the globe. Obviously, I cannot be with all of them at the same time. So movement consoles me. It makes me feel like I'm constantly moving towards them. It gives me the illusion that I never left, that I am simply in a perpetual state of circular motion.

Another recurring image/reference is to the importance of memory and remembering.

Only when we remember can we start accepting and repenting, and from that point, begin changing, evolving. We have to stand in front of the broken mirror, look at how and where it's broken before the cracks can start to vanish.

Tell me a little about the poem "Amrika," from The Lives of Rain.

In many ways it is a memoir-poem. It goes through all the places that have been an integral part of my journey: Palestine, France, Haiti, Boston, Miami, the Dominican Republic, London, and New York. But at the heart of the poem is exile. What it means to be displaced. I wanted to unite worlds within worlds. And it was important to use the Arabic word for America to echo the experience of exiles and immigrants; that's where they went, but that's not who they are. But also to demonstrate the contradictions associated to leaving ones homeland: the other place is a blessing and a curse, a joy and a profound sadness.

Tell me about The Neverfield. *Do you see this as a series of small, untitled poems or as one epic poem?*

The Neverfield is an epic poem. I was obsessed with mythology and folklore. I was also trying to articulate my journey. A life moving. Fields have always seduced me, especially the endless yellow fields I have seen in France, Palestine, and, yes, Iowa. I remember driving from Fairfield to Des Moines, and at one juncture could not tell the difference between the sky and the field. It was a real spiritual experience. And at the time, the Sufis really influenced me—the idea of oneness. I was on a continuous search. I still am, but I am searching for something different now. Then, I kept arriving but never arrived.

I hear you have a new book coming out called Poet in Andalucía. *By the time this interview is released in book form, your new volume of poetry will be a few months old. I'd welcome any general comments about it.*

Federico García Lorca lived in Manhattan from 1929 to 1930, and the poetry he wrote about the city, *Poet in New York,* was posthumously published in 1940. Now, 80 years after Lorca's sojourn in America, and myself a poet in New York of Mediterranean as well as Middle Eastern roots, I went to Spain to write *Poet in Andalucía.*

I recreated Lorca's journey in reverse.

Andalucía has always been the place where racial, ethnic, and religious forces converge and contend, where Islamic, Judaic, and Christian traditions remain a mirror of a past that is terrible and beautiful. *Poet in Andalucía* is a meditation on the past and the present. It is a voyage, cultural and personal, historical and creative. It renders in poetry a region that seems to hold the pulse of our earth, where all of our stories assemble. It is a meditation on what has changed and what insists on remaining the same, on the mysteries that trouble and intrigue us. It is about a poet who continues to call us to question what makes us human. Lorca left as part of his legacy a longing for homeland. My own longing stretches across four continents, due to a life made exilic by the political turmoil in the Middle East. His poems were about discovering a lost self. The poems in *Poet in Andalucía* confront that same loss, and resonate with that same yearning for a sustaining place. Richard

L. Predmore writes that *Poet in New York* is about "social injustice, dark love and lost faith," and the quality of otherness such forces produce. *Poet in Andalucía* explores the persistent tragedy of otherness but it also acknowledges a refusal to remain in that stark darkness, and it searches for the possibility of human coexistence.

Handal, Nathalie. "In January, *Amor y Lluvia,*" "Love and Strange Horses—*Intima',*" "History by Candlelight," and "Intermisión." *Love and Strange Horses.* Pittsburgh: University of Pittsburgh Press, 2010.

______. "Strangers Inside Me," "Bethlehem," and "Amrika." *The Lives of Rain.* Northampton: Interlink Books, 2005.

Poetry:

Poet in Andalucía, University of Pittsburgh Press, 2012
Love and Strange Horses, University of Pittsburgh Press, 2010
The Lives of Rain, Interlink, 2005
The Neverfield Poem, Interlink, 1999

Plays:

2 John, produced, 2011
Hakawatiyeh, produced 2009
The Oklahoma Quartet, produced 2009
The Stonecutters, produced 2007
Between Our Lips, produced 2006
La Cosa Dei Sogni, produced 2006
The Details of Silence, produced 2005

As Editor:

Language for a New Century: Contemporary Poetry from the Middle East, Asia, and Beyond, Coeditor. W. W. Norton, 2008
The Poetry of Arab Women: A Contemporary Anthology, Editor. Interlink, 2002

Spontaneity and Surprise: An Interview with Stephen Dobyns

Stephen Dobyns is one of the best writers *about* poetry in American letters. ("Why bother looking elsewhere?" Billy Collins told me.) This achievement is all the more impressive when one considers Dobyns is a prolific and successful novelist, and also one of the most distinctive poets writing today. Often bold, occasionally shocking, but never sensational, he deconstructs the comic desperations of our age with a wry yet earnest voice. It's a challenge to excite most people through poetry. Dobyns knows this and structures his poems skillfully, without ever "pulling punches" or accommodating disengaged minds. In the discussion below, he outlines some of the aspects of his approach to composition and revision that enable him to strike a balance between the raw energy of an initial draft and the refinements of craft. Once a news reporter, he has spent much of his writing life teaching at various colleges and universities in the United States. He has also received fellowships from the National Endowment for the Arts and the Guggenheim Foundation. *Cemetery Nights* was a National Poetry Series award winner in 1987.

In your essay on "Pacing" in Best Words, Best Order, *you write: "All poems are visually finite. Part of the pleasure of surprise in any poem is its suggestion of the infinite within the finite, that even when all apparent possibilities have been anticipated, change is still possible." While you were referring to "all poems," this statement is especially relevant to your own work. Poems like "Tomatoes" or "White Pig" (from* Cemetery Nights*) and, more recently, "Napatree Point" and "Nickel" (from* Winter's Journey*), succeed in large part because you continue to surprise the reader, creating inventive turns from and unexpected returns to the chief narrative in ways that suggest a continuous tension between finite (a story with a foreseeable end) and infinite (a story* *that meanders in any direction it wishes for as long as it wishes or likes). Could you talk a little about your use of pace in the new book?*

I was worried about the length of the *Winter's Journey* poems, and if they could sustain interest, so I would seemingly change subject a number of times within it, alter it very quickly, and then come back to what I was talking about, then alter it again. Those kinds of surprises, I felt, were useful in making the poems seem spontaneous, as if they were just being spoken, and in order to give them an element of verisimilitude. In the attempt of doing that, again there'd be the changing of the subject, and so on. But I rarely knew what the end was going to be until I got there. I knew the kind of thing I was doing, certainly, and why I was writing that particular poem, but then much of the poem after the first quarter or so had to be discovered, which I found exciting, and ideally some of that sense of excitement got into the poems. But then they're all set more or less in the same place and make references to more or less many of the same things and ideas, and so that gave them an element of structure as well.

Other considerations of pace have to do with formal concerns. Obviously, my twelve long poems in *Winter's Journey* are not strictly formal poems, but in writing them I was still constantly looking at the relationship between stressed and unstressed syllables. And then there's the kind of syllables you use, whether they're short duration syllables or long duration syllables, closed syllables like "cut," or open ones like "through." The long, open syllables make a much longer line and, obviously, the short, closed ones make shorter lines. Another consideration is the relation of stress to unstressed syllables. Iambic pentameter can have four degrees of stress from one to four, with one being the primary stress. A one-four rhythm is almost a comic rhythm. And you can speed a line very easily if you have a more exaggerated rhythm coming after a long syllable line, where the iambs are closer together: one-two-three degrees of stress.

I see a real continuity in the poems from Winter's Journey. *Many of them, for instance, seem more overtly political than one might have expected from you based on poems in previous books. What prompted you to address politics more prominently this time out?*

I've wanted to write political poems for some time, and there are a few political poems I've written, but there's just such artificiality to most of the ones I've read. It's very difficult to write about politics because it's too easy to become polemical. And it's very easy to show bias. I remember all those poems from the Vietnam War: very few of them worked. And I thought, if I could use a tone that seemed uncertain then I would be asking questions instead of making assertions. And when I did make assertions, the tone would criticize itself. And then using those shifts in appearance of subject matter, moving from a political statement to something that was completely different—a cat for instance—and then coming back to the politics in some way, but always in the interest of moving towards some lyric idea.

So the political subject matter in these new poems functions as a springboard for deeper considerations?

Exactly. "Napatree Point" was the first poem. I was pleased with it and thought, "Maybe I can do that again." So, I continued. Sometimes, I began with a definite idea of what I wanted to write about. Others began with an image. In "Rabbits" it was the sun coming down in the morning, touching the steeples and the trees, and so on. A few others began in image, too. Still others begin by surprising themselves, like "Werewolf": "Last night I dreamt a jumbo jet fucked a werewolf bitch, / changed for the event into half-human form. Forgive me / if I begin on a personal note." That's a startling beginning, although I did have that dream. One of my ambitions in that poem was to begin with an absurdity and then move it to the complete extreme of emotion, ending with Baudelaire quotes and a note of sadness and nostalgia.

This movement is one of the most pleasurable and distinctive features of your work overall—the ability to leap from the base to the exalted, a fluid mix of high and low cultural references.

Yes, I think this establishes an element of surprise in a poem, but it has to be introduced very early on because if it comes in later it disrupts the tone. I prefer to use the simplest words, though they have to have some texture. Most good poets writing in English try to avoid using a lot of polysyllabic words because a polysyllabic word has maybe one stress and three unstressed syllables, so their appearance can make a line seem flaccid. But when you do use one, it should be the most resonant word in that area of the poem. I also try to keep the poem to one theme and repeat certain things about the rhythm and sound while creating variations within that repetition, so nothing really feels the same. We read by anticipating what comes next. The writer, then, is always deflecting that anticipation, sometimes rewarding it, sometimes frustrating it.

"How to Like It" is one of your most widely enjoyed poems. On the surface, it appears to be a straightforward poem about a man's midlife crisis, manifested in the poem's narration through the persona's extended debate with his dog about how the man should satisfy his hunger and restlessness. But I also see this poem as a brilliant rewriting of "The Love Song of J. Alfred Prufrock." Could you talk about "Prufrock" and its possible influence on your work, particularly in this poem?

Your observation absolutely never occurred to me! I like "Prufrock" probably better than any other Eliot. I've certainly read it a lot. But I didn't have it in my mind when I was writing "How to Like It," not consciously anyway.

Some poets begin their careers writing poems they will later think are wordy, overstated. Put another way, some evolve towards an increased terseness in their later work. Your poems, however, appear to be getting more expansive and more intricately developed, as if the comparatively early brevity of poems like "Song of the Drowned Boy" (from Heat Death*) cannot contain the breadth of your vision. Although the first and last poems in* Winter's Journey *are brief little allegories, the rest of the book is subsumed in these vast, talkative poems that often exceed 150 lines. Can you talk about this tendency in recent work?*

I don't know. Maybe I've just become more verbose! Whatever the case, I try and make each book different from the one before. In many of the poets I admire, like Neruda and Apollinaire, there is that great difference between books. Clearly other poets I admire, like Zbigniew Herbert, don't have that. Charles Simic's poems are not always the same, but clearly always spoken by the same voice. There has been quite a change from Louise Glück's early work to her later work. Ellen Bryant Voigt has that, too. I have a terror of falling into self-parody. So, with each book, I try and follow a new paradigm. Well, this is not quite true of *Mystery, So Long* (2005) because I was working on those poems off and on while writing *The Pallbearers Envying the One Who Rides* (1999) and *The Porcupine's Kisses* (2002), both of which were clearly set around some idea. The *Mystery* poems almost seem like a kind of raggedy Selected Poems.

Some of your most celebrated poems read like chatty, long-lined monologues that do not have stanza breaks. Because you are so good at such poems, one might forget you are also a master of more recognizable poetic forms, such as the comparatively shorter poems using quatrains and tercets. How early on in the process of writing a poem can you guess the shape the poem will take?

Pretty early, actually. I mean there's something about the sound of the poem, something about how the ideas are working themselves out, something about the images that seems to break more easily into one shape over another. For me, many times a poem is just one long stanza; it will have a stronger narrative, albeit meditative, something that doesn't break up as easily, or I don't want broken up, something I want the reader to continue with as long as possible. I think I've written poems with stanzas of almost every length going up to ten, and they're usually stanzas of the same length. Stanzas can give the reader a sense of comfort: there's a suggestion that somebody's in control. The material can be outrageous in some way, yet there's this illusion of control supplied by the tightly constructed stanzas.

As if the sense of the poem as formal and unified chafes against an unfettered imagination?

Yes.

I'm repeatedly impressed by your handling of the line, and by your understanding of the complex, subtle effects good lineation can create in a poem.

My lines in a poem tend to be quite similar to one another. Between poems, they might run from six syllables to 16. The strongest places in the line are at the beginning and end. Through enjambment, you can discover nuance within a poem. Within formal poetry, nuance is much easier to create, as you reverse an iamb to trochee, or use rhyme to stress it. But in free verse it's much harder to create nuance. How the line breaks is one of the strongest ways to do it.

And then there is counterpoint. You have the rhythm of the sentence and you have the rhythm of the line. When I start the poem, I simply have that idea in mind. As I work on the poem, I fiddle with the sentences, sometimes up to a year or more, even when the rest of the poem is fairly set, and all because of counterpoint and the double rhythm it creates. Sometimes the sentence and the line work against each other, sometimes they can be right together, or start together and pull away, or any place in between. Counterpoint affects how we understand the line, how we move through it; it also affects our sense of knowledge, our sense of how clear or obscure it is.

You do generally write a much longer line than is typical of many contemporary poets. Who were some of the writers you emulated in this regard?

I suspect some of it was Wallace Stevens, some of it was Neruda, some of it was C. K. Williams, and some of it was Larkin—especially his handling of pentameter lines. Most importantly, however, I didn't feel I could build a rhythm I liked with a short line; it just made it too staccato. What I like in the line are undulations, basically, and stops or breaks within it.

You are, at this time, the author of 20 novels, one book of short stories, and 12 books of poetry. Unlike most writers working in both genres, you manage to sustain a successful career with both. In what ways has your prolific career as a fiction writer influenced your work as a poet? And/or vice versa?

Early in high school I wrote more stories, although they were dreadful, and then in tenth grade I began to write poems, though for the most banal of reasons. I didn't like the poems we read in class, but I liked jazz and started listening to records of poetry read to jazz, mostly Beat poetry, but Langston Hughes, also. What drew me to the poems was the jazz. But then I became struck by the poems because they were so often told in the way a person speaks, which was not how most of the nineteenth-century poems I read in school worked. I tried to pursue this in my writing.

I think where my poetry and fiction come together is my interest in narrative—although I never have something in the novel that I move into the poem or something in the poem I move into the novel. My narrative poems basically work to set up a lyric moment. Whatever story interest they might have is secondary, or the story interest is the hook that drags a reader towards the lyric experience.

I felt if I was going to be primarily a novelist I would have to come to terms with Modernism in some way. I didn't feel I could do this, or I didn't want to spend the time doing it. Most of my novels are mysteries, which is a nineteenth-century form: it sets up a problem and then marches through and solves the problem; it's not a bit like Joyce. I didn't adopt or embrace Modernism, though I did write a few novels that were more modernistic: *Cold Dog Soup, The Two Deaths of Señora Puccini, The Wrestler's Cruel Study,* and *Aftershocks/Near Escapes.* These novels, particularly *The Wrestler's Cruel Study,* come to terms with Modernism in a way I liked.

Although you make a clear distinction between your poems and fiction, many of your poems are architectonically complex the way a novel might be. Has your novel writing, which requires sustained attention to matters of plot and development, helped you build some of your more complicated narrative poems?

I suspect that is true, but I never thought of it before. There is an almost schizophrenic split in me between the poet and the novelist. Writing stories is difficult: I take a lot of time trying to work out the narratives. But what I have learned about the narrative in fiction I have certainly used in poetry. And probably vice versa.

I am intrigued by the sonnets you wrote about Cézanne (in Body Traffic*). There aren't many sonnets in your oeuvre. What led you to write about Cézanne and in this particular form?*

I never liked Cézanne. When I lived outside Detroit during college, I'd go to the Detroit Art Museum. In the early 60s they received a large body of paintings from a guy named Tannenbaum, and there were a lot of Cézanne works in that. I still couldn't see what all the fuss was. I didn't know how to look at them. As the years went by, it got so that

I could look at them the way I ought. I had read about him. He was a strange, more than eccentric figure. He began his life very much as a romantic who wrote romantic poems and was close friends with Zola. Everyone around him thought he was an idiot. His wife didn't respect him; his son didn't respect him. When he died, they sold his paintings as fast as they could because they thought they'd never get a better price than they would then—which showed *them* something important! The arc of his life was also a bit tragic. He was always an outsider. When he did become close with someone he wrangled with that person in some way. His sense of pride could show itself in the smallest of things: in one of the poems, for example, he claims, "Only I could paint such a red." And there's joy in this.

There's a letter by Rilke about sentimentality. He's comparing Rodin and Cézanne. Sentimentality is the artist pushing something forward and saying, "I love this." This is what Rilke saw in Rodin. But Cézanne pushes something forward and says, "Here it is." I began to see and appreciate how Cézanne's paintings were made. I made myself look at them. Years ago, I had one of those skiing machines that were popular in the 80s. I also had a slide machine. I went to the Syracuse library and checked out about a hundred slides of Cézanne's paintings and studied them as I listened to rock-n-roll on my skiing machine. Those slides would go round and around while I exercised; over the course of about a hundred hours I got to know those paintings pretty well. That's how I educated myself about Cézanne.

Cézanne's son once told an anecdote about his father. If he didn't like a painting, he'd throw it out the window. He would do this fairly often. One time he was walking down a path and looked up into an apple tree and saw one of the paintings he chucked out the window. He said, "That's no so bad after all!" So he sent his son up into the tree to retrieve it. I liked that. He was so tenacious. As I said, everyone in town thought he was crazy. The guy who ran the local art museum made sure no Cézanne paintings came into the museum. He could have had the best work! Instead, the Cézannes he did take were more studies than paintings, and they're all quite rough. His father was a banker and wanted his son to be a banker, but Cézanne just persevered. I admire that tremendously.

Why did you use the sonnet form for these poems?

I wanted for these poems the kind of restraint that a sonnet form could give. A sonnet is always a kind of argument that is broken so clearly into different parts, most clearly in Shakespeare with the "If . . . then" construction.

The turn.

Exactly. I felt if I were writing about Cézanne, I'd need a leash. I also liked the idea of writing something in form that didn't immediately strike a person as form. Some of the lines are iambic, but many are not, and there's off rhyme in them. I wanted to keep them colloquial and have some degree of verisimilitude. And yet the sonnet is obviously a formal poem—even as I was using it: it has that idea of the form being a glass and the content being that which you pour into the glass.

One of the poets I most admire is Bill Knott. He writes dozens and dozens of sonnets on all sorts of subjects. He writes upside down sonnets, he takes them apart. Some of them are rhymed and metered, others not. I admire that kind of perseverance. He's a poet who could easily become verbose but his work with the form keeps him to a definite shape. Many of them are beautiful. He's probably the best love poet of the twentieth century, though many would not think this of him. He appears to have no constraints. He just writes the poem. He doesn't have an ear that is worried about the critic or reader. He just does it, no matter how offensive or beautiful it might be. Obviously, there is a lot of originality in his work: he makes up lots of words, writes on subjects that you never possibly thought of before. I just admire him. He likes to play on his name, Knott/not, too. His last book, *Unsubscriber,* is an erasure, because he is "not." He wants the negation.

What brought you to Santiago, Chile, which figures prominently in a number of your poems?

My wife is Chilean and she was living there. It's a third-world country with those strange third-world stories. It has such an awful history, what with Pinochet and all that. Santiago is a place of tremendous smog. But walking around the town, I saw oddities I didn't see in first-world countries. Valparaíso and the mountains—those are gorgeous.

When I went there, there was still a curfew where you had to be in your home by 10 pm. After that you'd hear footsteps running, and every now and then a gunshot. You never knew what was true and what wasn't. The paper would say six extremists were killed in a car accident. And then next Sunday, a priest in the pulpit would say these men were taken from their wives' houses, etc. There was no place to go to get accurate information. There was no way you knew what was going on. That was an entirely new experience for me. I already had a slightly claustrophobic, paranoid nature. I mean, if you're a writer you have to be a little paranoid.

Why?

You have to believe that people are listening to you. Writing is a form of communication. You have to believe there is a reader. Poetry is not a form that is embraced wholeheartedly by many. So I have had to imagine that there is someone out there who is listening, which is basically a paranoid thought.

So many of your poems appear to be about failed masculinity.

Many of the characters I write about in poems are men, and there has to be some turn in the poem. Larkin says, "Happiness paints white." You don't turn someone ebullient or devil-may-care. There has to be a point in the poem—and this is something you see in the short story as well—where the character or the person develops a sense of himself that he didn't have before, that he clarifies a sense of himself that had not been apparent until that time. In playing with this, my characters discover the complexity of living. Some people fall victim to that, some endure it, others triumph over it. I don't like triumph poems. Poems where people fall victim to or endure the complexities of life—the psychology of these interested me. Maybe there's some autobiographical connection. I don't know.

In a number of the poems from Winter's Journey, *it seems as if there are two entities in the head of the character, the conscious will and the unconscious will that works against it. This conflict isn't necessarily trying to be Freudian, but what is hidden in the head and one's conscious thoughts are often at each other's throats.*

Add to this the fact that the state of the world is surreal. You think of how it is that people don't see things that they need to see—global warming is only one thing on that long list. People who don't want to think past the present moment. One of the things a poem tries to do is give the reader a sense of the arc of his life, where you're coming from and where you're going, and it doesn't do that in a way that is too pushy or too overt: it simply brings this concern into the mix, tries to get someone out of his complacency. In looking at how people live in this country, how privileged they can be, how anti-intellectual—The Tea Party becomes a dreadful example of that. They are the American form of the Taliban. I just hate to think of where some of these things could go. I try not to be too pessimistic.

But, yes, the world is surreal. You think of someone wearing a coat and tie. What an incredible absurdity! To wear this little bit of cloth around your neck like a hangman's noose, and then this jacket. You see politicians on a stage: they have their red ties for Republicans and blue ties for Democrats. Does that cloth keep them warm? No, it doesn't. What's the purpose of it? It's just a bit of male decoration. That's my rant about neckties. I'm done talking about them.

Some of the new poems remind me a little of Kenneth Koch's poems circa The Art of Love. *Was he an influence on your writing?*

I don't think so at all. When I was younger, I read some Koch. I had a teacher in high school who brought in Koch's parody of Frost's "The Hired Hand." I certainly liked that. Other poems I have liked, too. In the 90s, I reviewed one of his books and didn't feel strongly about the poems. Parts, yes, but I didn't feel the poems worked as a whole. I liked his humor, often. Maybe that has influenced me. The comic in a poem becomes an intellectual tool: you're not writing a funny poem, you're writing a poem that is using surprise in a way that energizes a certain part of the poem.

What was the impetus for The Porcupine's Kisses? *It's such a strange, wonderful book! In Part I, you have prose poems on one side, and aphorisms on the other. In Part II, you have this inventive dictionary.*

I was interested in exploring different ways of playing with metaphor.

I hadn't written prose poems before, with the exception of one, and I wanted to see what they were like. I wrote about 80 of them and used 50. And there are the aphorisms. A good aphorism is always a kind of a surprise. I think of Merwin's *Asian Figures.* They're nondiscursive; you leap from ignorance to knowledge, just like that [snaps his fingers]. All is grasped all at once. In writing them, I tried to create a sense of something that lies beyond reality, not a religious dynamic, but something else. Is reality all we have or is there a spirituality beyond that? Louise Glück's poems often have that sense.

At any rate, *A Porcupine's Kisses* is a bit like *The Wrestler's Cruel Study,* in that some people are just crazy about it while most people just scratch their heads.

In the course of this discussion, you have mentioned a few poets. Do you see yourself as belonging to a community of writers, or do you see yourself as someone who works pretty much privately, independent of community?

I think I work privately. I see poetry as an isolated act that you have to write without any constraint or thought of what someone might think of it, or what a critic might think of it. Many people write because they want to be liked or loved or admired or tenured. Those are all constraints: they cause you to pull your punch. I suppose I pull my punch in some ways, but it's something I hate the very idea of. I don't think my work is much like others' work. There may be points of resemblance. And I've tried to make my books different enough that they keep that separation. I've taught at Goddard and Warren Wilson, since January of 1980. I've taken time off, but I must have been there about 50 times. Many of the writers there have taught me—Louise Glück, Ellen Bryant Voigt, Heather McHugh, Steve Orlen, Tom Lux, and others. For a long time, when I'd go there, I'd see what someone was doing. Ray Carver was there for a time and it was exciting to go to one of his readings. You'd often see what someone had done over the course of a semester. Now it's really too large to do that. You have four or five ten-minute readings in one evening instead of one writer reading for an hour. But I still feel energized by the lectures and classes people give. So on one side, I feel very isolated. On the other side, I feel part of a community ten days or so a year, which is great for someone who is an isolationist because I can go to it and leave it at any time.

Do you see yourself as a poet who writes fiction or a writer who writes whatever he writes?

I definitely see myself as a poet who writes fiction. But when I get an idea for a novel I pursue it. The closer I get to the end, the more fanatically I pursue it. If I happen to start writing a poem in that period, everything stops, until I've got the poem in a temporary finished state.

So there's a willful concentration in writing poems you don't experience writing novels?

I suppose. Writing novels has been a way to give myself money so I could stop teaching for a year or six months and concentrate on something else that I wouldn't be able to do if I was teaching steadily. But I do love writing novels and I love the characters. When I have a character knocking on the door I have no idea who it will be when the door is opened. And there are other kinds of surprises like that, which I like. I wrote *Cold Dog Soup,* for instance, in Santiago. I loved writing that. It was full of jokes I liked, politically incorrect elements that I was very fond of. It's a peculiar book. Nobody likes it but the French. They have published it in several editions. They even made a movie of it. None of my novels are terribly successful, except for *The Church of Dead Girls*, which sold a lot, and was translated into twenty different languages. *That* made me feel like a novelist!

But to speak to your question, I suppose what I'd say is that the poem requires patience. You always have to forgive yourself for the awfulness of your first drafts and you can't be in a hurry to finish it. In the rush to a finish a poem you can force an intellectual ending on a poem that the poem doesn't deserve.

Dobyns, Stephen. "Pacing: The Ways a Poem Moves." *Best Words, Best Order: Essays on Poetry*. Second Edition. New York: Palgrave Macmillan, 1996, 2003.

Poetry:
Winter's Journey, Copper Canyon Press, 2010

Mystery, So long, Penguin, 2005
The Porcupine's Kisses, Penguin, 2002
Pallbearers Envying the One Who Rides, Penguin, 1999
Common Carnage, Penguin, 1996
Velocities: New and Selected Poems, 1966–1992, Penguin, 1994
Body Traffic, Viking, 1990
Cemetery Nights, Viking , 1987
Black Dog, Red Dog, Holt, 1984
The Balthus Poems, Atheneum, 1982
Heat Death, Atheneum, 1980
Griffon: Poems, Atheneum, 1976
Concurring Beasts, Atheneum, 1972

Nonfiction:
Next Word, Better Word: The Craft of Writing Poetry, Palgrave Macmillan, 2011
Best Words, Best Order: Essays on Poetry, Palgrave Macmillan, 1996

Selected Fiction:
Eating Naked, Picador, 2001
Boy in the Water, Henry Holt, 1999
The Church of Dead Girls, St. Martins, 1997
The Wrestler's Cruel Study, W. W. Norton, 1995
After Shocks/Near Escape, Penguin, 1991
The House on Alexandrine, Wayne State University Press, 1990
The Two Deaths of Señora Puccini, Penguin/Viking, 1988
A Boat off the Coast, Penguin/Viking, 1987
Cold Dog Soup, Penguin, 1985
Dancer with One Leg, Dutton, 1983
Charlie Bradshaw "Saratoga" Series, Penguin, 1976–98 (10 books)
A Man of Little Evils, Atheneum, 1973

By Way of Play and Accident: An Interview with Karen Volkman

Although Karen Volkman is the author of three well-regarded books of poetry, the following interview focuses on the contents of the most recent of these, *Nomina,* which was published by BOA Editions in 2008. As many critics have already realized, *Nomina* is a *tour de force* of formal innovation, a brilliant take on the Italian sonnet by way of Hopkins, Mallarmé, and Rilke. Like those writers, Volkman is inimitable, a singular voice in an age where so many poets seem indistinguishable from one another. Her sonnets contribute to a long tradition, and yet, by her own admission, they push that tradition "to its extreme limits." The result is a stunning collection of poems that seeks identification with and differentiation from the very form they celebrate. Given the degree of her sensitivity and the weight of her intellect, Volkman's considerations of her poetry—and of poetry in general—are as rigorous and satisfying as the poems themselves. Her first book, *Crash's Law,* was selected for the National Poetry Series, and her second book, *Spar,* won both the James Laughlin Award and the Iowa Poetry Prize. The recipient of awards and fellowships from the Poetry Society of America, Yaddo, and the National Endowment for the Arts, she teaches in the MFA program at the University of Montana, Missoula.

Let's start with a broad question: what intellectual and emotional impulses inspired you to write this sonnet sequence?

The sonnets came about in the best way—through play and accident. I anticipated going in the direction of a more spacious mode after the density and compression of the *Spar* poems, thinking in terms of a long poem or serial poem. Then I started reading sonnets in preparation for a forms class I was scheduled to teach. And not just English language sonnets. I'd just spent a stretch of time in Germany, and my German had developed enough for me to read Rilke's *Sonnets to Orpheus* in the original. These were poems that had been very important to me in translation, and experiencing them as formal sonnets was a shock. First, I experienced them as sound-structures in a very immediate way—with a foreign language, especially one you're new to, there is always a momentary disconnect between registering sound and meaning, so the material quality comes through more palpably. And second, I realized that this very subtle, complex thinking could be done in such a strict, constrained form. It was like rediscovering another character of poems that had been important to me through my whole writing life. I was moved by this to look at Mallarmé's sonnets in French. (My French was good at that point, and there were many poets I read in the original, but I'd always been daunted by Mallarmé's difficulty.) His brilliant, saturated musicality was a complete revelation. Again, the slight remove from the language made it even more purely an aural experience. Sound was so important a concern in *Spar,* and here I was experiencing it on a whole new level. I thought, "I want to make a poem that sounds like that. A wall of sound, totally overwhelming." I tried a few, and ended up writing about twenty in the first month, a number of which are in *Nomina*.

Why the Italian sonnet form over the English?

Largely, it was the greater constraints that the form imposes, a greater suffering, the awareness of that greater constraint, and the sheer sensuousness of the sound and musicality, that wall-of-sound effect, where you feel almost assaulted and overwhelmed by the recurrence of rhymes. In the Shakespearean sonnet form there is a more varied music, whereas I wanted the sounds of the poems to be engulfing.

I sense some of this engulfing you speak of comes about not only through the repetition of sounds but the way you build phrases, through a series of enumerations that are hypnotic. As a result, something beyond conventional meaning is being communicated through the sounds.

Yes, a frenetic quality, the way matter keeps happening, keeps mutating, the pushing of matter into different shapes. The material world is in constant motion, constant, compulsive making and changing. When

I was writing these poems I was thinking of constant motion and activity in the cosmos and in the elements around us, and wanted to make the furious activity of a material intelligence felt in the materiality and movement of the poems.

In poems 58–61, I saw an illuminating contrast between the building up into a whole or striving towards a whole and the dismantling of the whole, its destruction, its breaking down. For example, the stitching and splitting references in the poem "See the crack at the quick of the accident." There is a persistent idea of rupture and the scar and the "stitched divisibles." Thus, contrary energies seem to be at work where there is an attempt to bring things together and split them apart.

Well, that seems to me to be a central schism in the sonnet itself and why I find it such a compelling, compulsive and fascinating form to work with. There is a presumed resolution in the fixed rhyme scheme, so the regularity of pattern presents the sound structure under the sign of rationality and control. But that premise is contradicted by the nature of sound itself—once you're in the realm of sound association, there's a constant proliferation that's possible, which isn't fixed to the meaning of words. Once the form calls attention to the word as a unit of sound, the word seems to push against its own semantic boundaries. It almost seems to perceive itself as sound and be having a crisis.

On various levels the notion of both breaking open and the fixing in place are operative in the sonnet, particularly in its formal imperatives—but it's also in the language. We have charged fields of sound and the sounds are always pushing against the boundaries of words, and the idea of betraying the freedom of sound by putting the borders of particular reference on them is a kind of violence. We're trapped within a linguistic system of having our perceptions structured—on a deep level we experience the contradiction of wanting openness and needing a certain amount of closure in order to communicate.

You've explored this theme in your other books, too.

Yes. The sonnet is a different way of staging the argument and seeing how this tradition points to very deep contradictions framed in a particular set of terms.

Many of the sonnets in Nomina *are beaded throughout with what would seem like specialized vocabulary for the average reader.*

Some words I found in the dictionary. "Integral," for example, is a word that comes up in earlier poems of mine. Words fascinate me, not only by their sounds but the fields of reference that they open, the associations, the way they seem charged.

In what way do you think "integral" is charged?

To me, it conveys the idea of an essence, something pulling into itself—the charge is spatial in terms of the sensation of something compressed and tense with a quality that is held within but outwardly expressed. I get a feeling of a semantic space or motion being opened up by it.

Some of the poems deal well with the concept of ellipsis. In fact, the poems themselves are elliptical, brief snatches of sense or meaning that are deliberately—for whatever reason—cut off or withheld or never realized . . . for example, on page 25: "This ellipse, slip between seasons." I feel, in many ways, this statement is a kind of poetics for the book. Would you agree with that?

Well it certainly could be. I think there are a lot of places in the book that could be propositions for a poetics, taken on, shifted or turned around. Here, it is the idea of the ellipse and slippages between any certain positive meaning.

I admire your ability to choose words that are connotatively and denotatively rich, even elastic. The word "crux," for example, has a number of definitions, all of which are simultaneously possible in the poem "Yet, though. No one speaking, no one moves." Even better are the multireferential potential of words such as "occluded," "efferent," "apsis," "radix," and "lumen" in the poem "Blank bride of the hour, occluded thought." How do you consider your word choices in any given poem?

"Efferent," "apsis," and "radix" are all words I happened on in the dictionary. It's kind of a mystery how wandering into a certain word-field seems to create a magnetic attraction to other words—or how a particular word's field seems to draw others into it. Partly it's a matter of sound, but there is something else going on too. Several of the poets who most intrigue me have a certain near-fetishistic attachment to a lexicon that seems transformed by their attentions—Dickinson, with "circumference," Hopkins with "dapple."

What stays with me even after several reads is the mathematical imagery in the book. In a poem like "Never . . ." I was blown away by the play on the words "integral skin," "cardinal animal," "ordinal net": integral, cardinal, and ordinal each have several associations, all of which are working simultaneously in the poem. And yet you said you composed these rather quickly, so was most of the work done before the writing—did you research words beforehand?

Most of them came spontaneously without planning beforehand. There is far more spontaneity than study—the sonnets were mostly written very quickly, and the "sound chains" are basically musical improvisations. Getting into that space could take some doing, though, which is why there were often long lag periods between bursts of writing. And then there were many discarded poems that had a sonic cohesion, but were lacking in other qualities—that seemed merely formulaic. The 50 that are in the book are the most successful results of the diabolical experiment. I liked *cardinal* and *ordinal*; they have mathematical and sound associations.

Christian ones, too . . .

Being Jewish, I don't think much about that.

Do you see yourself as a Jewish writer participating in that great tradition of Jewish writers?

I haven't been a practicing Jew for many years, but I identify culturally as Jewish. I grew up going to synagogue—depending on how faithful my parents were feeling at the time—and we belonged to a conservative congregation, with services in Hebrew. It was strange to grow up hearing a language you're aware of as sacred, but don't understand—so the idea of holiness is bound up with the incomprehensible, a mysterious and coded speech. I remember experiencing these services as deeply sad, with the words often chanted or half-sung. My sense of sound as evoking mysteries and powers beyond the referential boundaries of language started with those services. I studied the songs in Hebrew school and looking at the letters on the page. Moreover, the mythology of wandering in the desert, of being dispossessed, the exodus, are foundational ideas in my work.

I wonder if that might have something to do with the fact that many of your poems are concerned with closing gaps, and attempt to achieve wholeness.

In my books, there is a constant awareness of, if not a divine force, a large annihilating force that's out there and can destroy at any time. The Hebrew God is a very dangerous god—very temperamental, very destructive.

At the same time, the Hebrew God frequently gives his people, not only second chances, but third, fourth, and fifth ones. He can be alternately terrifying and forgiving.

Yes, he's completely unpredictable. You never know what's going to happen. He can be benevolent, but he can throw a serious temper tantrum. The Lot's Wife tale was particularly horrifying to me when I was a kid. I remember reading an illustrated book of Bible stories for children and seeing an image of a pillar of salt, knowing it was once a woman—and it was horrifying, and uncanny. Why, of all possible punishments, a pillar of salt?

I read a fine review of Nomina *in* The National Poetry Review. *The author had insightful things to say about your work—particularly in regards to Mallarmé's influence on your work. But what struck me most was the writer's qualifiers. I came across phrases like "seems telling," "at the very least one feels," "could be," and "whatever the case," as if certainty with regards to your work were impossible.*

That writer, Douglas Basford, had the manuscript of *Nomina,* but was in fact specifically asked by the journal to explicate two sonnets, "Nice knuckle, uncle" and "That's what it says to the bloomingest more." He may have felt more bound to attempt precise "readings" of lines for that reason, which is no easy feat for these poems. I think his comments overall and especially broader observations on the book and currents in my work are quite brilliant. Comments on any difficult poetry are bound to require a lot of qualifiers—I seem frequently to say to my students, when we're talking about this or that line of, say, Dickinson, that I've been thinking about it for years and am still not sure what to make of it. I hope my readers will accept the experience of feeling like strangers in a strange land when they enter the poems, and not feel too bound to parse them, or abashed if they're not sure what every phrase means. Being lost is a feeling I personally enjoy, in a city or in a poem. The great thing about the sonnet is that a reader can't get too lost, because the form itself is familiar and provides a frame and orientation on a sound level.

As challenging as your poems are, they invite the reader to become intimate with them. I found myself working so hard at each poem that later, when I turned to another writer's work, that work seemed bland, shallow. Your work requires a good deal of commitment, but the payoff is enormous.

Here too, I don't think of it as work, but pleasure and play. Even with the most difficult poets, I just don't feel the engagement is "work." Reading Mallarmé isn't working, it's traveling, or it's being projected into peculiar spaces and states, or hearing sounds in your mind that create such an intelligent pattern, you feel your relationship to sound and word has entirely shifted. As far as "commitment," I don't ask readers to commit to anything but having an unusual experience—hopefully different than they've ever had before, hopefully pleasurable and strange, but not laborious! Intimacy is an interesting term to raise given the poems' "impersonality" and frequent lack of an "I." This too may be partly due to the familiarity of the sonnet form and the immediate connection that sound invites. It establishes a sensory relationship and allure that is "immediate" in that it doesn't require the mediation of sense; it skips past the meaning-making impulse straight to the pleasure of musical pattern.

You've admitted the influence of Mallarmé on your work. Could you expand on this?

His series of four sonnets called *Plusieurs Sonnets* were really pivotal. The density of language and sound, and the way he revolves certain images: the constellation, the empty room, mirrors, hair . . . some near fetishistic images that reoccur throughout his poems. Also, too, the ambiguity of syntax. All of this plays into how I conceived my sonnets.

This seemingly closed form, under the pressure of Mallarmé's brilliant poetic compulsions, is constantly fragmented by ambiguous syntax, so at nearly any point in these sonnets there could be multiple meanings and readings to his phrases and clauses.

One of the most arresting sonnets for me is the Orphic myth, the throat-flute sonnet.

This was one of the earlier sonnets. Some of the terms occur later in the book, such as the "claim," the idea of wakefulness and being aware and attuned, the sameness, which comes up in other poems, a lot of optimistic claims being made. Various propositions are made in the book, questioned and then turned around, seen in darker lights and sometimes more optimistic lights. This poem balances both the dark and light and makes some propositions about the "never-same" . . . the "throat-flute" is that utterance and audibility and articulation of a momentary self of language, which has so many possibilities . . . but in the end there is also so much anxiety about the possibility of failure: is this expression the magic of the ability to express and articulate, what happens when it is received? That's where the anxiety comes in.

Do you think some of the earlier poems, such as this one, determined or set forward the language that comes through in the later poems?

Yes, to some extent, though some of the later poems brought in new terms.

I was wondering if you might give a close reading of two of your poems, the pair that begin "I asked every flower," which I feel are among the finest in the collection. Would you be willing to walk through each one, explaining not only what they mean to you, but perhaps some of the considerations that went into their construction?

The opening two lines "I asked every flower I met / had they seen my palest friend" come from a situation in a chapter of the Hans Christian Andersen tale "The Snow Queen," which has been important to me all my life. The little boy Kay falls under the spell of the evil queen and is taken off to her icy palace. His friend Gerda sets off to find him and has various adventures. At one point, she wanders through a garden asking the different flowers if they've seen him. But the flowers are lost in their own meditations and only tell her their strange flower story—apart from roses, which are kind enough to report that they were underground and did not see Kay's corpse. Otherwise, the question isn't really responded to, so the speaker here gets more of a reply than poor little Gerda, though not particularly consoling ones. The speaker is a bereft Orphic wanderer in search of the lost beloved—and gets the bad news that the world doesn't care. Not only that, but "to search is only to same," so even the act of seeking is questioned. The desire for possession and location of a beloved might be just injury and distortion. A quote by Simone Weil that I've always found terrifying is "The 'I' leaves its mark on the world as it destroys." The implications for a lyric speaker are devastating. The poems are two of the earliest of the tetrameter sonnets in the book, at a point where I'd written many pentameter pieces and wanted to have a different sense of weight and movement, a lighter, more songlike quality, which seemed right for the fragility and strangeness of the "conversation." And the rhymes of course are the same in both, indicating how circumscribed the terms are, how repetitive the quest. I intended there to be a third poem using the same rhymes, but never could finish it.

In the second of the two poems that begin "I asked every flower I met" you conclude, "To search is only to same." In many ways this encapsulates the themes of the book, that the act of naming something is perhaps to shape that thing in a way we already understand, or shape it so that we can understand it.

There's definitely that anxiety in the claim. To seek something out and name it—is that a way to arrest it and therefore limit its meaning? In a kinder light it could be seen as a form of devotion or as a desire to encompass the expressive energy of the thing being named, to bound it.

But the notion of search is twofold: we search for things we've lost or we search for things we do not yet possess. Yet both of these notions would seem to be undercut by "same," which suggests that we're searching for something we already know . . .

In this particular poem, the flower is addressing the speaker's sorrow in searching for the beloved, the "palest friend." This beloved is a specific being who has been lost. However, it could be an unknown, a concept, or some object of desire that is undiscovered. So yes, there is a suggestion that the desire that leads to the searching is a reflexive desire to see what you have already seen or to have your memories reaffirmed.

You do tend to make universal statements in these poems. For example, in the poem "She goes, she is, she wakes the waters," the line "Her hands hold many or her hands hold none." To me there is, once again, that tension between wholeness and emptiness, presence and absence." Furthermore, there is only the choice between two extremes: many or none. Why not "some" or "a few"?

I think the sonnet is an extreme form that I've tried to push to its extreme limits in *Nomina*. And the poets who have most influenced me with regards to this form are poets of extremes, such as Mallarmé, who created incredibly dense sound structures in his sonnets, trying to push towards an extreme intensity—the words have these insights on the nature of the material on the expressivity—those occasions of intensity and extremity were the ones that seemed to charge me in the writing of my sonnets.

That is true of Hopkins, too. And like Hopkins you tend to employ the technique of enallage, recasting words in different parts of speech, such as making a noun into a verb.

Also in Hopkins even the smallest thing being observed became the center of the world; his meditative energies tend to charge the language, an intense awareness of expressivity.

The book is impeccably arranged. Did you compose these poems in tandem or did you write them and arrange them in a new order?

They were arranged this way after they were written.

In the final line of Nomina *you write, "the bride is fled." Not* has *fled, but* is *fled. One prevailing conceit of sonnet sequences is the idea of coming together, of unity that is achieved despite physical separation. Here, however, the final image is flight.*

And yet, another conceit of the sonnet is that the beloved is always out of reach. And even in Shakespeare's sonnets, the lover cannot always control the beloved; resolution and "mastery" of form is only apparent; the beloved can't be contained, as the word can't fully control its sounds. Of my three books, that line is the one ending I'm happy with, because I felt the other two books gave in to the longing for a firmer resolve. But flight and distance seems truer to the experience of poetry—always wanting. The energies of the sonnet often try to exceed its frame, just as the bride herself flees out of the frame of the sequence and the boundaries that are being put on her, including her categorization as "bride."

It's not total escape because, as you write in that same poem, there is an "endless loop." She has fled, but presumably into some other frame.

Yes, she is an elusive energy that is always trying to be pinned down. As a "bride" she is open and receptive to a degree; part of her aspect is a desire to marry, engage with experience, but she doesn't want to be contained in this structure.

Volkman, Karen. "See the crack at the quick of accident?," "This ellipse, slip between seasons," "Yet, though. No one speaking, no one moves ," "Never got, and never thought, and yet," "I asked every flower I met," and "She goes, she is, she wakes the waters." *Nomina*. Rochester: BOA Editions, Ltd., 2008.

Poetry:
Nomina, BOA Editions, Ltd., 2008
Spar, University of Iowa Press, 2002
Crash's Law, W. W. Norton, 1996

Poem as Gesture: An Interview with Kevin Killian

Versatile is an adjective that is often carelessly applied to writers conversant in more than one genre, but in Kevin Killian's case it is utterly appropriate. A prolific and successful novelist, memoirist, playwright, essayist, critic, and writer of short stories, he possesses emotional range and a vast cultural intelligence. Killian's fluency in several genres is only one way in which his writing is versatile, for even within a single book—and often within a single piece of prose or verse—he moves from high to low cultural points of reference, and from pathos to humor, with surprising agility. He is also one of the leading members of the New Narrative movement, which began in the Bay Area literary scene over three decades ago. "We wanted to infuse stories of our lives with the rigors of theoretical discourse," Killian explains. "We wanted to bring the body back to writing, by any means necessary, and so we employed everything from the litany of biology to the badlands of porn to get it there. From body it was a small step to hoping for community, to write for a whole, if limited, community, ourselves and our friends and lovers, and one or two benighted souls we imagined actually needed us in the hinterlands." Despite Killian's accomplishments in prose, he sees himself first as a poet, and his two volumes of verse—of very different quality and scope—are examples of ways in which his brand of New Narrative straddles the work of Language Poetry and the New York School Poets. Killian won the 2009 American Book Award for co-editing *My Vocabulary Did This to Me: The Collected Poetry of Jack Spicer,* and his collection of stories, *Impossible Princess,* won the 2010 Lambda Literary Award for best gay erotic fiction. A secretary at a top janitorial company in San Francisco, he is one of few American poets who does not primarily earn his living by teaching. Nonetheless, Killian is a much-loved mentor to many young writers.

You have over 2000 reviews on Amazon.com. That's a lot of time and investment, especially for an established, well-known writer such as yourself. What inspired you to write so many reviews for that site?

In 2003 I had a heart attack, which left me laid up in bed for a while. While I was recovering, I tried to write and it felt as if I had forgotten how. Dodie [Bellamy] suggested that I write reviews on Amazon as a way of learning to write again. "It's not like you don't have opinions," she said. "You just don't have the words to write them in." So I started writing one-word reviews, which eventually became a few words, whole sentences, and then paragraphs. Then the paragraphs grew into two paragraphs. And then little essays. By that time I could go back to my normal practice of writing entire essays.

That's an amazing story: Amazon.com functioned for you as a kind of writer's therapy. They could market that!

Yes, they could—and it would be true. I'm doing fine now.

Since this interview will focus primarily on your poetry, I was wondering if we could start with your first full book of poems, Argento Series *(2001). What's the story behind that book?*

I knew it was kind of a difficult book in some ways, so when Krupskaya published it I asked if I could put instead of blurbs on the back a timeline of what led me to write it:

> Kevin Killian, Long Island, meets Eileen Myles, Tim Dlugos 1979, San Francisco 1980, writing through cloud of sex, drugs, strong drink and then the curtain begins to fall on a fabulous world, death toll mounting, 1982 meets Bob Glück, 1983 meets Dennis Cooper, 1984 first friend dead, Reagan re-elected, 1985 marries Dodie Bellamy, first enemy dead, death of Rock Hudson, 1986 Grammy award Song of the Year "That's What Friends Are For," 1987, reign of terror, AZT approved by FDA, ACT UP founded NYC, 1988 death of Sam D'Allesandro, election of George Bush, 1989, Dennis writes "AIDS ruined death," 1990, empty, futile, importunate life, first boy Kevin ever loved dead Richmond, VA, 1991 Kevin frozen, unable to think of a way to write about AIDS crisis, 1992 Kathy Acker suggests films of Dario Argento as a prism through which to take apart horror of living and dying in AIDS era, election of Clinton, death of Steve Ab-

> bott, *Argento Series* born, 1993 death of David Wojnarowicz, death of Bo Huston, 1994 FDA approves wide range protease inhibitors, 1997 death of Acker, "I saw something important I can't remember."

Basically it was a feeling of frustration of living through the AIDS epidemic, losing so many friends, and not being able to do anything about it in writing. Every time I tried to write something it sounded ridiculous—hokey, sentimental, or as if I were posturing. In any case, it seemed the enormity of the crisis dwarfed any individual response. And yet I always felt bad about it. Sarah Schulman once said that in the future History will judge all of us by what we did during that time. I was like, "uh-oh!" because I had not done enough.

A form of survival guilt?

Yes, I guess so. I wanted to do more but I just couldn't think of how to do it. Writing big themes never worked for me. Maybe I'm not a heroic person. What could I have done anyhow? I stayed HIV Negative, so I never had to fret the way so many others did. Eventually, I took a tip from Kathy Acker, who urged me to look at Dario Argento's films. She herself had used Argento's *Suspiria* when she wrote *My Mother Demonology*, the first part of which, "Clit City," retells the story of that film. She suggested that Argento's films perform allegorical functions for the way that AIDS works in the body and in the social system.

So I began, skeptically, to look at Argento's films. It was true what she said. But not only that: the films themselves were very beautiful. *Suspiria*, for example, has this gorgeous photography drenched in saturated, unearthly-looking colors. You go into the film thinking you're watching a naturalistic picture of a girl's school, but the colors alone convince you that something really strange is happening. Every surface is treated in strange hues. Every time the heroine walks down a hallway, the walls are such bizarre colors! You'd be excused for thinking it might be light or shadow, but the source is in Argento's camera work. For me, this effect corresponded to the surrealism we lived through in the 80s and 90s.

I'm surprised the original idea was suggested to you, since your handling of this allegory is so deftly accomplished. Only someone who has an intimate knowledge and understanding of Argento's films could pull off such a thing.

I was shamefully unaware of Argento's films until Kathy Acker. But when I encountered them I immediately understood how to use them. A lot of what goes through *Argento Series* is the mystery of the origins of AIDS. The HIV virus: how did it come to be? Why was our generation cursed with this plague that destroyed so many lives and killed so many men? How could this plague make the curtain come down on our fabulous world? I remember the days before AIDS as a nonstop paradise of the senses. Despite what was happening in the outside world, the 70s in San Francisco were a fantastic time to be alive, to be a young gay man. For one thing, and actually it was nearly everything for me then, one could have sex constantly. That's how we said hello—without any kind of guilt or fear. It was a perfectly good way of getting to know somebody.

As someone who came of age in the 80s, I have never understood gay sex independent of fear and the possibility of death.

Yes, that's sad. I remember thinking having crabs was the end of the world—and you could get rid of them in one day!

Let's talk about the poem "Who," the one about Steve Abbott. In that poem, you begin with one context and then dramatically shift to another. It's stunning and yet very difficult to grasp if you don't understand how you're using Argento's films.

Yes, I withdrew some poems from the manuscript because of that obliqueness factor. Even I had forgotten what was happening in them! But in the poem about Steve I was wondering, "Where did he go? What happened to his actual body? What happens to the word when one person disappears? Who did this?" Of course the poem wasn't only about Steve. It was also about meeting David Wojnarowicz—he's in that poem, too. I met him in the early 90s when Wojnarowicz was already a big culture hero of ours. He was doing AIDS work that was not only appropriate but incredibly powerful.

In the first part of "Giallo" the voice is very much summarizing the kind of films Argento makes and their place in the industry. But midway through the poem, there's a sudden shift in context.

Yes. I am watching the movie, trying to describe it as I see it, but the real world keeps on intruding. I'm losing focus on what's happening in the movie because of the horrors of real life. In fact, I think that is what happens in Argento's films when you watch them. They don't make a lot of sense in themselves and you feel that in some way you are watching a derangement of the plot—or whatever is happening in the movie—and you can't follow it all the way in. There's a definite way in which these films want to fuck up your head.

I love the "Udo Kier" poem, especially the intertwining of the actor with a man named Rick Jacobsen. Who was Rick?

Rick Jacobsen, the man for whom I wrote this poem, lived here in San Francisco. He was an art dealer. When Rick came down with AIDS he decided to quit his regular straight job and open up his own gallery called Kiki, which became an extremely magical space in the San Francisco area. But he couldn't keep it open for very long because his health got so bad that he had to go back home to his family in Wisconsin to die there. The image that runs through the poem is of Rick going back to Wisconsin, sort of like deer who go elsewhere to die in the middle of the snow. So, like a deer, Rick dies in the snowy wilderness with only the animals to help him. In the end, he is put out of his misery by a hunter. Incidentally, I wrote a memoir of Rick and the Kiki era that Dennis Cooper published in his online zine, "The Weaklings."

The Udo Kier reference comes from another experience I shared with Rick. I was at Rick's gallery attending a show for the painter Brett Reichman and the real Udo Kier showed up! Rick asked, "Kevin, have you ever met Udo Kier?" I had not and was in awe. Not only had he acted in a few of Argento's films, but Udo Kier's image is that of one of the most evil men in the world! I had my autograph book with me and got him to sign it. He wrote, "I love you." All of that appears in the poem.

Did this experience happen before or after Kathy Acker suggested you use Argento's films as an allegory of the AIDS epidemic?

Before.

Wow. That means, on some level, you already were connected to Argento's films without realizing it yet.

That's what part of the book is, teasing out all of those connections that his movies made to my real life. And the book is, more generally, about death and loss from and beyond the AIDS epidemic. There are poems in there, for example, about Kathy Acker and Bob Flanagan, neither of whom died of AIDS.

Another great poem in the collection is "Testimone Oculare." It's not everyday that you read a poem, dedicated to the theorist Avital Ronell, with references to St. Augustine and Absolutely Fabulous.

Oh, yes. I remember meeting Avital when she worked at Berkeley. Dodie and I were in awe of her. She said something very beautiful to me one time. I'd asked her opinion about something and she said, "You should do what you want, of course," and then quoted Augustine: *volo ut sis*—which is in the poem.

A lot of times you evoke references to popular culture in ways that challenge our normal assumptions of them. The way you cite Absolutely Fabulous *in that poem, for example, is actually very disturbing. Often in* Argento Series *you transform such references, almost curate them in an unusual way.*

Thank you! To someone who works in the art world nearly as much as he does in the poetry world, that observation means a lot.

Let's talk about the poem "Suspiria."

I wrote that poem about Bill Aronson, the first person I knew well who had died of AIDS. He lived in West Hollywood. Actually I never met him in person, but we were both fans of Natalie Wood. He was the editor of *The Natalie Wood Fan Club Newsletter.* Under his editorship, the newsletter saw a dramatic change. It was no longer a traditional fan club newsletter but something much more creative and interesting. The Young Turks had taken over. Bill especially was dissatisfied with representations of Natalie. His take on her was more a postmodern one, as was mine. Therefore, he reached out to all kinds of artists and writers, instead of just the nerdy fans. When he died it was really a shock to me. Oh my goodness, his mother wrote me, answering all his unanswered correspondence piece by piece.

I sense the first line is a quote from some other source: "I know when he began to dance with me." Where does the first line come from?

"I only know when he began to dance with me" is the big number from *My Fair Lady*, when Audrey Hepburn is jumping up and down. The maids are trying to constrain her and put her to bed, but she can't settle down. She could have danced all night. I was thinking of that line when I learned Bill died. I imagined dancing with a corpse. I never got the chance to dance with Bill, to have sex with him, or really engage with him in any kind of way, because his virus kept us apart. I get incredibly angry in the poem, get a little sadistic against Bill, too.

The things you want to do to him are sexually aggressive—even violent.

Yes, I was angry because I was powerless in the face of this loss. I'd fuck him so hard he wouldn't be able to sit for a week. In the face of these images I was appalled at myself, and yet the poem unrolled from a place outside of my will.

And, as a way of interpreting this very personal loss, you conjure up images of Suspiria *the film in the final line.*

Yes, "the tear in the fabric, now the drop of blood" are both from Argento's films. But the fabric of this fantastic, creative relationship I had with Bill was torn, too. We would spur each other to greater creative heights. After his death, I thought there was something missing from that relationship because he never told me he was sick. There was a taboo about it. His mother didn't acknowledge he had AIDS either. He was only 29.

In your essay "Poison" you talk about how you wrote your book of memoirs, Bedrooms Have Windows, *as a love letter to someone who unfortunately died and would not be able to read it.*

In the book my lost lover is called George Grey, but in real life his name was Terry Black. He was a former boyfriend I wanted to reach out to. (Dennis Cooper told me he wrote one of his books for the same reason. Ironically, we each found out our muse figure had died before our books were published.)

It's hard for me to read *Bedrooms Have Windows* now because it has a lot of hope in it. I was counting on it locating my friend, bringing him to me in some unimaginable, magical way. A few years back, Terry's daughter, now all grown up, wrote to me and wanted to know details about what her father had been like when he was younger. She was living in Barcelona then and it was an immensely healing exchange for me.

I see a lot of your poems to Kylie as love letters.

Yes. Oh, I love her. I loved her from the beginning. But I loved her the way you love someone without talent.

Kinda like the way I have an unapologetic love for High School Musical III.

Oh, I *loved* that movie. Did you see I and II?

No, just III. I think you could just jump in there.

Yes! *HSMIII* was my favorite movie of the year. Some say *Synecdoche, NY* . . . but for me *High School Musical III* was the greatest film of 2008.

I notice there's a lot of collage work in your poems, passages from popular songs, images from film, phrases that celebrities might have spoken. Can you talk about your collage technique?

Collage is a good word for my approach. It's not just pop stuff but also the very fiber of the canon, the "great works," that I wind up tearing up and making my nest with, Shakespeare, Dante, Lady Murasaki, it's all grist for the mill. Modernism I guess. The heritage of Eliot, Pound, Mina Loy, H.D., a patchwork of "These fragments I have shored against my ruins." And also the surrealist touch, of counterposing images and lines familiar enough in context but which, when jammed together, produce the unexpected and awful force of an eight-car collision. And practically speaking, I always tell my students that they should try to employ three strands of material in everything they write, prose or poetry. Practically speaking, it precludes boredom in the poet or the reader, and it keeps switching just as if there were a third strand to DNA—mutations bulge and twitch into life from line to line.

The funny thing is I can often see how the poem will look in my head before I write it, see how it looks so I know how many lines it is, how many pages it is, and what's going to be happening on the page visually. So part of my process is filling in that canvas that I have already set up. Maybe it's like a weaving on the loom. I can see the pattern already. "I need a word that has fourteen letters in it to fit in there."

So sometimes strictly formal considerations determine what you put into a poem?

Definitely. Probably really conceptual considerations.

Do you see your connection with the visual arts informing how you write a poem?

I do think of myself as an artist in that high-flown way I associate with the visual arts: it's all in the gesture. It doesn't matter if the poem is good or bad. What matters is the gesture I'm making with it. It doesn't have to be great. Still, most of the poems in *Argento Series* and, I suspect, *Action Kylie*, are about writing.

One poem in *Action Kylie*, "Your Disco Needs You," is about Matt Greene, a painter friend of mine who lives in Los Angeles and, at the time I knew him first, showed at Perez Projects. He is a wonderful painter. When I met him, he said, "You're the one writing all those poems about Kylie. Did you know I met her? I was the art director of one of her videos—and I hated her!" He was the only person I've met who has had anything bad to say about her. In the video for "Your Disco Needs You," Matt reduces Kylie to this little figure so he can have thousands of her dancing across the screen. She spells out her own name in tiny little pixels of herself! Matt's work is very labor intensive: thousands of figures appear in one picture. And because he's so much in vogue, he would paint all night and complain the next day that his hand hurt. I confessed that I'd never written so much that my hand hurt, but I had, like every other guy probably, jerked off so much my hand hurt.

Let's go back to what you said about the gestural. I was talking to Bob Glück about this yesterday. He doesn't see himself as a very prolific writer, or as a writer who needs to write all the time. I suggested that you, by contrast, appear to need to be writing; for you, it's a form of breathing. Bob concurred. He said for you writing is a gestural act.

Well, I'm not a perfectionist like Bob is. And I do believe I should send it out while it's still wet: it's not going to get any better. But, like Bob, it takes me a long time to finish something. I'm finishing another novel, *Spreadeagle*, which I started in 1990. I managed to publish different chapters of it in various publications over the years.

Plus you work on several projects at the same time, so something's always coming out.

Yes. And working on several projects at once relieves my boredom. I get bored very easily, with people, things, writing. So, in writing many projects at once, I can always turn from one to another when I get bored with one.

What brought about the Action Kylie *poems?*

I had worked for years on Jack Spicer, and then another X amount of years on Dario Argento, and in each case the longer I worked on them the more I could see them rising out of the cult status to which they had been condemned, and attaining critical respectability. OK, *that's* a double-edged sword, but I did wonder what would happen if I found a muse that not only had cult status, but what if he or she had no appreciable talent at all? Would poetry still coalesce around such a figure? My feeling was "why not," but until I discovered Kylie Minogue I couldn't even come up with an example. Then in a magical confluence, during one week late in the 1990s, I kept hearing about Kylie from many different sources. An old "behind the music" special on MTV detailed the life and death of Michael Hutchence, lingering on a sad photo of Kylie at his grave, while a narrator said, "and there she came again, Australia's pint-size pop princess." I saw Edmund White in NYC and he happened to be telling one of his great bittersweet stories about a lover who had died of course, but what he remembered best about this guy was dancing the night away in a Rome disco to Kylie Minogue's song, "I Should Be So Lucky." These references were coming to me fast and furious and it was at a time when Kylie's stock was extremely low—she hadn't even a record contract. She was definitely over! Did she intrigue me because of that? Yes I suppose so. Then I heard her duet with the Pet Shop Boys, "In Denial," and I knew I had found my icon, the one with absolutely no talent or voice. Now of course I can safely say that "In Denial" is one of the greatest musical compositions of all time, and that she is like an angel on it. So I just started getting hooked, as I had on Spicer and then Argento.

Can you talk about "The Cats" section of the book?

Stalled and stuck and feeling I wasn't writing anything "important," I decided to embark on an ice-breaking voyage of little, gestural poems—the equivalent of playing *Jeopardy!*. Each of them would embody some cliché about cats, "what the cat dragged in," "kitten on the keys," "raining cats and dogs," etc. I was surprised to discover that, as I got comfortable with the form, the form itself was allowing some other part of my mind deeper access to my feelings than usual. Do you know Robin Blaser's *Moth Poem* from 1964? Similarly a series of disparate poems in which a moth flies through each one. When I was done I was quite proud with what had happened.

The epigraph came to me quite suddenly, for I flashed back to a piece I wrote for *Artforum International*, interviewing Larry Rinder and Nayland Blake who were then preparing a show of gay and lesbian art at the Berkeley Museum. To illustrate the interview, *Artforum* got Bobby Neel Adams to come by my apartment and snap the three of us pretending to chat. Back then I had two cats, Blanche and Stanley, who just loved the hot lights Adams was using, and from what I gather, when the contact sheets came back, one or both of the cats was in every picture, lounging in our laps or across our shoulders or just, you know, hanging out. Except there was one shot in which miraculously no cats appeared. They had to use that one catless photo because, or so it was relayed to me, the editor squawked that there would never be cats in *Artforum*. (That was many years ago; there's a new editor now, and it always surprises me how many cats show up in *Artforum* under the present regime.)

In what ways are the Action Kylie *poems different than* Argento Series?

Argento Series was, as I said earlier, a way for me to (belatedly) address the complex emotions stirred up by a worldwide AIDS epidemic and the disappearance, on a personal level, of a whole slew of my friends and idols, by juxtaposing them with the savage slash murders of Argento's films—and their eerie, implacable beauty. I keep telling myself that *Action Kylie* would have been lighter, except that George Bush Junior was president and America plunged itself into a new Gulf war—while still doing nothing about AIDS. My own identification with Kylie became near total during this period, and while she recovered from cancer, I recovered from a heart attack just as valiantly and touchingly, don't you think?

And the deaths of two public figures anchor the book, the murder of Gwen Araujo, the East Bay teen who, raised as a boy, lived life as a girl until her "real" identity was discovered by the gang she hung out with, who killed her in October 2002. And also the death, from AIDS, of the musician Arthur Russell, with whom I was briefly involved in the late 1970s in New York City. So in a way it's the same book, but *Action Kylie*—a title borrowed from a once-active website devoted to pleading with Kylie Minogue to visit New Zealand—is lighter and more romantic I think, it's the book of a man who has had a second chance to do over everything and start anew. "There's a dark secret in me," Kylie sang. "Don't leave me locked in your heart. Set me free." Her amazing comeback, which occurred over the years that I was writing this book, led to a state of affairs where everyone in the world who loves pop now knows all about Kylie, and for once I'm not resentful.

You were a longtime editor of Mirage. *Can you talk about the goal of this publication and perhaps how the poems you published in it contributed to the vitality of poetry in your community?*

Mirage #4/Period[ical] came about when Dodie Bellamy and I were visiting Vancouver in the spring of 1992. I was impressed by the intense energy of the Kootenay School of Writing and the whirlwind of activity made by what was actually a very small group of poets, writers, and artists. We decided we could publish a magazine using the tools at hand. It didn't have to be fancy like *o·blēk* or *Sulfur* or *Conjunctions;* it just had to come out fast and often. It didn't have to be a hundred pages, as long as it came out just as fast as people could write for it. It was, in fact, modeled on the magazines Jack Spicer sponsored in the late fifties and early 60s, *J* and *Open Space*.

From the beginning, *Mirage* distinguished itself by its cover art. Perhaps no other literary journal had had so many unusual covers and gotten so many fine visual artists to execute them. We were able to get all these people usually by failing to tell them what they were really doing when we asked them for autographs, to "draw a little picture for me," et cetera. Thus by stealth and subterfuge *Mirage* has had gorgeous covers by the likes of John Baldessari, Matthew Barney, Jennifer Bartlett, Louise Bourgeois, John Cage, Vija Celmins, Chuck Close, John Currin, Jeremy Deller, Tom Friedman, Ellen Gallagher, Nan Goldin, Robert Gober, Michael Graves, Thomas Hirschhorn, Jess, Chris Johanson, Mike Kelley, Ellsworth Kelly, Jeff Koons, Sol LeWitt, Meredith Monk, Tony Oursler, Raymond Pettibon, Pierre et Gilles, Jack Pierson, Richard Prince, Charles Ray, Bridget Riley, Peter Saul, Carolee Schneeman, Kiki Smith, Torbjorn Vejvi, Bill Viola, Sue Williams, and dozens more. In conversation, Charles Bernstein called this practice the "absolute low end of high art."

Mirage also went into the archive and sponsored first publication of work by writers such as Spicer, Robert Duncan, Djuna Barnes, Marianne Moore, Robin Blaser, Christa Wolf, Allen Ginsberg, Helen Adam, George Oppen, James Broughton, William Bronk, Philip Lamantia, John Wieners, Joe Dunn, et al. In the nature of zines, the stakes are low. It was easy to take risks. We wanted to recontextualize the work of prestigious writers by jamming them up against unknown, beginning, or, frankly, nonwriters. We could print the Goth-death poems of the security guard at New College next to Jackson MacLow or Barbara Guest—to invent a new economy of reading.

Could you talk about the origins of the New Narrative movement, of which you are a part, and what its contribution has been to literature?

New Narrative started as a loosely-joined group of North American prose writers united in opposition to structuralist theory and its view of narrative as inherently corrupt. When I moved to San Francisco in 1980 I met Steve Abbott, Bruce Boone, and Bob Glück, each in his own way active in rehabilitating narrative from the aspersions of Language Poetry and, frankly, from its own embarrassing shortcomings. It was a fun time, and I think all of us in the New Narrative approached the idea of being in a movement, of working collectively, with various degrees of seriousness. Instantly AIDS was upon us—and AIDS activism, and to this day these apparently disparate campaigns—the fight against AIDS and the struggle for a new narrative—are linked in my mind, stubbornly as my cats. In recent years an impressive number of studies have been done on the impact of New Narrative, and Dodie and I are compiling a New Narrative Anthology for Nightboat Books, which will, I hope, answer your question about its contributions to literature.

Jack Spicer is an important poet to you. Can you talk about ways in which his poems have had an impact on you as a writer?

Oh, Tony, what a big question! I came to him first through the daring impersonations of his first book, *After Lorca,* which, as you know, involves some more or less "straight" translations of Lorca, mixed in with a number of original poems in the style of Lorca passing as his, as well as a third group of poems openly exuberant in their freedom from Lorca's influence. And mixed in with those poems, a number of prose works—letters written by Spicer to Lorca's ghost, and some material by Lorca responding back. It is a book that guarantees nothing, certainly it does without the bottom line I had been used to sinking down to in poetry. You know, there'd always be some sort of formal gesture that would reveal the whole thing as poetry. But with Spicer, that didn't seem to be the case.

His theories of dictation have also been important to me and, even though they have been under question, I still imagine that that is exactly the way I write poetry myself. I just tune down all the other noises until the voice of the "other" can be heard—the voice of what Spicer calls the "invisible world." Spicer compared the poet to a radio through which transmissions find an audience, but the origin of these messages remains unknown. Or sometimes he said that one's own experiences and memories and talents and education might well be thought of as "furniture" in the attic of one's mind and yet the ghosts seek to write poetry by using that furniture, shoving it about till it means something, or at any rate conveys something. Yes, I do happen to know heaps about Kylie Minogue, but will that see me in good stead? Will the Martians be able to mash up what I know to get any poetry out of me? You be the judge. That's just the beginning of my continual changing relationship to Spicer's work. I sometimes imagine that if he knew I was his devotee, or claiming to be one, he'd—oh, what do my students say?—he'd throw up a little in his mouth.

Killian, Kevin. "Suspiria." *Argento Series*. San Francisco: Krupskaya, 2002.

Poetry:

Wow Wow Wow Wow, Belladonna, 2008
Action Kylie, ingirumimusnocteetconsumimurigni, 2008
Argento Series, Krupskaya, 2001

Fiction:

Spread Eagle, Publication Studio Books, 2013
Impossible Princess, City Lights Publishers, 2009
I Cry Like a Baby, Painted Leaf Press, 2001
Arctic Summer, Masquerade Books, 1997
Little Men, Hard Press, 1996
Shy, The Crossing Press, 1989
Desiree, e.g. Press, 1986

Plays:

Island of Lost Souls, Nomados, 2004
Often, (with Barbara Guest), Kenning Editions, 2001
Stone Marmalade, (with Leslie Scalapino), Singing Horse Press, 1996

Nonfiction:

Screen Tests: Collected Film Writing, Fanzine Press, 2012
Selected Amazon Reviews, Volume Two, edited by Jason Morris, Push Press, 2011
Selected Amazon Reviews, edited by Brent Cunningham, Hooke Press, 2006
Bedrooms Have Windows (a memoir), Amethyst Press, 1989
Poet Be Like God: Jack Spicer and the San Francisco Renaissance (with Lewis Ellingham), Wesleyan University Press, 1998

As Editor:

The Nightboat Anthology of New Narrative Writing 1975–1995 (with Dodie Bellamy), Nightboat Editions, 2013

The Kenning Anthology of American Poets Theater 1945–1985 (with David Brazil), Kenning Editions, 2010

My Vocabulary Did This to Me: The Collected Poetry of Jack Spicer (with Peter Gizzi), Wesleyan University Press, 2008

The Wild Creatures (short stories of Sam D'Allesandro), Suspect Thoughts Press, 2005

Bat Logic: An Interview with Dara Wier

"The story of an idea is as dramatic as the story of something we typically call anecdotal." This assertion, made by Dara Wier in the interview below, is a useful portal into her strange and wonderful poetry, for Wier's poems are filled with ideas, and some of her finest ones show us how a particular idea emerges from a state of fog as something solid and clear. One of her particular obsessions is death, her awareness that we are "creatures with an expiration date." However, she is an endlessly inventive poet whose sense of form and "deadly serious" linguistic play have allowed her to find fresh ways of exploring that theme time and again, without ever resorting to angst or cliché. What is more, her quirky humor, terse yet precise phrasing, and ironic sensibility make her an important link to major twentieth-century Eastern European poets, such as Wisława Szymborska and Aleksandar Ristovic. A permanent member of the MFA Program faculty at the University of Massachusetts Amherst, she is a founding editor of Factory Hollow Press. Her many awards include the Jerome J. Shestack Poetry Prize and a Pushcart Prize.

Many of your poems appear to embrace surrealist procedures, especially in how you explore logic in unexpected ways. What, if at all, is your relationship to surrealism? Do you see a vital strain of surrealism in your work?

I don't believe I've ever thought of my poems or how I go about writing as remotely related to something so particular as surrealist. Alternative logics, however, are important. I've always believed that to deeply look into something very literally produces some of the most beyond-realistic effects and understandings. Ever since those first self-conscious relationships with language took hold, what's fascinated me most is how we invent logics. To this end, Edgar Allan Poe, for one, was such an important discovery. He exposes the irrationality of what appears, or tries to appear, rational. I loved him and still love him so much for that. When I first read him I felt, "Oh, here's somebody I can understand! And who might understand me." Going further back into my life than that, I was also fascinated with fairy tales and stories of all kinds and nonsense nursery rhymes, (and lots of these are anonymous and, in a way, that is a good thing: it is all of us writing to all of us if it is anonymous) and taking pleasure-a-plenty from the kinds of playfulness your imagination is invited to celebrate in all those things. Those are a few things—and the simple existence of words and what we make out of words—that inspired me. The music of two words rubbing up against one another, that's wonderful.

And since every word tells a story, is a logic, reveals a point of view, drags around its history, proposes its future, adjusts to its various contexts, just paying attention to what words do gives us plenty to work with. So when you refer to "surrealism" and whether I feel I practice its explorations to find "logic in unexpected ways"—aren't we all exploring logic?—I can't really say for sure.

And, in fact, sometimes what looks very expected is shockingly jarring.

I like to think that what it means to take something strictly literally is a liberating fiction. All stories do this. All combinations of sound and word and all syntactical arrangements. So when I say that when I was around twelve I found Voltaire's *Devil's Dictionary* inspiring, this will later relate to how much I've loved Flaubert's *Bouvard & Pécuchet's Dictionary of Received Ideas*. I like the deadpan delivery and the addled way treating something literally can be so explosively revealing.

Voltaire's playfulness is dead serious. It often happens that you run into something that you need to run into. Early on, for instance, I ran into Ionesco by accident, just because I was hanging around in a library. And a title such as *The Bald Soprano* intrigued me. And I vaguely recall an illustrated edition of it. I was excited to follow that logic. And there are many surrealist writers I love but I've approached them not in any programmatic kind of way. For instance, I'm just getting around to reading William Carlos Williams's translation of Phillippe Soupault's *Last Nights of Paris.*

Almost all of the poems in Selected Poems *fall into one of two formal categories: block-shaped poems that are lineated but without stanza breaks; or carefully-lineated couplets. How early on in the process of writing do you determine whether or not a poem will be organized into couplets or proceed without any stanzas? Why is each of these formal shapes important to you?*

I started writing when I was young—really much too young to be writing. But as soon as I could write I tried to make things that looked like poems. I love the way poems look. It's surprising that I haven't done more exploring of just the look of poems on the page. I don't do very extreme kinds of things with that. But I am drawn to couplets primarily because I appreciate how sane they look. Their peaceful appearance can contribute to a poem's tone, and yet I can do all sorts of interesting and complicated things with logic in a couplet's disguise that I can't do as well someplace else. Couplets seem controlled and rational, but the kinds of logic I can explore in them might not be all that routine, so there's a good tension of playfulness and complication in there, sometimes.

And there is the nine-line/nine-stanza form I do throughout all of *Reverse Rapture.* That was an adventure. I was very happy doing that writing.

You are able to strike a unique balance between playful and sad. In fact, some of your poems, like "Interview" and "Company," are, though heartbreaking, so ingeniously and cleverly constructed that the effect is a mix of devastation and play. Can you discuss this?

Oh yes. The things I've written about are life, love, death. We are all in the same boat when it comes to the fact that we are creatures with an expiration date. The fact that we are still able to have love in our lives and are sometimes happy is all mixed in together with this knowledge of our eventual death. We all know this. Somebody who makes a good joke at a funeral is either awful or a savior. The first time I ever realized how serious death was I didn't start weeping and weep forever. I had to find other ways to live with that. Poetry was the refuge.

It's magical that we are alive. That's obvious. When our minds are active, we walk around in life and change things by lighting them up in various ways with our imaginations. This makes us feel as though we have more in our lives than we literally have. And so in fact we multiply and add to our experiences. You go inside a book and access a whole other life and a whole other world. And I do mean whole. You look at a painting and get incredible things from it that you never would have gotten on your own. This is why I've loved living so much in art all my life.

Poetry has other purposes, too. If a loved one dies, a poem is a good place to grieve. If you're trying to get someone to fall in love with you, a poem can be a great place to flirt, or hope to seduce. The uses of poetry are inexhaustible. And poetry is very forgiving. Sometimes I think it is the most forgiving thing on Earth, maybe in Existence.

Insofar as your poems strike this ironic balance between the playful and the serious, your poems remind me a bit of Wisława Szymborska's. Was she an influence on your work?

This comparison has been made before, and it's a complement. She hasn't been an influence since I discovered her pretty late in my life, but when I did I was immediately drawn to her. We tend to gravitate towards the imaginations and the intellects that are compatible with our own. You want to have a conversation with them.

I am struck by how irony permeates your work on so many levels, especially in your later poems. Irony is obviously an enormous concept that applies to a wide range of expressive possibilities. Can you discuss ways in which your poems embody various forms of irony?

Irony exists in our human interactions as something we observe. I can't force irony on anything. God forbid, I'd ever do that. It's just there. When it shows up in an attitude or tone, it's probably just a natural part of Human Nature. Maybe if I tried to articulate this a little more clearly when I'm walking around in my life, when I'm not writing, I would say I probably enjoy coming up against something that is naturally ironic, kind of rare; I don't much care for fake or forced ironies.

I've interviewed a number of poets for this project who cite Whitman as a strong influence on their work, and more precisely Whitman's earnestness, his tendency to say things unironically. Although your poems are not dishonest, they seem less concerned with earnestness and more inclined toward irony, the magic of riddle.

If you were to put me next to someone in that particular American time, it would more likely be Emily Dickinson than Whitman. I love them both. Some of Whitman's outtakes that he never published in *Leaves of Grass* are rants and raves *against* humanity. But he chose to not let that be part of his public persona. The fact that he made choices like this to me makes him a much richer poet. He was creating Whitman in poetry as fiction, as he was doing his work, making his choices. But I don't think there are as many tonal shifts or changes in his work that come quickly. You have to read him several times to sense them.

While, with E.D., you're being taken for swiftly insistent tonal rides. And that requires one's brain to behave with agility. But all writing that's engaging delivers passages that challenge our personal, private, habitual ways of thinking. Both Dickinson and Whitman let us in to get good strong doses of human brains at work. So of course they'll be doing very different kinds of thinking. And so their rhetoric, syntax, language, subjects, manners with logic and attitudes will be wildly different. I think poetry shows us who we are and we are infinitely many.

So many classical rhetorical devices have been named and defined because they have been seen to exist—like paradox: it's there. We don't create it out of thin air.

Or, say, sometimes we can stare into moonlit water or we can notice wind-blown hair or shadows or clouds creating strange illusions, and we can feel disoriented and good about that. And, say, sometimes this is why ventriloquism might be exciting. Something is coming from where we know it isn't originating. That's play, that's something that invites our imaginations to kick in. Anything that invites imagination to roam is necessary for us, as we live, as we write. When you're a kid and you can play as if you're dead, or pretend you're a horse, or be water or fire, or be someone else than you are altogether.

The presence of horses is strong in your poems. Can you talk about this?

I think it comes from my childhood, lots of pretending I was a horse, a lot. I grew up on a farm. We had a mule, not horses. I wanted a horse. But when I was having a make believe life as a little kid I *was* a horse. Coincidentally, at the same time, when I saw my father his bedtime stories were sometimes about a horse. A beautiful, good, and heroic horse. Probably the presence of horses in my poems is the result of a lot of little spaces in my brain having horses in them put there back then. Horses are also majestic animals that can be romanticized when one describes how they appear and what they do. Horses are figures of transportation, and they enable us to feel transported.

I've pretty much lived my entire life in the country or in a small town. Right across the street from my house here in Amherst are horses. I see them everyday. If I lived in NYC, there'd be horses pulling people around Central Park and maybe I'd sometimes see them. It's kind of amazing that horses are everywhere.

That's true. We often describe them as wild animals, but they're everywhere in our civilized world. They're liminal creatures insofar as they bridge for us those two worlds—the untamed and the tamed.

Yes, they're marvelous in that way. I also can't help but think of Pegasus. And carousels, flying horses—those are amazing! They exist because we can see the wonder of them as they travel around and around in circles. With music!

I also noticed a recurrent image of fog in your poems.

I don't know what to make of this. It's probably very useful to think of oneself in a state of uncertainty as "in a fog." I grew up south of New Orleans, and we had some serious fog down there.

You also play with images of blurring. Whether it's fog or a blur, I see in your poems the self's not-always-successful attempt to pass through fog, be it literal or metaphorical, towards a point of clarity.

I think that's accurate. I'm most of the time and sometimes often baffled. Who's not often baffled? I know I know very little. I guess some people would call this being in a fog.

What's interesting about this is that often, by the poem's end, the self is still in a place of confusion.

I think that's one, just one, honest way to end things. It's hard to end poems. If you don't have some kind of help—such as getting struck by lightning—then it's hard to know when and how to exit a poem. You're not drawing a conclusion. You're not theorizing anything. You might have made some discoveries along the way without having made any ultimate discovery. But it's kind of in the interest of writing a poem to hope for as many possible moments of discovery as possible. Some will come because words have a way of pointing at other words, and any music that eventually arises from combinations of words has a way of pointing to feelings, and then you know how it goes, one thought has a way of pointing to another, sometimes it seems all with minds of their own. That's definitely one of the thrills of writing a poem, feeling you could not possibly recreate the chain of events that led to it.

I'm surprised to hear that exiting a poem is difficult for you, since I am often impressed with where you stop your poems.

Well, sometimes! When you think about exiting anything, leaving life, leaving a party, saying good-bye any time, anything you leave, there are all sorts of variations on how one can do this. The same with ending a poem. I've often had more than one idea about how to exit a particular poem and have done a lot of moving words around to find the best possible way. Sometimes the process is awkward and difficult. I thank you for thinking that the endings are doing okay but that is the scariest place to be in the poem. If you can't exit the poem well you've wasted the whole poem!

Form can be a consolation in this way. Knowing a certain number of lines or syllables or whatever in advance has its own challenges, but it can help you create the gesture for the exit when the time comes, whereas a freer poem can go on and on without providing a clear indication for the termination point.

Exactly. I recently finished a book of sonnet-length pieces in which after a while I started to feel, really feel, the power in the end of each poem coming. You see the end coming and you know you have to get out of there. It's a bracing feeling.

Many of your later poems seem to be the result of your working with a seed idea or a premise, an approach that enables you to develop a poem thematically instead of through narrative.

Well, the story of an idea is as dramatic as the story of something we typically call anecdotal, like coming across a dead body in the park and trying to play detective to figure out how that happened. You can also come across dead love and do a little detective work to see how this happened. Ideas and how they develop are so oddly obvious, but only after they seem to have been found.

Both an early poem, "The Direction to the Left of Sunrise" and a later one, "After the Birds Learned to Count to Eight" refer to the self's struggle to locate a center. In "Direction" you write, "What is central to our direction?" whereas in "After the Birds" you write that the geographic center "was never where / we thought it was." Care to discuss?

Change is one of the essential elements in our existence. Change in directions and not knowing where the center is as the center is moving is giving me a chance to think about change. Oh, and you know that old saying about God whose circumference is everywhere and center is nowhere. That kind of thing. Pascal. Borges. So many writers have liked to or needed to think of this circumstance. I guess because it seems an awful lot like the situation we find ourselves in.

A flux idea?

Yes. And what is more, change is always directly connected to time. Time is another central obvious thing: it has to exist for everything else to exist. So all these concerns are connected to a sense of center. It's amusing to me that we are stuck with ourselves and our place in space and our kind of mind, we have those great little inferotemporal neurons that allow us to read, and our very tenuous appreciation of what time is doing, and what do we want to do, or what makes us feel most alive, getting out of the center of ourselves and shooting around the universe like some crazy hellbent comets . . . I don't know.

I read a rather cranky review of Selected Poems *that claimed the poems didn't add up to much. It was clear the reviewer based this conclusion on the assumption that poems have to mean in certain ways, or that they have to tell stories, be about big themes, and generally assert their own importance. However, what makes so many of your poems fascinating, and your* Selected Poems *a good indication of the substantial body of your work, is that your poems in fact consciously do not set out to "be meaningful" or "important" in traditional ways.*

Ouch, yeah, that's too bad, sometimes people just don't like you or your work. And sometimes this dislike doesn't have anything to do with poetry or poems. Yeah, well, I think my poems matter. Big surprise! I write about death, life, love, sex, beauty, truth, time, change, pain, politics, commerce, animals, water, and the sun and the moon and the stars—all the big stuff. I'm not writing about how to make omelets.

Some people who write about poems expect certain things from poems and if they don't get what they expect they don't want to get anything else. I don't want to get into that rut. I want poems to surprise me.

In my experience so far, a lot of times people who are not writing poetry but love poetry and want poetry to be in their lives sometimes only need one poet. And that poet, if they pick a really good one, satisfies all their needs.

Then there are other people who are basically doing the job of being police authorities in this thing called poetry and their job is to determine what is right and wrong. That's who they are.

Observations about poetry often have a whole lot to do with what someone is doing when they're sitting there at home writing about poetry, and a whole lot to do with what experiences they've had with poetry. You can see how variously complex this gets to be.

When I am listening to someone read their poems to me, I'm right there listening to them and following their thoughts. I'm more intimate with their mind's workings than I am even if they are my closest loved one. And then—and this is a good thing when this happens—they're saying, "Go and live now, get out of here and stop staring at my poems."

Discovery of the endless ways human brains work and the infinite combinations ideas and feelings take—Poetry is this, and this happens to be the closest thing to omni-everything we can ever come close to knowing. We are a greedy, searching, needy, desperate, funny, beautiful tragedy. For a musician, Music is this. For a painter, Painting is this. For a mathematician, Math is this. For a saint, Prayer is this. For a builder of bridges, Bridges are this. For an architect, Building is this. For a cook, Cooking is this. And so on.

I've recently thought that sometimes when I read a poem the biggest thing that affects me is what I come to understand about what a poet thinks and feels about us, and what a poet thinks and feels about poetry.

I've never thought I didn't understand a poet's poems. I've always thought that a poet's giving me something to understand.

I'd like to talk for a bit about the strange but charming poem, "I Remember Rilke."

I had been reading lots of Rilke's letters when I wrote that. I was thinking, "Oh, man, he is such a big-time flirt, always sweetly trying to seduce someone, always trying to get what he wants." Not so different from most of us. It's charming to watch someone behave this way. I wondered what it might be like to want to do everything one can do to make one's self attractive to Rilke. I guess you can say I was teasing Rilke. One day when I was reading these letters, I had the luck of seeing a spider trying to walk up on my wrist and that spider sort of became Rilke, the spider transformed itself into Rilke, and the spider is the spider who appears in the poem you mention.

Another poem I wanted to talk to you about is "Company," which seems tremendously sad to me.

One thing I want to say first: any I in any of my poems isn't me, I'm free (shocking!) to say any I and let any I take on any character or mood or political or everyday purpose. I've never been inclined to give up using I even when I is/am not me. I don't have to be any I, right?—and I'm usually not. Pardon my touchiness here; I have been accused!

I didn't assume you were, actually. I was really more taken by the relationship between the "I" in the poem and his or her friends, who insist, "we must uncomplicate our lives." Why are we running away from complication? That seems heartbreaking.

I think you're right. The tone of that poem is set up early in the poem when I talk about a conversation about taking care of horses on their way to slaughterhouses. Why are we trying to make a lot of complications that are false complications (which would involve feelings) when we have real complications—and complexity is to be desired almost always? Although Faulkner did say, "Life is simpler than people think." That's perfect for Faulkner to have said that because the several meanings of that are pretty good. Literally, life is simpler than how we think about it. But how we think about it and what we do because of how we think make it all so complicated!

Before the beginning of every poem you could practically inscribe over the threshold of it, "What if?" What if this is the way I am having to think right now? This is how I'm going to have to be thinking now. Now what will this require? What might this determine? Who will this let in? Where will this take me? Do I want to go there? Will it be terrifying there? Will anyone love me there? Will I hurt someone there? Can I ever get out of there? Is it dark in here? Will there be music in here? Will I be able to find a match or a light switch? Who else is in here? Will I want to stay here forever? How will this change me? How will this change everything? What can happen in here that can't happen anywhere else?

My favorite poem in Selected Poems *is about Henry Adams and is called "A Secret Life." In that poem you write, "My thoughts have hidden themselves // from everything available / which might have made them visible." Can you talk about this?*

You know, when someone dies you can pretend they're just hiding. When you don't know something you can pretend that there is something that you know, even if you are unable to know it. So when I mention thoughts being hidden I am talking about potential, about possibility.

Things are hidden. Everything one wants to know is hidden. There is so much that is hidden from us, we've had to make up games that involve hiding, just as a way to make the idea of being hidden or hiding not so frightening. And to lend us the idea that we might be capable of hiding something. We gain a little agency. Remember when you were little, and you were hiding, it might cross your mind—the possibility . . . that what if you are never found! I like to think about things that we suppose are there, literally *there*, but where? We don't know. Either because it is in their nature to be hidden or because someone, perhaps, thought it might be best to hide them.

Oh, no! We are right back in that terrible old Garden of Eden story! Sorry about that! Aren't lots of games made up just so we might not be so afraid of what the games involve? The sweet little girl angel dressed up like a demon isn't so scary as a real honest-to-god Demon. And so on.

To cite an idea you explained earlier, hiding, in the sense you are using it, seems like an interesting exit strategy.

Yes. The ending of "A Secret Life" is an example of the good fortune one can stumble into when two activities cross paths at the right time. When I was writing this poem, I had just finished reading Henry Adams' biography. The ending of the poem is a literal representation of an anecdote in which Adams spends the evening telling his niece all he knows precisely because he knows she won't understand a word of it and therefore won't be able to repeat it. That was so remarkable to me: it was beautiful and heartbreaking.

And it reminds me of how and why we talk to animals.

In that same poem, you write: "We dream of what we really are / and spend lifetimes denying it."

A literal way to take that statement is that we are human animals who are doomed to die, though we spend our lifetimes denying that fact, which is a good thing. We need to act as if we are living, not dying. It's dangerous to fall in love with someone. It's dangerous to fall in love with a place. It's dangerous to want anything. All of that has to do with time and our earlier-mentioned expiration dates that seem to haunt me without end. This danger is connected to daydreaming, thinking, pretending, and imagination being the thing that saved my life basically. And probably why I fell in love with poetry.

At the same time, our dreams return us to that reality.

Yes. We need both the dream and the denial. We need to know this truth about ourselves and we need to act as if it weren't true.

In "Hypnagogic" you say, "They were training me to wait and not want / what I'd lose if I asked for it. // I had to pretend I didn't care / and this was against my nature." Could you first identify the "they" and then talk about the rest of this?

They—all that would be life and the gods. That would be, I guess, *everything*. What does this passage mean? I guess I sound like a broken record: once again, our lives are so short and we need to pretend that they're not. I pretend not to care about that, even though I do care desperately, so as not to be the most forlorn, sobbing, grieving, sick, and possibly boring person ever. A note about my life: I grew up in the middle of nowhere, south of New Orleans, so my family had its own cemetery. I grew up playing there. A dead giveaway, as they say!

A constant memento mori?

I would lie on top of my great aunt's tomb and look up at the sky and daydream. It was a very important place to me, but I didn't know that at the time.

In southern Louisiana the tombs are above ground, because of the low sea level. Maybe, metaphorically, your poems are like those tombs, raising what other writers might push underground.

Well, I don't know about that. Isn't it just our universal way of dealing with death? I feel in writing about such things I'm participating in a tradition.

In "Gullible Mosquito" you say, "A false door stays a false door / saying exactly what it was / put up on purpose for."

False doors are both architectural motifs and archeological elements you will find, among other places, in ancient Egypt and in the Etruscan times. Some architects/builders have made this image more literal, where one might think you could actually open the door, but you can't. False doors are symbolic doors, in a sense. They represent—as they would for you if you made one for yourself—our idea about the ultimate separation between life and death. There is a door. In tombs, false doors were where all the inscriptions would go, all the writing would be put on the doors. In writing that poem with a false door in it, I was thinking about the paradox of the false door—what a great concept. And I was thinking about how wonderful it is that we build physical representations, objects, that directly say something about thoughts, actual thoughts, being able to travel through physical barriers.

Interesting! The fact that poems or writing was placed on the false door suggests that one finds escape through the language.

Right! Or if not escape, transportation. In vampire lore, a door can be open, but the vampire can't cross your threshold unless you, with words—I'm assuming, I guess, a really strong and clear gesture would do!—you invite the vampire to come in. Taking the idea of "you asked for it" or "be careful what you ask for" to happily eerily literal regions.

And the notion of the false door itself, as you've described it, can be understood as a metaphor for poems themselves.

Yes. In a sense you need a false door, for example, to create the illusion that there's an ending, and a beginning, that you are leaving the poem and going somewhere else.

Wier, Dara. "The Direction to the Left of Sunrise," "After the Birds Learned to Count to Eight," "A Secret Life," "Hypnagogic," and "Guillible Mosquito." *Selected Poems*. Seattle: Wave Books, 2009.

Poetry:

Selected Poems, Wave Books, 2009
Remnants of Hannah, Wave Books, 2006
Reverse Rapture, Verse Press, 2005
Hat on a Pond, Verse Press, 2001
Voyages in English, Carnegie Mellon University Press, 2001
Our Master Plan, Carnegie Mellon University Press, 1999
Blue for the Plough, Carnegie Mellon University Press, 1990
The Book of Knowledge, Carnegie Mellon University Press, 1987
All You Have in Common, Carnegie Mellon University Press, 1984
The 8-Step Grapevine, Carnegie Mellon University Press, 1980
Blood, Hook & Eye, University of Texas Press, 1977, 1980

Poetry Steeped in Intellectual Matter: An Interview with Bin Ramke

In a recent discussion with his Omnidawn Editor, Rusty Morrison, Bin Ramke explained why he believes poetry has value to its writers and readers: "The poem is shaped by the preconscious aspects of Mind in ways that teach us who we are and how we connect to each other and the world." This statement is especially relevant to Ramke's oeuvre. Often cerebral yet deeply elegiac and emotionally charged, his poems expose the workings of the mind in ways that reveal his obsessions—notions of home, loss and death, theological and mathematical languages, and the nature of reality—and invite readers of poetry to reflect upon their own mental processes. As the poem "Reminded" from *Aerial* (2012) demonstrates, the author's focus on Mind is connected to ethics and action: "Mingling over the years growing / vinelike into vascular awareness, an // arrangement of anxieties into what we call *Mind.* // To mind is to care." Writing and reading work of such quality requires sustained concentration. Perhaps this is why Ramke, who began his career by winning the much-coveted Yale Younger Poets Series in 1978, has followed a more singular, hermetic path than most of his contemporaries. Each of his concept-driven books is the result of an incredibly hard-won labor of love. A Professor of Creative Writing at the University of Denver and the Art Institute of Chicago, he has also received two Iowa Poetry Prizes (1994 and 1998) and four Pushcart Poetry Prizes.

Theory of Mind: New and Selected Poems *is your tenth book of poetry in 31 years. In that time your poetry, perhaps more than the work of most poets, has undergone some fairly radical evolutions in style and conception. Can you discuss some of the more prominent changes in your work and your reasons for evolving the way you have?*

Yes, I suppose the work has changed quite a lot. At first it was such an exciting experience to find language shaping itself in recognizable patterns on a page that my earliest work was just a kind of ebullient celebration of itself—and I just sort of cast-about for reasons to write—hitting most easily upon what was probably a callow version of my own experiences of the time with slight interventions to make myself sound literary. As an instance: because my family did in fact have a horse that died on Christmas Eve, and the experience was not one I had seen dealt with literarily, I played with that in an early poem. And since I am a Southerner—born in east Texas to a Cajun mother and farm-raised father from the bayous of Vermilion Parish Louisiana—the things I wrote about (if not the actual process of writing) said I was a Southern writer.

The volatility you identify probably has to do with my education in and into poetry. I began writing poems while learning to read Wallace Stevens (and other canonical figures, but they were new to me) under the tutelage of then-graduate assistant John McNamara at Louisiana State University. Stanley Plumly was my first official teacher of creative writing—I was in my fifth year as an undergraduate, having weaved back and forth between Baton Rouge and New Orleans, and while I had then been writing poems for a couple of years I resisted any actual formal coursework. Plumly is now and was then a brilliant teacher, charismatic and commanding. He spent only a couple of years in Baton Rouge, and his assigned readings were mid-sixties midwestern at that time—which is to say, I began as a Southerner having his eyes opened to the contemporary through the works of, for instance, James Wright and John Berryman, with forays into the "deep image" of Diane Wakoski. In some significant sense, this allowed me to wander among possibilities, not indebted to any particular ideology or school. On my own—and I still vividly remember picking up copies of Clayton Eshleman's *Caterpillar* in a New Orleans bookstore—I began reading West-Coast writers with little understanding but some sense of the new energy (new to me) they made available. I suppose when I was in graduate school, having followed Plumly to Athens, Ohio, I began to assimilate Ashbery and O'Hara into the mix. My point is, I had no idea where I was going, or that I was going anywhere. I was aware of poetry generally as a kind of permission to make sounds and sentences in all kinds of ways, and I would return to earlier ways of making poems (ballad stanza, sonnet, et al.) simultaneous with trying out the next new (to me) thing. In some ways this practice continues.

In terms of selection, Theory of Mind *is really more of a sampling than a full, representative chunk of your poetry. It must have been hard to select only a few poems (though some of them quite long) from each book to include. What were some of the factors that went into your decisions about inclusion?*

Others have complained about the selection, too. Craig Morgan Teicher, in *Boston Review,* made much the same point. But I have no idea what a "full, representative" sampling would be, short of a Collected Poems. The major factors that went into my choices had to do with which poems I could stand, which I could stand by. The flaws and naïve assumptions of so much of the first four books have been noted in print and in person to me and I have a hard time arguing for them. So I looked back from my current position, from my sense of what I can usefully work with now, what I can defend. I see my possible usefulness as a poet in these ways: the poem is a representation of consciousness itself, and an experiment in that phenomenon; and the poem can be a semisecret vehicle of significance—i.e., it can say more than the poet knows in ways that readers (including the poet) with time begin to recognize and appreciate. So when I started to look again at my old copies of those early books, I looked for surprises. I found few, but what I began to value were the poems, which seemed to anticipate my later concerns. If there were a minimum of embarrassingly awkward lines and images, then I included those poems in the final selection.

I have pretty much since the second book tended to work with the idea of a book as I write individual poems—that is, selection goes against the basic principle of these investigations that ultimately make individual fragments (poems) into books. But then it was my idea to do a selected, so I should have known better.

The new poems in Theory of Mind *are grouped under the section heading* Anomalies of Water. *Water is a recurring image in many of your poems, especially in your later work. Can you discuss why this is the case?*

I grew up in a sort of swampy, humid, water-infested environment that is probably unimaginable to many people; that is, on the Gulf Coast. And my father's work was often with water treatment—the analysis of waste water from the chemical plant where he worked, as well as the study and the treatment of ground water in the region—watching for encroachment of salt water into the fresh water aquifers, for instance, a job I accompanied him on a couple of times, which involved taking a boat into swamps where test wells had been drilled. I heard him talking about these matters, and I "helped" him at times, learning to do some chemical analyses with a little chemistry set he made for me. But then later I became sort of obsessed with Heraclitus and other pre-Socratic philosophers—as much because they are so little more than names, and yet they maintain a presence in even contemporary thought. The attempt of these thinkers to understand, come to terms with, the physical world around them still strikes me as terrifically exciting. Anyway, Heraclitus is credited with some interesting statements about change, about water and the shapes it takes as not merely images but instances of the constant alteration of Reality. Further, I did sort of understand earlier than some (because of my father) how crucial and terrifying our relationship with water is. Floods and famines and such. Then when I moved to Colorado twenty-five years ago I encountered the same issues inverted—western water concerns have more to do with scarcity than surplus, but are no less critical. And the fact that my roof leaks because of ice dams whereas in the south my worries were about molds and mildews and rot does not mean water in its various forms is not still the issue.

I could go on, and quite often I do. About all the clichés, about the bodies of all us animals being largely water, about the grandeur of clouds and oceans and rivers and streams.

And I do consider *Anomalies of Water* to be its own book, even though I have continued it in some sense in my current project, tentatively titled "Conspiracy," which is a group of poems arising out of my thinking about clouds, those most transient of forms of water.

Richard Hugo chose The Difference Between Night and Day, *your first full-length collection of poems, as the winner of the 1978 Yale Series of Younger*

Poets. Hugo saw in that first book poems "so honestly rooted in isolation that they suggest a man with no way of reaching others except through his writing." Would you agree with this assessment of your work? And do you think themes of isolation have persisted throughout your books, despite radical changes in style and conception?

I suppose I do agree and that the themes have persisted, even though I cringe a bit. The current dogma is all about community, about poetry being of the here and now, there is no such thing as "transcendence"—all of which is no doubt true. I, on the other hand, grew up at a time and in a place where a certain kind of isolation was the norm, and another kind of isolation was the goal. I am moved to speak of a summer experience I had, studying mathematics at the University of Texas. It was a National Science Foundation event for high school students, in 1963, and among the things we homesick students discussed late at night was the isolated thinker versus the corporate (not the word we used) team-player. Oddly, the intervention of computing was part of this discussion—we had limited access to the school's CDC 1604, one of those giant rooms with cables beneath the floor and amazingly accurate air conditioning, all to keep going a machine with far less power than this laptop I am typing on. But the fact that calculations were soon to become mechanized raised questions about thinking; and the value or reliability of an individual computer (the word, as used by one of the "fathers" of the digital computer, Alan Turing, generally meant a person, not a machine) as opposed to some organized group doing Big Science, was cause for consternation for us. Some of us. In some way my turn to poetry later on may have been an attempt to hold onto that Romance of the individual against the demands of uniformity and normalization that the twentieth-century American was subjected to.

The individual mind is connected to the species through language, language as a sort of external nervous system. Unselfconsciously I did begin connecting through writing, but without very much faith that the connection was strong on the other end. I believe not so much that I can only reach others through writing but that only through writing (on the physical solidity of paper, not blogs, not telephones, not texting) does that connection suggest confidence (with faith, with trust).

Some of those poems in that first book, such as "Summer 1956: Louisiana" and "To Bury a Horse in Texas" are rooted in place and, at least as far as the titles are concerned, would have seemed perfectly in context in a table of contents for one of Hugo's books. In those early years was Hugo's poetry influential to you in any way?

As to the poems of *The Difference Between Night and Day*, no. In fact, had I known Hugo was to be the new reader for the Yale Series that year, I would not have bothered entering, since I thought at the time we were so different as to make entering pointless. I had given up on that manuscript shortly after entering it (and forgot it was there—the call from the publisher was quite a surprise since I really had forgotten) and was already sending out a different book when it was selected. But when I got to know Hugo the person, as well as the poems, I did pay attention, and learned some things. So his influence no doubt is at work in *The Language Student*, possibly in some of *White Monkeys*. I would say his influence would come from his letter poems, which struck me as strangely and liberatingly casual (I was caught up in formality of a different sort at the time), and *The Right Madness on Skye*, because he was writing those at the time I got to know him. (To know him a little. That is, he was quite guarded, and after I pestered him for a while with letters abusing his kindness he made it clear he had issues of his own to worry about. Soon after, as it happened, he died.)

But your question about the place of place in the poems is not so much connected to Hugo as it is to a kind of Southernness, and just a kind of curiosity I am heir to. I am fascinated by where my students are from, what experiences of landscape, urban and otherwise, they have. I like to experience regional accents. And yet I do very little traveling. Go figure.

White Monkeys *(1981) remains one of my favorite books of your work. Poems like "The Magician" remind me a little of the terse, surreal world of Gregory Orr. Was Orr an early influence?*

No, not really, and I am not sure why. That is, I came to his work rather late, and always considered him far beyond me, far more established and successful in his work. I was using personal childhood experiences in my writing, but in a sense didn't want to, thought I was disguising them, and intended to stop as soon as I had developed the skill necessary to move away, to move on toward . . . well, I didn't know what. But I have always in all my attempts at poetry known that something bigger or better or more beautiful or more humane might be possible, and in some sense I felt Orr's achievement, significant as it was and is, would misdirect me. It might have been that, in the poems I first encountered of Orr's, the experience he used (the accidental killing of his brother) seemed so much more significant than anything I could tap into that as a writer I had to turn away.

Also, and this is moving into a different focus, there was my simple ignorance. I did not know the work of many poets, and only encountered Orr's work late. And this is all part of an oddness about who I was at the time. My first three books were probably read, if they were read, as located in the American South, as I was. But I suspect that I was seen as a highly suspect Southerner. That is, while the poems were often located in a specific place, and that place was often the south Louisiana-east Texas nexus of the Cajun Diaspora (forgive the use of the term, but it was a Diaspora, and involves a fairly horrific history), I think the poems were disappointing to those looking for some sort of Southern street cred.

The poem "Eclipse" from that same collection seems, from a retrospective standpoint, to be a particularly important early poem. It's there that one can see many of the features of your later work—fused sentences, deliberate lack of punctuation, the deconstruction of narrative, and repeated pronoun shifts.

I always thought it was about seeing, and connectedness. So I did play about with boundaries of sentences and of the elements of narrative (small as the narrative is). I can't say much about the actual specific decisions, but I do know that I was caught up in a concept of seeing with such intensity that the eye itself would be seered into singularity—blinded. And I liked the notion of, the drama of, nighttime subtleties of light versus the nakedly viewed sun.

"Seeing" was from my earliest awareness a constant concern and worry for me, probably because two of my uncles were blind, one from birth, one from a childhood accident. One became a musician, the other a historian—these facts are not obvious in the poem you cite, but are part of how I think so much and often about vision.

"Syllogism" from The Language Student (1986) *is a terrific poem. It exemplifies perhaps a tad more explicitly than elsewhere, your poetry's longstanding affiliation with philosophical concepts and language. Can you talk a little about "Syllogism" first and then, more broadly, about how philosophical discourse has nourished your work throughout the years?*

I am pleased that you like the poem. I do too, and it is rare that I continue to like any of my own writing past the first few months or minutes. The origin of this poem is in hearing a cousin of mine recite the mnemonic, "every good boy deserves favor"—I always wanted to learn to play some musical instrument and envied all who had learned, and I had been questioning her about her lessons. And for a time in my childhood milking a cow before school was one of my chores, and the changing tone of the sound of milk spraying into the bucket was part of the experience. In fact, then, the poem grew out of an intensely physical, specific set of circumstances. The syllogistic form, and the title, was part of the poem from the beginning, and in some sense was a deliberate imitation of what I thought of at the time as a habit of composition learned from Wallace Stevens—an imitation of the form of conscious thought, always being undermined by the emotional weight of experience itself.

I read philosophy and theory, but from an amateur's untrained perspective. Outsider philosophy? Folk philosophy? I read mathematics (the history of mathematics, and logic) with a slightly more formal sort of training, and I have always enjoyed the philosophy of mathematics and logic even without knowing much about the discipline itself. I think I can do two things well—make connections between disparate ideas or images or words; and patiently wait for connections to occur during the process of investigating. This is somehow connected to my firmly held faith in the relationship between mathematics and poetry—that both are concerned with what it could possibly mean to claim one thing is another thing, or even "like" another. And both concentrate on the difference between as a way of knowing the thing—why is one thing not another thing.

"Life Raft" from The Erotic Light of Gardens (1989) *is an intriguing poem about pain, desire, and art. In the poem's hair-raising conclusion, you ask, "what does any art consume / if not its own maker and maker's flesh?" What does a conclusion such as this mean for a poet who makes poems? What does this say about the relationship between the creative drive, which may be partially physiological, and the body?*

I have much, too much, to say about this. For one thing, the poem was almost completely a response to my watching a television documentary about Géricault. I taped the documentary off-air and watched it over and over (I still have the tape). And these things started happening in my imagination: Théodore Géricault produced this painting as a documentary, even if imaginative, even if after the fact, of a specific historical event. I became aware of it through a documentary, and then I began a poem as a documentation of my response. Questions of fact began flying around my head—questions about what a fact is or can be. The very word is derived from the word for make—from *facere*, which means "to do" or "to make," just the opposite of what we usually mean by a fact, which is a thing not made, not made-up. Anyway I was also fascinated by Géricault's nearly obsessive artistic practices of examining the body, its various parts, even those parts such as amputated limbs. When I finally saw the Géricault painting of a severed head in the Art Institute of Chicago, years after this poem, I was immoderately happy about it.

But to your question specifically: I find this conclusion, that a thing of art gets made out of the very flesh of the artist, and the physical being of the art itself, I find that exciting and promising. I am reminded of the Mass, the Roman Catholic ritual, which Catholics are bound to believe, is the actual eating of the flesh of God (the bread is transformed into the body, the Body of Christ, and the blood). Consuming and being consumed is not just the stuff of B-movies.

In "A Tree Full of Fish," from Massacre of the Innocents (1995), *you employ a strategy which is carried over into many of your later poems, namely the inclusion of quotes and paraphrases right in the body of the main poetic text. What were some of your reasons for using this technique?*

I was in love with epigraphs early on, and I was and remain excessively respectful of scholarship. I wanted to be smart, and I collected bits of language which struck me as especially apt, or beautiful, or for whatever reason. I often would use this language as a starting point, or as a way to further an attempt at a poem, usually finding some way to camouflage the quote, to remove it and allow it to have been a catalyst but no longer part of the chemical construct. At some point it occurred to me a more honest presentation of the process of the poem was to leave these passages, to allow the actual engagement of the mind of the poem with the world to remain obvious. (I might point out here that much of what seems to a reader to be obscure in my work is the result of attempts at directness and clarity, leaving in all the steps.) Also I had been realizing for some time that I was not going to be a real scholar, but that I could make use of some of the techniques and attitudes of scholarship in these things that still looked like poems.

A corollary to this is an embarrassing admission: I am the only person I know who always appears to be more intelligent than he is. (This applies even if other people think I am not smart—I am even less intelligent than that, I assure you.) I grew up in a situation which suggested I was supposed to be a good student, highly intelligent—I played the role. But I have never had confidence, never am able to argue my intellectual position in the face of opposition. I know a lot ABOUT intelligence, I know what it looks like and sounds like, and I can do that. But in the end—and here is where the use of all those quoted passages is relevant—I am always an outsider looking in, so what I have to offer is my appreciation of other people being smart. And sometimes I see connections between them that even they don't see, but that's about my only contribution.

"Wake" from the book of that same title (1999) is one of the longest poems included in Theory of Mind. *So many of your poems are about sleep and dreaming that I find its title interesting! The poem itself seems a bit like a collage of literary allusions that flow together and into one another like water. Can you talk a little about the composition process of this poem?*

I can, and I surprise myself in this case. The composition of "Wake" remains vivid for me. It began in highly structured, formally divided sections, more or less a sonnet sequence, rhymes and all. But after a month or so of collecting these pieces I began to think I had a larger sort of thing going on than I had intended. Incidentally, I have from my earliest days of thinking about poems been semi-obsessed with Ezra Pound. Not always admiringly. But I have some notion of Pound being able to move with impunity among and through the material of consciousness, of being "aware" that the bits and pieces which fall off are part of the process (what process? life?). Anyway, I used some made-up events of my life, plus a bit of my obsessive examination of the lives of my aunts and uncles (especially my Uncle Kenneth, former merchant marine, who let my brother and me spend summers with him on the Mississippi, in a houseboat), and let my readings of Heraclitus, of Lucretius, of Pound all swirl around while I was trying to work out a form. In the end what I wanted was a singularity, I wanted everything to happen at once. The poem is intended to happen all at once, hence instead of being divided into neat sections it is all a blur, a mass of words with very little punctuation. I have only tried reading this thing through in public twice, and each time was physically taxing—I am sure on the audience, but also on me. I mean, it isn't all that long, but I am actually not supposed to even take a breath, theoretically. And I always stumble over the quoted Greek (which I quote because Pound quoted it.)

I must admit I am surprised you find many of my poems to be about sleep and dreaming. You are no doubt correct, it just hadn't occurred to me. I do not remember dreams well, at all, and go through spasmodic efforts at recalling them—notebooks beside the bed and all that. Why I want to remember them is so as to reclaim as part of experience that one-third of a lifetime spent asleep. In regard to "Wake," however, I was thinking about blurring the distinctions, awake and asleep, living and dead (i.e., the practice after funerals), but also the shape of water behind a boat as evanescent record of movement. Plus the verb usage of "wake" is related to "watch," so it is about vision again, about how to see.

It's interesting that "Wake" began as a sonnet sequence. You have mentioned before that in your apprenticeship as a poet you turned to traditional forms. And then there are the "Cold Sonnets." You seem to return to the sonnet form periodically. Could you talk about your relationship to the sonnet and why this form is important to you?

I think about the "received forms" nearly constantly because they offer a continuation of the innate structure of language—of how "meaning" depends on a multidimensional placement of its atomic parts, of the letters contained in words contained in phrases/sentences and so on. That "and so on" takes us to one possible split between poetry and prose—whether one moves then to paragraphs or stanzas, or in some other way into units which have a history, or which appear to be nonce, newly formed for the occasion. The sonnet simply happens to be convenient in my mind for such moments. Early in my mumbling toward a poem I am nearly always tempted to round-out some set of sounds by finding a shape and calling it quits, and this can easily be at fourteen lines. I can even have fun with sounds and suggest those rhyme schemes, or with rhythms and tease out a sort of iambic pentameter. But for me this is usually a sort of holding pattern that allows me to keep the matter of the poem (I am thinking of the entire complicated etymology of "matter," which involves maternity as well as trees) alive in my mind. The other great usefulness of (the idea of) sonnets for me is the tradition of sequences, which means one can move outward in little quantum leaps (a quantum is a very small measure) into a second sonnet, a third, and onward.

My experiences as teacher have an effect on all this. Primitive students often come to the *writing* of poems with this peculiar ahistorical notion, that poems differ from prose in that poems have no formal restrictions (they are accustomed to the five-paragraph essay, I suppose, which is for their prose an onerous formal restriction). But in literature classes they approach the *reading* of poems with quite the opposite expectation—that the poem will be recognizable and predictable visually and aurally, whereas prose is a trackless desert. My reason for mentioning this in answer to your question is simply that in my thinking, formal issues of language are always tense, full of tensions and paradoxes that provide much of the energy that poetry requires.

With Airs, Waters, Places *(2001), I begin to see a more forceful use of scientific language surfacing in your poems, a language that fuses with philosophi-*

cal references and terms in the dazzling poem "Water." Could you talk a little about "Water" and what some of your aims were with this poem?

I love your question, partly because it jolts me into a new view of it. The poem "Water" was, to my mind at the time I was making it, a response to stories my mother told of her family caught in a flood, and it was an attempt to consider the flooding and dissolving of the very land where she (and all my family, including me) grew up. What I mean to say is, it felt to me very personal, very emotional, very much an exposing of vulnerability. My aim was to recover some of the dignity and despair of the people of the region. But I cannot help but be fascinated by the processes: a related matter: my paternal grandfather's house, which my father helped build, is now nearly at the edge of the Vermilion Bayou, since commercial boats plying that waterway have through their wake washed away 30 or 40 feet of land during my lifetime. The hydrodynamics of the river and its boats have caused the land on that side of the river to dissolve and then be deposited on the opposite shore—the river is moving; the river IS alive and dangerous.

That is to say, I was surprised because your question would suggest a more distanced, scientific approach is at work in the poem. And you are certainly correct that philosophical references and terms are all over the place. But they arose out of one of my most emotionally specific poetic acts.

"Scientific language" interests me, of course, for several reasons. One is that any sort of language connected with defined activities is fascinating: the terms associated with carpentry, or plumbing, or genetics, or hydrology. The other fascination has to do with the continuous failure of any language, any grammar, any diction, to say what we want it to say. Momentarily a new coinage seems to enable a new vision, but soon it falls into habitual uses, and begins to blur and to bleed into other ways of thinking and seeing and soon we are off looking for another, newer . . . word or phrase or way of being. So I do try to be faithful to the technical terminology, to how the experts understand and use the term, but as much as that I am attending to the corruption of the usage.

A student of mine in Chicago brought my attention to Tom Stoppard's *Arcadia*, to a comment by the character Septimus (which I quote in "Computational Origami"): "We shed as we pick up, like travelers who must carry everything in their arms, and what we let fall will be picked up by those behind." When Erin showed me those lines I saw with greater clarity how it is that the language of various activities can fall off, fall out of hands, then be used by us gleaners of language, us poets, who then shed—find what we do being used by others in surprising ways, and so on.

Some of my favorite poems of yours come from Matter *(2004). I am especially impressed with the three prose poems "The Tender Grasses of the Field," "Where the Famous Wish They Had Lived," and "On the Origin of Language." Because I am so used to considering you a verse poet, one who exploits lineation in innovative ways, the amount of prose poems that appear in* Theory *overall surprised me. What kinds of considerations are at work when you decide to work in prose instead of verse?*

Another quite intriguing question. There are times, there have been several times which have lasted months or even years, when the whole notion of "lines" and "line breaks" seems preposterous, seems even pretentious, to me. During those times I tend to want to "make statements," to argue, or tell stories in a kind of language that seems unavailable to me during my more lineative months and years. I don't really know why it happens, and maybe I am wrong about this altogether since I see that I have a number of poems that switch back and forth (it does cause anguish to typesetters) between lineation and prose paragraphs. But then my "final" products are often the result of smaller pieces being joined, divided, reassembled over months and years, so those final products, such as "The Naming of Shadows and Colors" in *Matter*, include work from my anti-line episodes, as well as those times when it feels useful to echo, however faintly, Milton and Lucretius and Margaret Cavendish (to put it as pretentiously as possible). I think maybe an answer to your question does have something to do with my slightly pathetic hope that poetry can continue to connect with those grand moments, monumental, of the history of language. The paragraphs are from the times when I am more withdrawn into a presentness, which feels safer.

I was reading Amber Ahlstrom's biographical essay on you. She states, "The poetry of Bin Ramke might best be described as unsettling because of its disturbing themes. Ramke's poems offer a vision of a world characterized by empty relationships, doubt, and disillusionment . . ." Would you agree with this?

Yes but. *Doubt*, absolutely yes. But I find doubt to be a positive, engaging, even energizing condition. Disillusionment is also a source of clarity and knowledge—after all, if there was illusion, then now there is enlightenment. And as to "empty relationships," if there is relationship then there is no emptiness—but I do know what she means. To some extent, from the perspective of my distance from most of the poems Ms. Ahlstrom had to work with at the time, I see exactly what she meant, and she was right. But I no longer think those poems were "about" relationships in the sense she probably meant but I think they used human relationships as instances of variable connectedness.

I find this an oddly appropriate place to provide a biographical note, a follow-up to something I alluded to before. Up to my sophomore year in college, mathematics was my chosen medium. I mentioned earlier that my father was involved in chemistry—my older brother was an electrical engineer with NASA, my younger brother a technical writer and software tester, and many of my uncles (there were many of them) were involved in technical and scientific fields—aeronautical engineering, forestry, as well as plumbing and carpentry. All this in a generation of sisters and brothers who grew up on a rice farm, who were able to go to college at all only because of the efforts of Huey P. Long. At any rate, one of my most formative experiences was the national science foundation summer program in mathematics at the University of Texas when I studied with a famous topologist, R. L. Moore. Moore was actually most influential as a teacher, and his methods of teaching mathematics were (as I think about them decades after the fact) reminiscent of writing workshops. (I am saying all of this in retrospect—at the time I was unaware of his fame, aware only of how frightened I was of him and his methods). He and John Ettlinger would set theorems and then forbid us students to use outside help, including books; if one of us thought he had a proof, he or she would present it to the rest of the class and it would be open to discussion, oddly similar, as I recall, to the discussions I hear now of student poems in workshops. But the point I want to make is, even though I failed as a mathematician I see mathematics as essentially similar to poetry, as being "about" relationships. One can argue that mathematics and poetry are about similarity and difference, about challenging the boundary between one thing and another and about the exploration of what that boundary then does—how they reveal previously hidden connections and disconnections. And both work with "material" which is much misunderstood—mathematical objects have a strange relationship to so-called "reality," as do the significations of words in poems. "Aboutness" is most curious when you ask what a poem or a theorem is about.

Ahlstrom also astutely notes that such themes are "put in perspective by [your] humor and sheer joy in language." I definitely see this working through your poems. And when humor and joy are less apparent, there is always intellectual curiosity and wonder, which seems to undermine some of the alienation. Can you talk about the presence of humor in your poems?

I welcome humor, and leave it there when it happens. Strangely enough, it can arise at the most gloomy of my considerations, and usually the elements of a poem that strike me as funny are not recognized as such by listeners at readings. But I sometimes stop and point out that something I just did was funny, and THAT act will be heard as funny. What are you going to do?

How would you characterize yourself, in terms of a "school"—if indeed you feel you belong to one at all?

I don't, but would be happy to join if invited. Quite seriously, I suspect that to the extent my work has been noticed by anyone in a position of authority in/with any school, I have somehow managed to alienate her or him. I noticed a few years ago when my name came up on Ron Silliman's blog he did seem annoyed that the word "experimental" was applied. It was clear that he, as an influential figure in a recognized "school" of poets, wanted it known that I was nothing like a language poet—I am one of his "quietists." But then anthologists of various stripes gave up on me long ago—I was once a younger Southern poet, but now no longer either young or Southern. It may be that I am not really a poet. That sounds strange, but what I am aware of wanting to do with language is not so much making recognizable "poems" as, . . . something else. Something to help me engage with a world, real and imaginary, as I encounter it. When poetry is no longer able to help me do that I will try to find something else that will, and maybe that is what I am already doing, just calling these things poems for lack of a better term.

Some may call you an "academic" poet insofar as you are working from within the academy and your poems are steeped in intellectual matter. Do you see your work beyond this?

Beyond this? For 35 years I have taught for a living. Lots of freshman composition for a decade in Georgia, less of it in Denver, where I do some graduate teaching along with "general education" duties, but lots of fairly basic work on how to read and how to write. I am recognized in this institution for my poetry publishing, but I have only recently been involved in much exchange with colleagues about poetry itself. That is to say, working within the academy does not necessarily mean working within a supporting network of like-minded people, (whether fortunately or unfortunately). This is the situation for every writer I know of in "the academy."

And I don't see how poems could be other than steeped in intellectual matter. As conscious animals we are inexorably caught in a body aware of itself in a most shattering, anxiety-producing way. Since we are all pretty much in agreement that the old Cartesian split was an erroneous imagining, we are all, all of us, body-minds with varying degrees of pain to remind us of how fragile this thing is, this "self." We do not wear our bodies, we do not live within them; we do not house our minds. So what goes on in my place of work results in self-consciousness about all of these issues. More than in most other places of work, I assume, but I would say that poetry is not much more appreciated by "the academy" than it is by "Wall Street" or "the fourth estate" or any other imagined and named sanctuary of similarities.

There are some poets whose work is well known outside the smallish community of university employees and small-press publishers. So there are alternatives to the situation I am part of. But I would suggest that even the word "academy" is not very useful, since so-called "higher education" in this nation is so amazingly varied, from community colleges through graduate schools. I do with language what I am able to do, for reasons I probably do not understand, and there may be moments when other people read those things I write and there is a kinship among us. That is what happens for me when I read things—poems by Nathalie Stephens, or the occasional posting that I can understand on arXiv.com, or a story by Brian Evenson—and feel connected.

Ahlstrom, Amber. "Bin Ramke." *American Poets Since World War II: Third Series.* Dictionary of Literary Biography Vol. 120. Ed. R. S. Gwynn. Detroit: Gale Research, 1992.

Ramke, Bin. "Life Raft." *Theory of Mind: New and Selected Poems.* Omnidawn, 2009.

______. "Reminded" in *Aerial.* Richmond: Omnidawn, 2011.

Morrison, Rusty. "Interview with Bin Ramke." Press Materials for *Aerial.* Omnidawn, 2012.

Poetry:

Aerial, Omnidawn, 2012
Theory of Mind: New and Selected Poems, Omnidawn Publications, 2009
Tendril, Omnidawn Publications, 2007
Matter, University of Iowa Press, 2004
Airs, Waters, Places, University of Iowa Press, 2001
Wake, University of Iowa Press, 1999
Massacre of the Innocents, University of Iowa Press, 1995
The Erotic Light of Gardens, Wesleyan University Press, 1989
The Language Student, Louisiana State University Press, 1986
White Monkeys, University of Georgia Press, 1981
The Difference Between Night and Day, Yale University Press, 1978

A Poetry of Expansiveness: An Interview with Mark Doty

Mark Doty is a gay-identified writer whose poems and books of prose reach well beyond the perimeters of the gay community. A recipient of the 2008 National Book Award for poetry, he is in fact one of America's most distinguished, versatile poets. Passionate and often transcendent, his poems are descriptively precise, richly detailed, and distinguished by a strong sense of craftsmanship. They are also the creations of a humble and courageous spirit, one that in "Nocturne in Black and Gold" admits, "I've been no one / so many times I'm not the least afraid." As the quality of his observations makes clear, Doty is generous and possesses remarkable powers of concentration. Other honors include awards from the American Library Association, the Lambda Literary Foundation, and an Israel Fishman Award for Non-Fiction. He teaches at Rutgers University.

Your groundbreaking poem "Homo Will Not Inherit" was anthologized in Cary Nelson's Oxford Anthology of Modern American Poetry. *In his introductory notes to that poem Nelson writes, "Doty has a rich and complex relationship to the work of several other American poets, including Hart Crane. In Crane's case, one might say that Doty has set out to write the poems Crane himself could not have written in his own time." While there is no question, you are writing poems Crane could not have written in his lifetime, I was wondering if you agree with Nelson's claim about your complex and rich relationship to Crane in particular.*

Crane's a hero of mine, and a poet I carry with me—that is, I seem to be in an ongoing conversation with him, and his poems are touchstones that I go back to in relation to particular kinds of experiences. (Whitman and Bishop, Stevens and Lynda Hull are certainly members of that internal company as well.) I'll talk about him first on the level of content. He is a great poet of exuberance; his work overflows with his energetic encounter with the city, with the twentieth century, and with the erotic life. "Voyages" is one of modernity's great love poems, nearly boundless in its faith that sex will transform the speaker—and even if he's left with a mere artifact of memory, a poem instead of a beloved, by the end of it, well . . . it's the intensity of erotic encounter in that poem that anyone would remember. And passion is of course also the signature of Crane's relationship to language; he's intent on a charged density of music, on a line that makes a charged little explosion of music and sense all by itself, and who could ever manage to braid so many lines of thinking into a single phrase? I spent a few pages in a recent book, *The Art of Description,* talking about the first two lines of "Voyages V"; they invite you to unpack them, to consider—in the poem's context—the multiple ways they can mean.

And finally Crane, like Whitman and O'Hara, is a lover of New York City, a man who loves men who finds permission and possibility in the great human field of possibility New York is. In this way these poets are anti-Romantics; transcendence is maybe more likely, for them, to be located somewhere in the grid of the numbered streets, or under the shadows of the Brooklyn Bridge.

Crane is for me a type of expansiveness; his opposite, Cavafy, is my hero too. He was equally brave and enraptured, but his temperament was entirely at odds. In his hands, less actually is more.

Other, more obvious affinities exist between your poems and Mary Oliver's. Rereading Fire to Fire *for this project reminded me how extensive some of the similarities are. Rather than my listing them, I was wondering if you might be willing to comment on your relationship to Oliver's work and—by extension—the work of her mentors who also appear to be yours: Elizabeth Bishop and Marianne Moore.*

Do you think so? There are a lot more people in my poems, and many urban settings. And my work has sex in it! But Mary and I have both been citizens of Provincetown, and that compelling landscape has been crucial to our work. And we're both poets who do turn to the world for instruction, as though we're knocking at the door of whatever image it may be that fascinates us and asking it to teach us something. We are inheritors of Emerson in that way, students out to read the book of the world. I think Mary is much more certain in her stance toward reality than I am; I'm inclined toward speculation and qualification, while Mary, at least in her poems, really does know what the wild geese are saying, or how to read the message of the moss on the stones. I love her work, and I wrote a longish essay about it for *Provincetown Arts* a while back in which I tried to point to its canny intelligence, its sly strategies, and some of the subtle ways it incorporates self-doubt. I think people sometimes read her as a sentimental pastoralist, but there's more going on there than that.

Bishop and Moore are of course essential companions for me, especially the former. Her way of revealing the self not only through *what* she chooses to look at, but through *how* she looks—that continues to teach me so much about seeing. Again, in *The Art of Description* there's an extended discussion of "The Fish," which is a remarkable model of the perceiving mind at work, an inexhaustible poem. Both poets have such firm allegiance to the individual character of perception; they are entirely committed to their way of seeing and saying how they see.

Although you have lived many years on the Atlantic coast, you were born in Maryville, Tennessee. To what extent does that geographical and cultural landscape inform your writing?

I was born in Maryville. Then my family lived in many towns in Tennessee because my father was an engineer and, for whatever reason, we moved very frequently for different jobs of his. So I lived in a lot of towns in Tennessee until I was seven years old. After I finished first grade, we moved to Tucson, Arizona, and from there on out lived in lots of Sunbelt places in the Southwest and the West—and even back to Florida for a while. Tennessee has, for me, a sort of magic about it, because it is landscape to which one does not return. Part of that is about cadence and voice: my relatives had these rich voices and a distinct vocabulary that didn't appear in other places I had lived. One place that really showed up was in singing. We would sit out on the porch swing on warm nights and everyone would sing these old hymns like "Rock of Ages," "Swing Low, Swing Chariot," and "He's the Lily of the Valley,

He's a Bright and Shining Star." I loved the imagery of those songs and they come from an otherworldliness that became important to me as a kid. Also there was Tennessee food, which was really different from what you would eat in other places. Those flavors still seem to me very relevant to my past.

I think the Christian thing was important. My father's mother was a Fundamentalist who thought the end was coming soon; she really believed these were the last days, that the world we saw in front of us was a veil for what lay beyond it. That kind of thinking was very influential, that one could somehow see through things to a deeper level of reality. I was mostly young enough to escape the conservatism and the prohibitions of religions. I got a little bit of a sense of hellfire, but I didn't feel I was born a sinner. I felt, if anything, God's eye was on me as it was on the sparrow, and that was a lovely thing.

Because you moved around so much and in very different geographical locations, do you feel you developed an eye for seeing changes in landscapes, more so than if you had stayed in one place?

Probably, yes. It gave me a sense of being in a position of unfamiliarity, not expecting things to be the same, which is a very different point of view than what most of my classmates grew up with. If you stay in one place you get a sense that "This is what the world is" or "I can predict the world will look a certain way." I never felt that. There was always something new and I was always trying to find my way. In this regard, I was also influenced by my mother who, when we moved to Arizona, took up painting. She loved to paint the desert landscape, loved to pay attention to its color and light. She was totally enchanted by it in a way that was new to me. Before this, I had never seen someone fall in love with a *place,* and it was very interesting to me.

In many of your poems from Atlantis *I have noticed a persistent tension between the singular and the plural—the one and the many. In a poem like "Mackerel," for example, you ask "would you want // to be yourself only, / unduplicatable, doomed / to be lost?" Whereas the mackerel would prefer to be "multitudinous." Could you talk about how this struggle between the many and the few relates to the book's more general thematic concerns?*

That particular obsession has occupied me so long that it feels like it's always been on my mind, but I guess it did first emerge in *Atlantis*. Those poems were written in Provincetown, in the crisis years of the epidemic, and because I was surrounded by demonstrations that the self could disappear, I found myself thinking a lot about what a self might be to begin with. I'd always written about the evanescent, about disappearance. And now that I think about it there's a poem in *My Alexandria* called "Becoming a Meadow" which suggests that it's not so bad, that an individual wave breaks against the shore, since the steady oncoming waves continue. That's an attempt to seek consolation for mortality—an attempt that, at least in my book, is bound to fail, but that doesn't mean you stop trying. The mackerel poem is an outgrowth of that, and it wants to suggest that perhaps the real shining life is in the group, in the life of the flock or the tribe, and that perhaps we aren't as individual as we'd like to think. That idea appears, in some form or another, in every book of mine thereafter.

Another interesting tension occurs between our "ongoingness" ("Atlantis") and the "trajectory" ("In the Community Garden") of our mortal (and therefore terminal) lives. Could you talk about this?

It's the same opposition really. The sunflowers in the "Community Garden" poem seem to be dying even as they're blooming: you can see through the radiance of the flower to the dry structure of the seedhead that will be fully revealed later. But they wouldn't be sunflowers if they lasted; their nature is this wild rapid coursing up into bloom and seed and ending. Stillness vs. speed is, I guess, the temporal parallel to the one vs. the many.

People want to last, and how do we do that?

You are not afraid to ask questions in your poems, which is a risk insofar as this often indicates a certain degree of vulnerability and searching. Could you discuss the prevalence and importance of questions in your poems?

It was a crucial thing for me, when I found the nerve to pose questions in poems, and to allow them to remain, often, part of the finished text. I had been interested, from the poems in my first book, in a poetry of expansiveness: how could I delay closure, and thus avoid shutting off a more complicated sort of meaning, allowing the poem to dig in, walk around its subject, build a larger sense of the real. I'm mixing metaphors with abandon here because that feels to me like what I wanted, in widening my embrace: to open, to dig, to explore, to construct. I felt when I wrote a poem that was mono-focal, in a single layer as it were, I couldn't get the sense of dimensionality I was after. I began to incorporate other scenes and frames of reference, and to braid narratives. And to pose questions, which could serve as points of entry into deeper levels of the poem. By asking questions, I could push against the given material—the image or perception that had engaged me in the first place—and try to figure out why it mattered, why it might demand being written.

Questions have the advantage of feeling like an invitation to participate; there's a certain humility in them, a nod to the presence of the reader. It's wonderful, for example, that in one of Whitman's great visionary moments, section six of "Song of Myself," just as he is about to make one of his grandest claims, he turns to his audience and asks, in a separate stanza, "What do you think has become of the young and old men? / And what do you think has become of the women and children?" Then, having thus relinquished or shared his authority for a moment, he can go on to say the most shocking thing, that to die is "different from what any one supposed, and luckier."

Of course this can be manipulated. Rilke uses questions to make very bold assertions seem acceptable, and though I am usually aware that he is disguising his pronouncement with that interrogative mark, he's so charming that I don't mind. I myself am trying not to let the question become a mannerism, an easy gesture; I like them so much that I have to be a little hard on myself in revision.

You are also not afraid to discuss the process of writing a poem as you are writing it. Matters of poetics are confided in ways that challenge the traditional practice of remaining mute on one's aesthetic technique.

Writing a poem is an act of making or discovering order. I'm interested in how we make knowledge, how we map the world, constructing a sense of our relation to what is. So when I talk about "the poem" in the poem I'm writing, I'm really thinking about this action of meaning-making, of how we manage to know anything. I've certainly heard it said in workshops or among teachers of writing that poems shouldn't be "about" poetry. And I've been taken to task by a reviewer identifying myself as a "poet/professor," which amazed me—as if it were somehow more authentic to work in some other field. Well, either all of my poems are about poetry, or none of them are: that is, they are self-conscious acts in language of making pattern, attempting to represent something of subjectivity, and part of my subjectivity *is* that investigation of language.

An example might be my poem "Source," which is a kind of gloss on James Wright's unforgettable "A Blessing." Wright's poem ends, of course, after the speaker has encountered some horses by the roadside, and then he gives us one of those quintessential James Wright moments, an epiphany that comes barreling out of nowhere with a mysterious rightness, its power resulting from an emotionally charged, somewhat ambiguous image: "Suddenly I realize / That if I stepped out of my body I would break / Into blossom." The poem goes on reverberating in the mind long after you've finished it. Or more accurate perhaps to say you can't finish it—it's an open-ended, thrilling assertion, and while it feels like a precise description of the ecstatic we also are left thinking about what it might mean to step out of the body, and not just to bloom but to break into bloom.

My own tender encounter with some roadside horses was informed by this poem—how could it not be, as I've been reading "A Blessing" for 40 years! And when I began to write, I found myself thinking about what might lie beyond that epiphanic moment; what if you arrived there and kept writing? Wright's poem is completely transparent; what I mean by that is that it doesn't want you to be conscious that it's made of language, doesn't ask you to think about the fact that it is a poem. So I've done the opposite, in a way—favored expansion and exploration over compression, and allowed the poem to become reflexive, contemplating its own project. One reason you might want to do that is simply in order to construct more of a portrait of a mind at work; a poem like "Source" wants to give you both a report on an experience and to study the consciousness that is framing and ordering and making meaning of that report.

One of the most salient features of your poems is the richness of their details. This "welter of detail" (from "Pipistrelle"), this "density" (from "To the Engraver of My Skin"), is often juxtaposed with conspicuous attempts to draw conclusions and generalities from the particulars. The poems, in other words, often move between the concrete and the theoretical. And you even remark upon this with doubt in "Description": "I'm not so sure it's true, / what I was taught, that through */ the particular's the way // to the universal." Could you talk about the relationship between the general and particular and how your commitment to treating both of them affects your compositional process?*

Detail is there to make the world seem real to the reader, but of course every really good one does more than that; and as I mentioned above in relationship to Bishop, those chosen details are also comprising a portrait of the one doing the looking. This is entirely the subject of *The Art of Description* and is, in a less direct way, also the subject of my long essay *Still Life with Oysters and Lemon*. I think I went through a period of enjoying a kind of precision and exuberance of the descriptive, taking pleasure in how sensuously I could evoke the physical world. Sound becomes part of that too, as rhythm, assonance, and consonance lend texture to speech, and sonic play often subtly mimics that which is being described, or begins to create a sonic environment that subtly works on the reader to physicalize the poem.

I've been inclined, since *School of the Arts*, toward a more compressed poem, and sometimes I like using a minimum of detail, wanting more of the sense of the quick sketch or the notebook entry than the highly-wrought made thing. Of course they are very worked in their dashed-offness, but I don't want that to show!

To answer your question, I suppose my process would usually be something like allowing every detail that interests me into the poem, early on, and then, as it becomes more clear to me what I'm actually talking about—assuming I'm lucky and that *does* become clear—then I can let the unneeded ones go.

Dreams are prominent in many of your poems. What do dreams mean to you? Do you record them? Do you have a theory of dreams?

I don't remember my dreams all that much, so when I do I like to think them over and consider what they might be suggesting. I used a number of dreams—both of my own and other people's—in *Atlantis* because I was trying to get something of the community of those brought together so forcefully by the epidemic onto the page; I wanted some sense of conversation, shared struggle, exchange. In Wally's case, how could I come close to his subjectivity, when he was undergoing such a radical process of change, paralyzed, his brain changing daily? His dreams could offer a bit of a window in, and my own dreams could point to the terror beneath the daily surfaces.

And then there are those dreams that come with extraordinary clarity, where you know you aren't having any ordinary dream but something more along the lines of a visitation. Those are few in a lifetime, I think, and crucial.

Your poems about loved ones and friends suffering from AIDS were among the first to gain a wide readership in this country. Most of these poems were written in the 90s and early 2000s. But we need poems like this more than ever now, especially when a surge of younger people who have unprotected sex do not understand the risks involved and the extent of the losses we remember so vividly. Would you care to share your feelings about this?

Well, I don't think that poems will keep anyone HIV-negative, and it's hard to know quite what form of education around safe sex is actually effective. For people who've grown up with the idea of protecting themselves, there's often an aura of transgression around raw sex that's alluring. How could it not be? I'm really interested in reading poems that represent younger men's experience around HIV—how it feels to be positive now, or to stay negative, how sex and desire are shaped. I've read some wonderful work in this direction from Randall Mann and Tom Healy, Aaron Smith and Patrick Donnelly. But not enough yet! And I can see why; the subject matter is slippery and daunting.

Slippery in what way?

In the early 80s through the mid-90s the epidemic took on a particular kind of character. We understood that AIDS was a disease that struck gay men and intravenous drug users, and that it had a particular kind of trajectory—from infection, through various really recognizable opportunistic infections, like KS or wasting disease, and then death. In 1995 that all changed with the development of protease inhibitors which began to keep people alive longer and truly make HIV—at least for people who had access to the drugs—a kind of chronic manageable disease like diabetes. So now there are lots of people who are positive and aren't sick, and that represents a difference. As a result, we have a culture now around HIV that is not pretty well articulated, in part because one no longer knows who is infected or not. And people may or may not talk about this because there still is a sense of stigma or lack of acceptance. That's one of the difficulties. If we don't have a common understanding in the language how do you write about such a condition?

Another part of the slipperiness in writing poems about HIV is that poets don't necessarily know how to proceed in defining . . . Let me think about this . . . Hmmm. If there isn't a preexistent body of work about what it means to be infected or to seroconvert, and what it is to live with this disease, if there is no tradition, it's difficult to think of ways how such writing becomes inscribed. One has to plunge into the unfamiliar and make it up. That's hard for anybody.

And I think, too, if one writes honestly about HIV and AIDS, one has to write with some degree of familiarity about medical conditions. That requires a vocabulary a lot of people—poets included—are not used to using.

That's true. Such terminology can really resist the lyric tone. One can try to use euphemisms or veils or metaphor, but these conceal more than they express and are not quite adequate to the subject matter. It's just too easy for a conventionally lyrical language to be sort of ratified: we agree that certain terms or a certain focus is the territory of the lyric.

In writing about HIV and AIDS, it may also be more difficult to move out of the personal realm into looking at HIV within the community or state of the world. That's one of the characteristics of American poetry: we're much more able to describe personal experience than we are to reach outside of ourselves; we lose our sense of authority and confidence when we move into the sociopolitical realm.

Do you think "gay poetry" is a dead term? That poets are poets who write what they write, as opposed to being defined or framed by identity politics?

Good question! I love reading poetry that in some way speaks to my own experience of desire. It's just inevitable that poets who write about same-sex desire, particularly male-male desire, are going to come closer to the realm in which I live. Here's the paradox: I want to be able to read about experience which touches directly upon mine, but it's also true that what we define as gay can become a very limited set of elements that may simply leave other things out. So, to be called a "gay poet" suggests that you might be dealing with a smaller subset of experiences—which is absurd. Cavafy is a splendid example of a poet who manages to talk about absolutely everything in the world—time, memory, desire and history, to talk about the possibility of transcendence, to talk about what it means to live to old age—without any feeling of limitation. Everything is there in his work, and yet it's always very focused on a few elements. Identity politics is always a paradox. It can be maddening. As a gay poet you might be shoved off in a corner, or you could be told that you're not gay enough. I was hurt that way pretty recently in a review of mine, startled by it actually. How can I get much more gay, I ask you!

On the other hand, I recently went to speak to this great group in New York City called The Wilde Boys. It's a sort of loose association of younger gay poets who have salons where they talk about particular poems or invite people to come and speak. Just this fall, Frank Bidart has been, as has John Ashbery and myself. I was so knocked out. They'll put more than 50 people in the room, and they're clearly writing very different kinds of poems and have very different ideas about poetics, but there was such a sense of vigor and life there. And I don't think they want to be cordoned off in a gay bookstore or in a gay section of stores like Borders and Barnes & Noble. They want readers but they also want to find ways to wrestle with the particular stuff of their own lives and the circumstances of those lives. I think probably the era of the gay bookstore as a place where you would go and find like-minded souls is gone and that our literature will be intermingled with everything else, as it already is with writers like André Aciman, Michael Cunningham, Colm Toibin.

Many of your poems are deliciously erotic insofar as they revel in the body and the physicality of desire. At the same time, the voice in your poems is striving for something beyond the physical, such as in poems like "Theory of Soul" and "Theory of the Sublime." Do you see the attention paid to the physical as a byway to the spiritual, towards the transcendent? Is there a point in which one must distance oneself from the pleasures of the flesh to arrive at transcendence?

Thank you. I wouldn't want to think of the physical as a byway, because that would make the destination seem more important than the road. My desire would be to take pleasure and delight in the body, and to come close enough to see that it is, as Whitman would have it, not distinct from the soul. That's my dream. But I know that I have always been drawn to the ecstatic erotic, to a sort of boundless and timeless communion—as my partner Paul would put it. I'm not so much interested in sex as a narrative with a beginning, middle and end, but rather in the extended lyric state. This, my adult self knows, isn't sustainable, and the limits of the flesh are always real, even if we seem to leap over them sometimes.

I sense that you are as much a storyteller as you are a lyric poet. Do you see yourself as a storyteller? Is narrative a vehicle by which you reach lyric apprehension—or is it pleasurable for its own sake?

I love stories, and they are fun to tell. A good poem is never simply a story; if it is, it becomes like a joke—you hear or read it, you got it, you need never encounter it again. Narrative in poetry, to my mind, is a means to an end, a way to arrive at a lyric moment, a means of traveling toward a question or a crux of meaning. I enjoy the technical process of structuring a story, finding a way to lend tension and energy to narration through formal means. That's probably one reason I'm a memoirist; memoir is entirely dependent upon finding narrative strategies that make a story resonant and taut.

In "Fog Suite" you write, "Every poem's / half erased." How does this admission apply, in different ways of course, to some of your poems? Perhaps cite one or two of your poems to illustrate?

I mean that in a few different ways. First, by the time you complete a poem, you've thrown out a lot. Either what you actually wrote down, or what you thought and didn't pursue. You make choices along the way, and each one eliminates other possibilities.

Then there's the partial nature of any report on experience, or of knowledge itself. How complete can my discourse on the nature of fog actually be? The poem is "half erased" because I can only see so much.

And then, of course, the physical presence of white space on the page; you can't see letters or lines without the negative space, the field on which they stand. The full requires the empty, the present needs the absent, maybe the living need the dead. Sound needs silence. And on we go: the poem's a song with a lot of emptiness inside it. Or is that open space?

You've written not one memoir but three. Do you ever feel "Gosh, I've said it all!" or do you think other memoirs are bound to come?

Well, these books aren't autobiographies in the sense of covering a whole span of a life. They're quite particular. *Heaven's Coast* is concerned with the illness and death of my partner Wally and the time thereafter; *Firebird* is about growing up; and *Dog Years* is about 16 years of living with four-legged creatures. These are books that choose a particular lens through which to look at aspects of a life. I'm actually working on another one at the moment, a book about reading Walt Whitman that also concerns sex, death, ecstasy, and body issues Whitman helps me to think about. So, yeah, I think nonfiction is going to continue as a part of my life all of the time. Writing these memoirs is comfortable for me because they give me a kind of center or spine that lets me know what to leave out. Each memoir has a particular question it's addressing, each proceeds from a specific point of departure.

There are so many books of Whitman published each year. What's your angle?

If I start thinking about my little contribution to the library of books on Whitman it's thoroughly daunting and makes me want to shut up! But I feel an affinity with Whitman that has grown deeper and more obsessive over the years. I have come to live more profoundly in his work and to talk back to it. Whitman opens the territory for me as a writer. What I have to say is indirectly about him. I don't think I can give anything new to Whitman scholarship, but what I can do is talk about my own history as a reader of Whitman and the ways that my experiences intersected with those texts. It becomes a way of talking about a friendship between writers, a way of talking about Whitman as a spiritual guide to the erotic, which really interests me enormously. And I'm not sure *that* book quite exists yet.

Doty, Mark. "Nocturne in Black and Gold," "A Display of Mackerel," "Description," and "Fog Suite." *Fire to Fire: New and Selected Poems*. New York: Harper Perennial, 2008.

Nelson, Cary. "Introduction to Mark Doty." *Anthology of Modern American Poetry*. Edited by Cary Nelson. New York: Oxford University Press, 2000.

Whitman, Walt. "Song of Myself." *Leaves of Grass: 150th Anniversary Edition*. New York: Oxford University Press, USA, 2005.

Wright, James. "A Blessing." *Above the River: The Complete Poems*. Farrar, Straus and Giroux, 1992. (See Permissions Page.)

Poetry:

Theories and Apparitions, Jonathan Cape, 2008
Fire to Fire: New and Selected Poems, HarperCollins, 2008
School of the Arts, HarperCollins, 2005
Source, HarperCollins, 2001
Sweet Machine, Harper Flamingo, 1998
Atlantic, HarperCollins, 1995
My Alexandria, University of Illinois Press, 1993
Bethlehem in Broad Daylight, David R. Godine, 1991
Turtle, Swan, David R. Godine, 1987

Nonfiction:

The Art of Description, Graywolf Books, 2010
Dog Years, HarperCollins, 2007
Still Life with Oysters and Lemon, Beacon Press, 2001
Firebird: A Memoir, HarperCollins, 1996
Heaven's Coast, HarperCollins, 1996

Poetry in Present Tense:
An Interview with Billy Collins

Billy Collins is the most popular American poet writing today. It is not difficult to see why: concise and urbane, his poems are endlessly inventive within traditional—and accessible—procedures; they are also distinguished by a playful, often piercing satirical edge that tempers his obsession with the universal theme of death. As much as Collins's work resonates with readers on the page, his stage presence is even more alluring. His casual demeanor, well-timed wit, and self-effacing sensibility have ensured Collins an enormous non-specialized readership. For many, his books are a gateway to poetry. Collins has received fellowships from the National Endowment for the Arts, The Guggenheim Foundation, and the New York Foundation for the Arts. A former teacher at Columbia, Sarah Lawrence, and the State University of New York at Stony Brook, he was the U.S. Poet Laureate from 2001 to 2003.

I understand your book Ballistics *has been translated into Italian. Congratulations. What were some of the difficulties your translator, Franco Nasi, faced when recasting your poems in that language?*

Having your poems translated into another language can be a bit frightening because if you are external to the wonders of that second language, you have no idea if you're being mishandled or distorted. I see the labors of the translator as an honor and an act of trust, but something, of course, is lost in translation. The best metaphor I've heard to explain what is lost and what is saved is from a friend of mine, Eamon Grennan, who translated the poems of Leopardi, the Italian Romantic poet. He said translation is like walking in a mountain stream on a beautiful sun-shot afternoon, you're admiring these stones lying on the bottom of the stream, and you pick a few up and they're gorgeous, full of roseate patterns and striations, and the like. One is so gorgeous that you take it home with you. The next morning you wake up and there it is on the shelf, only now it's just this gray stone, completely unremarkable. The reason for that is that you have lifted the stone out of its native waters, its native language, and so it has lost its luster. You have the stone, but you don't have the luster. I think that's a great metaphor for it. The luster of the original language is what's lost in translation.

I'm lucky to have Franco Nasi as a translator. This is the second book of mine he's done. When he said he wanted to translate my poems, I told him I thought that would be fairly easy. I use fairly simple diction, and my line breaks are predictable insofar as they follow the breathing of the grammar of the sentence. Indeed, what I was trying to say is that my poetry is extremely conservative. He said, yes all that's true, but getting the right tone is the challenge. He told me in Italian poetry the tone is usually somewhat elevated. Certainly way above street level. He said my poems are closer to street level, so in bringing them down from the expected height of Italian poetry, there's this danger of bringing them down too low; the challenge lay in making adjustments so as to find a midground between the tone too elevated and too common. Once he explained this me, I immediately trusted him. And I know enough Italian to know he's not completely crazy. And you have to love the title of the book: *Balistica*!

Tone is so important to your work. Your poems are often ironic and funny.

When I was starting out in poetry, I was afraid to use humor because in school I was raised on nineteenth-century poetry written by dead males who had long beards, three names, and no sense of humor—William Cullen Bryant, Henry Wadsworth Longfellow, and the lads. Then in college and graduate school, we entered high Modernism, and I studied Wallace Stevens, Hart Crane, Pound. There is high linguistic play in Stevens, but it is still a stretch for most readers. Of course, I had a taste for this. I have a Ph.D. in English Literature, so I obviously had a fondness for explication and difficult texts. Otherwise, I would have dropped out and opened a little frame shop in town. At that point I was desperate to be a poet. But what I was getting out of poetry was that poetry was difficult to understand and it was written by men who were miserable, or at least deeply vexed about something. So many hard to understand poems that gave off an aura of anxiety. So because I wanted to be a poet, I wrote really obscure poems in which I lied about being unhappy: in fact, I was a fairly happy youngster. I wanted to be in the game.

It wasn't until I started reading poets like Thom Gunn, the New York Poets, such as Kenneth Koch and Frank O'Hara, and particularly Philip Larkin, that I realized it was possible to be funny in poetry without being inane or merely entertaining; you could be funny and serious at the same time. In the case of Larkin you could be funny and *deadly* serious, a kind of ironic despair. I also realized at some point there was something authentic about being funny. Anyone who has ever had a job or sat in a classroom knows how to pretend to be serious. It's easy to pretend to be serious, but you can't pretend to be funny. Either you're funny or you're not. You can't just put that on. There's something indisputably real about laughter. After all, it's an involuntary response, like sneezing, only someone else causes it.

If you like, I can give you a "Humor in English Poetry 101" course in 30 seconds. Humor always had a place in English poetry: Shakespeare wrote comedies; Chaucer can be a barrel of laughs; then there is metaphysical wit and Augustan satire, basically having fun by making fun of other people. But something happens when we get to the Romantics. Basically, Coleridge and Wordsworth go into a back room somewhere and strike a deal that we are going to rid poetry of sex and humor and substitute landscape, which, I think we can all agree, is not a good deal. But, indeed, it worked. It really wasn't until the 1950s, with Larkin and others, that humor regained its rightful place in poetry. Prior to that, it was assigned to a ghetto called "light verse," which made humor just silly.

Humor is very much back now. There's a new anthology called *Seriously Funny*, edited by David Kirby, which is a collection of contemporary poems that use humor but as a way into more serious stuff.

We live in ironic times. Some of those "serious" Romantic poems are unintentionally humorous, even campy.

Well, Shelley is seriously lacking irony. Not too many poets these days could say, "I fall upon the thorns of life. I bleed." I think it was Richard Howard who said in any poet's career you only get three exclamation points. If you comb through Shelley you'll find hundreds of exclamation points. Because Byron had a sense of humor (and a taste for debauchery) we really have to classify him as a late Augustan, not a Romantic. Byron was never consoled by landscape.

I'm struck by the degree to which imagination has a strong presence in your work. Many of your poems begin with mundane, unsurprising observations, but as they progress they move towards increasingly odd or imaginative contexts.

Poetry is, among other things, a sort of playground for the imagination. Any pleasure I derive from reading poetry has to do with observing an imagination at play. Lyric poems tend to evolve from the mundane towards the odd, the eccentricities of the imagination. So the poem has the shape of a pyramid that you read from the top down and end up with something bigger than what you started with. The poem is really a traveling from something local to something general, or from the obvious to a moment of revelation. My favorite analogy for that kind of development is the eye chart. You have the big "E" at the top of the chart—and pretty much we can all see the "E." As we go down the lines we eventually reach some level of illegibility and we give up when we start guessing the letters. I don't want the poem to end in illegibility, but I want the reader to strain a little bit more in the end, to be somewhat challenged imaginatively or maybe just surprised. Stephen Dobyns, who is one of the few really good writers on the subject of how to write poetry, says if you get the reader to accept something simple in the beginning of the poem, he or she will be more prone to accept more complicated things later on. I have very little patience for poems that start out by making uncalled for demands on me, and the demand is usually that I am predisposed to be interested in the psychic misery of the poet. Of course, I am not. Who would be? Starting small is very dependable as a seductive device. I enjoy beginning with something that is indisputable. If you say, "I am sitting here looking at a bird," the reader can't say, "I don't believe you." The reader has to buy in at the beginning if the poem is going to engage his or her attention. If my poems get more imaginative as they go along, it's probably because I'm getting bored looking at that bird. Bored staying in the same place. I want to jump somewhere if only to escape from the wheel-spinning of monotony of staying in one place.

I rarely know where I am going when I begin a poem. Like most poets, I think, I don't want to know too much at the outset. Like William Matthews, I want to "preserve the benefits of my ignorance for as long as possible." Frankly, if I knew where I was going, I wouldn't bother writing. Surprise, of course, would be impossible. The pen is more than a recording instrument; it is also an instrument of discovery and exploration. That's where the imaginative traveling comes in. My persona has nothing to do but sit around and get imaginative. That's his job. I wish I were my persona. He just walks around being interested in his thought process.

So many of your poems are about a persona writing the poem as we the readers are reading it.

I want the poems to have a present tense, even if the poem is not *grammatically* in the present tense. I like to give the impression that the poem is happening as you read it. I guess one way I do that is I pretty much write all of my poems in one sitting. I obviously go back and fix things, but it's not so much revision as fiddling. The conceptual run of a poem would be written in one sitting: it could be twenty minutes or three or four hours. I want the poem to be a single compositional experience for me. I write until I discover the ending. I sense that by doing that, the experience is recreated in the reader's experience of reading the poem. The reader has a sense that I'm making it up as I go along, which is what all poetry does; it's just a matter of how obvious you want that to be. Yeats said something—I'm going to misquote him, but—*all our stitching and unstitching is for naught if it does not seem a moment's thought*. So, no matter how much you revise, you're always trying to make it sound spontaneous. In fact, that is the aim of revision: to make the poem sound improvised. So, yes, I will begin a poem by saying I'm just sitting here writing and then we see where we will go from there. It's also an example, once again, of starting small. The fact that the poem was written at a certain time is not a bad thing to admit to. I think also that so many of my poems refer to writing a poem because I'm still very self-conscious about being a poet. There's something ridiculous about writing poems and not just because of the gap between how seriously poets take themselves and how little the public is even aware of their labors. There's something ridiculous about the word "poetry."

I think it would surprise a lot of people to learn that your first book of poems didn't come out until you were in your forties. So you came to poetry later—

Well, *it* came to *me* later!

Does this fact contribute to the self-consciousness you speak of?

I suppose. Like most young writers, I was insecure. Also, I just had a lot of bad poetry in me. It's been estimated that we're all born with about three hundred bad poems in us, but I was blessed with about four or five hundred. High school, by the way, is a great place to get rid of these poems. It's actually *designed* as a place to get rid of them. Also, back then, I wasn't really taking poetry that seriously. Wanting to be a poet began a very romantic idea with me. Ever since I came across a picture of Edgar Allan Poe when I was an adolescent, I wanted to be a poet. I'd never seen anyone who looked like that in my life! My parents didn't look like that, that's for sure. It suggested there was a realm inhabited by people completely different from the ones around me, that is, middle-class, suburban people. I wanted to be with them, find out who they were. But, as a poet, I was sort of hobbled by doubt, so I didn't run with the pack. I didn't go to poetry readings very much; I didn't hang out with poets; I've never taken a workshop. And frankly, it just took me a long time to figure out how to write the kind of poems I couldn't wait to show others.

I think the development of a poet is all about influence. No one makes any progress in poetry without being influenced by others. Creative writing, as it is called, must be preceded by creative reading. And don't worry, young poets: reading poetry you didn't write will *not* compromise your originality. That's just a poor excuse for not doing the work of reading. When I stopped trying to "express myself" and came under the influence of other poets, the influence was so direct that I ended up writing travesties of their work. In high school I was writing really bad Ferlinghetti and Ginsberg, then really bad Wallace Stevens, Richard Brautigan. Bad Thom Gunn. Bad Nemerov. I had a whole crew of literary models, but the influences were so slavish, I was just producing knockoffs. You have the brand name and then right next to it in the cereal aisle you have the supermarket brand. I was writing the supermarket brand, which is cheaper but not as good. Then, at some point, I figured out how to combine my influences. That's really what happened. It's a long story, but eventually I figured out how to write poems that were closer to my personality. Eliot says poetry is the elimination of personality. It's beyond personality. I unfortunately bought into that, which is one reason it took me so long to allow my personality into my writing. Frank O'Hara is the best counter-example to Eliot's chilly removal of the poet's ego.

A lot of your poems deal with animals, especially domesticated animals like dogs and cats.

I don't know, animals . . . I mean, they're *there*. And there are so many of them that they're hard to avoid. They're just in the way sometimes! Seriously, there's a horribly lost connection we have with the animal world, and I think dogs and other domesticated creatures are an attempt to recreate that linkage, if it ever really existed, just as the garden is an attempt to reclaim a linkage back to our physical, natural environment. The garden is like nature in quotation marks, and the dog is like the animal kingdom in quotation marks. I mean unlike wild animals, the dog has a name, like "Sparky," and a collar! When you think about it, there are basically two kinds of animals: animals that we're afraid of, like grizzly bears, and animals that are afraid of us, like squirrels and birds. Ultimately, poets are all just looking for metaphors, and dogs happen to be a recurrent one for me. Readers often feel they have detected a theme in a poet's work. "What's with all the berries in your poems?" Or "what's with all the clouds, or storefront windows?" Well, if you write long enough, certain preoccupations will surface. I have a ton of mice in my poems (if mice can be measured in tons). But there's nothing terribly obsessive about these subjects, whether it's jazz or the weather or dogs or whatever. They're really just metaphors, angles of approach. Poets have available to them only a handful of basic human themes. The only originality is finding a new metaphorical path into these old statements. Animals are one of them.

You and John Ashbery are among the most well-known poets in America. Yet there aren't any obvious similarities in your approach. Besides your enormous popularity, what else might you and Ashbery, as poets, have in common?

Well, I guess one reason not to be puzzled about our mutual popularity is that we draw on very different audiences. It's not like I'm taking readers away from John Ashbery or that he's taking readers away from me. Personally, if a poet reaches a wide audience, which means selling a lot of books, the way John Ashbery and I do—we have *that* in common—people get resentful. The same people who wring their hands about how no one reads poetry are the first ones who turn against you if you achieve some popularity. One of the lovely paradoxes of the writing life. I think some poets think that I'm stealing their readers. No, I'm creating my own readership. The people who read me—I've created that readership. I'm not taking anyone else's readers. As Wordsworth says, a poet has to create the taste by which he is enjoyed. As far as Ashbery goes, I guess we have irony in common. I make more sense, but that's because he doesn't want to make sense in the way I make sense. I used to be very puzzled by Ashbery because I was making the mistake of trying to understand him by making ordinary sense out of him. Then I realized that wasn't the point. Now I enjoy him tremendously; I love his poems for being sort of ironic rides through the tones of written and spoken English. I enjoy his campiness, his appreciation for American figures of speech, cliché, little bits of dialogue, how he jumbles all this together into a new entity. One of the things about learning poetry in school is how to deal with not knowing how much interpretative pressure to put on poets, because you can't know right away; it takes years of reading. You can't approach a Robert Frost poem and a John Ashbery poem with the same interpretive machinery, or with the same expectations. It's really only after reading a lot of the poet's work—a lot of Emily Dickinson, a lot of Ashbery, etc.—that you really learn how much pressure to apply, because it's easy to make the mistake of applying too little or too much pressure. Initially, with Ashbery, I was exerting the wrong kind of pressure, trying to get a paraphrasable meaning out of his poems, which was a dismally wrong approach.

Your poems have often been called accessible, but there is still room for ambiguity in them.

Ambiguity is not desirable in normal life, because we often need clarity. For example, in a political speech or instructions on how to assemble a piece of furniture. But in poetry, ambiguity is a good thing. Meaning more than one thing results in a thicker texture. Poets, you might say, are people who find it impossible to say one thing at a time. (Teachers are people who never say anything once, as Joseph Epstein put it). That's one aspect of poetry that's hard to get when you're a student, I think. Ambiguity is a source of frustration. How can the poem mean two or three things at the same time? Is everybody right or is just the poet right? These questions are rattling away in the classrooms of America as we speak. But the more poetry you read, the more you come to appreciate ambiguity as a sign of depth, a thickening of meaning.

In a wonderful interview with George Plimpton for The Paris Review, *you talked about your growth as a writer in very frank terms. You said, "There's an expectation that the artist must grow, must expand and change . . . Yet there's also a strength in doing one thing well." You cite Emily Dickinson as a prime example of a writer who has "learned to do one thing well and to find variation in it." Then, in reference to your own poetry you admit: "I don't envision any great creative breakthrough. My hope is to continue to do good work . . ." Do you, like E.D., write the same poem over and over again?*

I suppose. I'm not really all that interested in my own development or growth anymore. I really just want to keep writing pretty much the same kind of poem, but each one a little different. One of the odd things about writing poetry that differs from fiction or writing plays—apart from its superiority to those lesser genres!—is that if you're a novelist, whether you're Kurt Vonnegut or Charles Dickens, or a playwright, Eugene O'Neill or Ibsen or whoever, you're inventing characters. That's your job: you're inventing one character after another. Some minimalist fiction writers have only a handful of characters, whereas the prolific ones, like Trollope or Balzac, have hundreds. By contrast, a poet need only invent *one character*, for life. A poet needs to come up with a persona, that is, a voice that sounds like you, but is not you exactly. And then you stick with it. We don't expect Emily Dickinson to change. Even if we could get back into her room in Amherst we wouldn't say, "Emily, really, could you just write longer poems?" We don't want her to change. We want Emily to keep singing that beautiful song over and over again with all those variations. We want Whitman to be Whitman, Thomas Hardy to be Thomas Hardy. There are a few poets who do develop many different voices, such as Browning in his dramatic monologues, but generally poets find one voice. It takes a while to find that gear. And you find it through getting influenced. Then you might as well stay in that gear; finally, you get to some point where the only person worth imitating is yourself. It's sort of like autodidacticism—you're learning from yourself. I just want to write more poems like me, only a little better.

However, the new book, Horoscopes for the Dead, *feels a little different from the others. The poems in it struck me as deliberately less playful. Not depressing, but a bit more serious than I was expecting.*

Well, one does *age*. But I am still trying to maintain that voice I mentioned. There are these two faces that we have in theatre: the face of comedy with the big rictus smile and the downcast face of tragedy. I'm usually trying to navigate the poem away from those extremes into some middle ground. There is no third face in theatre. The third face would probably be the face of irony, which would be more a smirk or something. Maybe some of the poems are now leaning towards the darker, downcast face. I suppose maybe I'm running out of comic gas. But then there are some poems in *Horoscopes* that are just downright silly. Do you recall "Hangover"?

Good point! I was thinking overall, as a collection.

The thing is I never think in terms of a volume or a collection. I just write this poem and then that poem, and when I get a hundred of them, I look at them and think maybe it's time for a book. I don't have a special, overarching theme for any particular book. It's not really even a book. It's just enough poems for a book. The theme of my poetry is basically me . . . and death. *Me and Death* might make a good title for the next one.

Plimpton, George. "Billy Collins, The Art of Poetry." *Paris Review*: No. 159, Fall 2001.

Poetry:

Horoscopes for the Dead, Random House, 2011
Ballistics, Random House, 2008
She Was Just Seventeen, Modern Haiku Press, 2006
The Trouble with Poetry, Random House, 2005
Nine Horses, Random House, 2002
Sailing Alone Around the Room: New and Selected Poems, Random House, 2001
Taking off Emily Dickinson's Clothes, Picador, 2000
Picnic, Lightning, University of Pittsburgh Press, 1998
The Art of Drowning, University of Pittsburgh Press, 1995
Questions About Angels, 1991, (reissued: University of Pittsburgh Press, 1993)
The Apple That Astonished Paris, University of Arkansas Press, 1988
Video Poems, Applezaba Press, 1980
Pokerface, Kenmore Press, 1977

As Editor:

Bright Wings: An Illustrated Anthology of Poems About Birds, Columbia University Press, 2010
180 More Extraordinary Poems for Every Day, Random House, 2005
Poetry 180: A Turning Back to Poetry, Random House, 2003

Balancing Images: An Interview with Carol Frost

More than most poets, Carol Frost strives to reduce the presence of narrative in poetry to its essential elements. "I usually shun narrative or see how little I can get away with," she explains below. "I'm sure this is a preference I hold because of the way my mind works, which is by association and ellipsis." Although often understated and matter-of-fact about her process, Frost is an outstanding versifier whose contributions to lyric poetry have improved the state of American Letters. What is more, each of her books demonstrates her willingness to tackle formal challenges. Possibly the most rewarding of these experiments is "Abstractions," a series of brief, long-lined, unrhymed poems that embody the compression of sonnets and make surprising, often startling, associative turns. Sensual and lyrically dense, these poems—along with much else in Frost's work—are essential reading for anyone interested in exploring how to balance metaphorical richness with minimum discursiveness. Currently living in Florida, Frost is a Professor of Poetry at Rollins College of Arts and Science, where she also directs the Winter with the Writers Festival. She has won fellowships from the National Endowment for the Arts and three Puschart Prizes.

Genesis, particularly the story of the temptation and the fall, is clearly a source text for a number of your poems. Could you discuss your relationship to that text and articulate ways in which it has sparked your creative imagination?

My initial sense of language as ceremony may have come from the Bible. I grew up Episcopalian, though as a young child was sent summers to Bible school—a free day camp run by Baptists. I gradually lost my sense of biblical truth, but the beauty in language and in myth continued and continues. Journey, losing one's way, and return are only secular versions of temptation and fall and the possibility of redemption. Another way to say this is that the parts of the Bible that have resonated with me are stories of a natural world—gardens, stars, flesh. I imagine that if I'd been told Homer's stories first, my imagination would have been sparked by the vivid and lasting physicality of that moral universe.

Many of your poems are ekphrastic. Others reference specific paintings and the artists who create them. Could you explain why you have so often turned to the visual arts for material?

How can one *not* turn to painting and works of architecture? Many of my aesthetic lessons when I was young came from looking at art and, to some extent, listening to classical music, which probably makes me sound elitist. When I was 19, for instance, I left school to travel in Europe—it was my money, after all. I wanted to look at Roman architecture and to see the grandmother in Vienna I had last seen when I was three or four. I hitchhiked through Western Europe and then settled in Paris in a tiny apartment on Rue de Senlis. I took classes at the Sorbonne, and one afternoon chanced meeting a Canadian friend near the Luxembourg Gardens. We were bored—it was our job to be bored at that age—and wondered what to do. On a kiosk we found that the Hotel Meurice was having a showing of Salvador Dali's painting *Tuna Fishing.* Woefully underdressed we went, and I remember being surprised and perhaps disappointed that there were many other artists represented in the show, considering who they were—French and Spanish Realists. I loved surrealism; it was my job to love surrealism (and existentialism). Then Dali came into the room. Yes, he had the cape and cane and wonderful mustache. I happened to be carrying a copy of Sartre's *Nausea.* I had been holding the book behind my back, and the curator of the show noticed the cover. He asked me if he could show the book to Dali. After a few minutes Dali turned toward me and motioned me over. He asked me where I'd gotten my copy of the book. I told him I'd recently bought it at Shakespeare and Company, and Dali asked his assistant to get him a copy. The painting had been pirated. I said, in my rather poor French, that he could have my copy. In return he gave me a copy of the beautiful program, a book with illustrations of the paintings in the show, and he signed it for me. He *drew* my name, I should say, then signed the program. I poured over it when I got back to my place and found a sentence of his that really did teach me my earliest lesson in aesthetics: "Je ne renonce à rien, je continue." The whole trip through Europe became a time of figuring out the art continuum. Years later I did the same for poetry. Last year I saw the Brueghel and Bosch I'd missed in *Tuna Fishing*. I found Dali's copy of Vermeer's *The Lace Maker*. Don't get me started on what writers I've seen in other writers! I take from writers and I take from art.

You seem genuinely excited talking about the importance of the visual arts in relation to your work.

Yes, I have had such vivid and extraordinary experiences that as much as anything else made me want to be a part of the world of art. Since I can't draw or paint or sculpt, or anything like that, I've done what I could with words. My husband has some fondness for the few watercolors I've attempted, but I think that's mainly because he is my husband. It's freeing to paint badly—I haven't any sense I *need* to paint well. I paint when the mood strikes.

Michael Waters has called the 35 poems that comprise the "Abstractions" section of Love and Scorn, *and which originally appeared in* Pure *and* Venus & Don Juan, *truncated sonnets. Would you agree with his term for the form you've created for those poems?*

I've always found the word truncated to be ugly, and in truth some of the Abstractions are longer than the traditional sonnet of 14 lines or 70 stresses (14 x 5), but the number of lines has less to do with a sonnet being a sonnet than its lyric movement. Is not a curtal sonnet a sonnet? Are not George Meredith's sixteen-line poems in *Modern Love* sonnets? The Abstractions are lyrics, and there are enough of them to seem to be in their own form. I can tell you the aesthetic principles and even a few rules—which I feel free to break—that inform the poems.

The abstract title, usually one word, must appear in some form in the poem. The poems ought to be eleven lines long, and most of them are—but not all. The metaphoric equivalent for the abstract title ought to be surprising: "Her beauty no longer catches glances like small animals in a gentle snare . . ." for example. I try to suppress narrative and to keep changing directions. I try to write in long lines, though it's hard to write a long line that isn't a few short lines spliced together. I was also experimenting with pace and with where to put the "turn." They were brain-breaking to write at first, stayed challenging, then became so much a part of my thinking and metaphor-making that I had a hard time quitting writing them. It took me two years.

In a prior phone conversation, you told me one critic dismissed your Abstractions as mere imitations of the condensed, long-lined poems C. K. Williams wrote in Flesh and Blood. *On the surface, your Abstractions and his poems look similar (they both favor the long, syntactically complicated verse line and rarely exceed 10–15 lines per poem) but your work is, in your own words, far less discursive than his. Could you elaborate on the nonnarrative and nondiscursive elements of these poems and alternative methods of development?*

I like metaphor; it's my mind's worst or best habit. In writing the Abstractions I was trying to write a short lexicon based on metaphor for abstract terms. I like the leaps one makes in thought and association, and I wanted to create a poetic which would make that part of the experience of the imagination in early form, before story intervenes or discursive thought waters down the effect of sensory perception associated with another sensory perception. Then, in revising, one measures the distances between the perceptions and sees what new meanings are possible. It's certainly not the only way to write poetry, but I read a lot of John Donne and Gerard Manley Hopkins when I was young.

One of the chief pleasures I get in reading the Abstractions is seeing how you build up an often-stunning density and concreteness. Each abstraction, for instance, is condensed to a specific context, and you subject that context to remarkable shifts of thought and perception.

I'm gratified that you see this. The shifts were willed at first. We are remarkably linear in thought when asked to be, and I wanted to break free from that social behavior. I'd seen for a long time, probably since childhood, how logic perverts the truth; I lived in fear of hypocrisy and rationalizing. The way for me to trust language has been by balancing images and in this way shifting the moral and emotional ground toward honesty.

Hunting imagery is common in your poems. I understand that you are a hunter as well. Could you talk about the hunt's importance to you and how participation in this ritualistic act informs your poetry?

For me, hunting has less to do with ritual than it has to do with the quality of attention you must bring to the hunt, being very much in a physical relationship with wind, earth, sun, trees, bird call, and wanting to take responsibility as carnivore for the flesh I could more easily buy in the supermarket. The truth is that packaged meat is animal.

I have noticed the prominence of extended similes in your poems. Can you talk about the simile in your work?

I don't have a theory about simile. In "Lies," for example, the people I'm talking about are self-conscious, so why not write a self-conscious simile? That can be a kind of precision. I don't think that all similes need be natural. And I do think that the attempt to get to something that can't quite be found or said is benign, even if the result seems a bit obscure. A fair attempt must be made. I take pains to try to get it right, but sometimes "it" is out of reach.

In "Secrecy" you write, "It was scarcely explainable / and could not be kept a secret." Ironically, that which cannot be easily articulated insists upon articulation. Would you say this is a statement of your poetics? If so, how do you see the proposition quoted above working through your poems?

That's a wonderful question. I suppose a way to answer you is to say that I've never been particularly interested in the obvious. Oh, I try to work toward clarity, but mystery often exerts a stronger force in my thought. I may even be psychologically unable to fasten on one answer to a question or one resolution to a problem—political, emotional, social, philosophical, epistemological, etc. I mean, I vote. I voice my opinions to friends and colleagues—sometimes. But poetry seems the realm where something more complex, beautiful, and truthful exists and changes in every little shift of experience or syntax. As for "could not be kept a secret," isn't a writer one who cannot not write? I cannot not write. The universe would be overwhelming.

In many of your poems, something or someone is being ruptured or torn. Why does the image of tearing resonate so strongly in your work? What does it mean to be torn?

I hadn't noticed. There are poems about surgeries. I'm more interested in other evocations in the poems.

Okay. Let's focus for a while on your newest book, The Queen's Desertion, *and in particular on the section in that book called "Voyage to Black Point." What was the impetus for writing these poems?*

Some of those poems were a continuation of poems about Florida that I started maybe three or four years before and published in my previous book, *I Will Say Beauty.* But the more time I spent on the water in Florida, the more it seemed to me that writing about Florida would require some additions to my usual syntax. That realization was finally as much a part of the project as anything else. Subject matter is always important to me, but coming up with a syntax that would represent the fecundity and richness of the experiences I had on the water along the nature coast and around Cedar Key is what especially pleased me when I was done writing them.

It wasn't until I had ten or so that I began to see this section of the book as a voyage or a journey.

What kind of voyage did you see here?

First of all, there is a genuine physical and literal journey from the cove where I have a cottage north to Black Point. The backwaters and marshes are tricky to navigate. I had to pick my way around shoals and sandbars. I had to be aware of the shifting tides. The experience of being on the water by myself, lonesome and in some danger of going aground, losing my way, or hooking a fish as large as my boat, has been thrilling. I'm often out all day and I have had the opportunity to think about a lot of things—the internal journey.

Your decision to create a triple spacing between each line here works wonderfully. As a reader I was inclined to pay more attention to what was happening in any given line, rather than thrusting vertically towards the end of the poem.

Good! I have an idealized notion of the line. I think of it as a unit of integrity. Although grammar, the coherence of the sentence and the way syntax carries meaning are of initial importance, the line itself has the possibility of being any number of things: one I suppose is a thing of beauty. I wanted to isolate the line in these poems. I'd tried something like this in *I Will Say Beauty,* when I justified the poems on the right side of the page, instead of the left. That was a way for me to work against print culture. The print culture is, I think, an aid to reading quickly. I thought I could find some ways of slowing the reader down to regard the line in fresh ways. The line can help to create the ceremony of language poetry aspires to.

The "Voyage to Black Point" poems are not only distinguished by your decision to triple-space between each line. You also punctuate these poems in unusual ways. The prevalent colon in particular.

The colon is for me a very interesting punctuation point. It can be used as a formal introducer, of course. It can be used between sentences almost as an equal sign. I think of it also as an arrow: this leads to that. The double colon, which I favored in many of the poems, is not only a stronger stop, but also a way of sending you forward *and* backward—and this goes back to the heightening of items in a page of poetry.

When I came across the double colons I tended to value the word that appeared before and after it more than I might have if the punctuation mark were absent.

Just as I prize the line, I prize the word. This comes from my early reading and loving a poet, for instance, like Gerard Manley Hopkins, who created his own lexicon. While I wasn't creating new words, I was trying to reinvest very ordinary words with something new. A good way for me to try this, I figured, was to find a way to isolate those words.

But then, of course, so much diction having to do with the natural world in Florida includes interesting words. The vocabulary is already enriched. The names of fishes, for instance, like "mako" or "hammerhead." "Sheepshead" is a good case in point. You think of the word as the name of something and not itself. Why would this fish be called a sheepshead? Does it look like a sheep's head? Is it woolly? What does an actual sheep's head look like? One can find this sort of elemental language play in William Carlos Williams's "The Red Wheelbarrow" where he writes, "a red wheel / barrow." There, he broke the word "wheelbarrow," which allowed me to see for the first time that a wheelbarrow was not just a thing that I could picture in the garden, but a construct of a barrow and a wheel.

Words are, above all, signifiers, not necessarily invitations to contemplation—or even pleasure. Like Williams and Hopkins and countless other poets before me, I had to somehow value the word in a way that would allow it to be appreciated beyond that first function.

Do you have a name for the form you've invented in the "Voyage to Black Point" poems?

No idea. How about "High Lyric with Double Colons and Triple Spacing"? (laughs)

I can tell you this: in the interest of saving space in their magazines, editors or typesetters would want to remove that extra spacing, perhaps thinking it was merely an eccentricity of mine. I had to be insistent. It made me think, "Is this just an effete gesture. Will it be read as effete?" I decided to stick to my guns. I doing so, I had some satisfaction that I managed to do what I wanted with these eccentrically spaced and unusually punctuated poems, which had to do with what I initially said about trying to capture the essence of the Florida landscape. It's almost an onslaught of experience when you're in the very hot and humid weather, out on a boat in the beating sun, and suddenly a ten-foot diameter ray will leap out of the water! I needed to find a way to get across that astonishing surprise. I very much prize the experience of looking at that ray alone, with no social obligations, just for itself.

In these poems, I was also getting a sense of how the mind constructs a language in order to understand that environment.

Yes, I think that is right. And the journey does take on an interiority: how the mind functions (which is something that has always fascinated me, and which I'm sure I get wrong); how we feel and think; how we are in the world; how we process the information that comes to us, and how we create language out of it. I wanted to be able to talk about the landscape as if there were no intercession of word or thought, which is a paradox because the poems think and there is language. But somehow I wanted to see if I could give the *impression* of transparency, a lack of human intervention. All of these considerations were part and parcel of the project, part of the journey.

You allude to Elizabeth Bishop a few times in the "Voyage to Black Point" poems. Do you see yourself connected to her in some ways?

My relationship to her is complex. As a graduate student, I started out really disliking her poems. I found most of them too transparent and simple. But then I began to appreciate some of the more metaphysical poems. "At the Fishhouses" comes to mind. Enjoying the metaphysics, I returned to simpler poems, more ready to appreciate them.

Later I found she and I had a lot in common—and I don't mean to say this by way of praising myself. We both liked to fish. We both lived in the northeast and in Florida. Her interests in maps, in flora, and fauna matched mine.

I've been drawn to the syntactic complexity in poems like "The Weed" and "The Monument." Her whole idea of geographical mirroring (G M in her notebooks) is interesting to me—basically writing out of a sense of place. I now own 1/9 of her grandparents' house in Nova Scotia, as sort of a literary legacy project. Because I've done some research on Bishop and possess all of the drafts of "At the Fishhouses," I decided I would go and try and find where those fishhouses were. I found, for instance, the hotel where she stayed: The Ragged Islands Inn. It's now a private residence. The woman who now lives there told me she thought the fishhouses were near Lockport. Nothing's left of them, but I recently had a letter from a woman who knew Bishop that confirms the location.

Great Village was a rather large port during the time she lived there. I decided to try to find the wharf and the shipyards, which now are grazing ground for cattle. You can't see or get to the wharf from the road anymore. Everything's grown in. The only way for me to find the wharf was to wade along Great River. I saved a small piece of the caving in wooden structure for the Bishop place.

Your interest in flora, fauna and animal life connects you not only to Bishop but to Marianne Moore and May Swenson.

I feel connected to all writers. One of the loveliest things about writing is this sense of literary continuum. As a writer you are part of tradition and a conversation, and it's very sweet to try to fix yourself somewhere along that line. I suppose what saves us from arrogance in doing so is that the process takes a lot of work, a lot of reading and trying to find out the connections between writers. I have certainly read and enjoyed both Moore and Swenson, but I know less about them than Bishop. I know a lot about Bishop and Berryman because I have written about them. I have also learned about Moore through her correspondence with Bishop. Those letters are fascinating and wonderful.

Yes. The collection of Bishop's letters in One Art *shows her to be an excellent and prodigious letter writer.*

And now the complete letters of Robert Lowell and Bishop is out. I can't wait to have the time to read the whole collection.

She had a bit of a crush on him, didn't she?

Yes, and he on her. And they both wanted to be fishermen. Actually, she wanted be a sea captain and he thought he would like to have a fishing trawler. He once sent her a copy of *The Compleat Angler.*

You, too, are fascinated with fishing. Do you see this as related to your interest in hunting?

I suppose so, in the sense that both are activities—like the writing of poetry—you can do by yourself. I don't hunt or fish with other people. I like to have no interference with my experience of being in the natural world, which is the main reason why I fish and hunt. I suppose I could just walk around in the woods or I could just row my boat or take a kayak out and still be in the natural world. But for some reason my attention isn't as focused when I don't have a task. When you're fishing you have to know everything about the tide and the wind and the bottom. Is the bottom sandy or muddy? If it's muddy, you're more likely to catch catfish, which is not a prized fish in the salt waters. By fishing or hunting, I'm required to pay closer attention, which I love to do.

Let's talk about another poem in The Queen's Desertion, *the beautiful dramatic monologue called "Relación of Cabeza de Vaca." This poem is very unlike anything I've ever read of yours before.*

I had read Cabeza de Vaca's *Relación* and had also taken a trip down to that area in the Florida Keys with an outward-bound group long before I had any idea I would be living in Florida. The group was a writing class I devised. I joined my student writers on the boats. One of our activities that really fixed for me a connection with Cabeza de Vaca's notebooks was walking through the Everglades swamps, trying to find a shell mound, and having to climb over mangroves and mangrove trees, where there were tree crabs all over the branches. This helped to make alive for me what it must have been like for him and the other survivors of the shipwreck. Only four companions and shipmates of Cabeza de Vaca's lived and made it to Mexico. I was so compelled by his story that I thought I'd try writing a long poem about it. Also, when I started going to Cedar Key, I learned there was a possibility that he might have gone by—and probably right through—the place. That was another connection for me.

I imagined some of his story, but portions of that poem were simply handed to me by experiences I had that, at the time, I did not realize had anything to do with a literary activity but ended up being important to writing this poem.

I will tell you that I went back and rewrote and repunctuated the first section of the "Relación" *after* I had written the poems in "Voyage to Black Point." I use a lot of ellipses and a few colons. There, I was imitating interior states through the varying length of line. I wanted to start out the poem in an authoritative-imitative way of establishing someone's thought.

This dramatic monologue is a real contribution to early settlement literature. It reminds me of Robert Hayden's "Middle Passage."

Oh, yes, that's a favorite poem of mine and far too brilliant for you to see any parallel.

I don't see your poem as derivative. But they both seem to be participating in a similar project, which is an attempt to reclaim the distant past and reshaping it through the contemporary imagination.

That's interestingly put. The Hayden poem, as you know, is very different from the rest of his work, as well. It's a much more heightened language.

Your poem too has heightened language, but it also has a richness of narrative you do not use in most of your other poems.

Yes, I enjoy this poem because of its narrative, which is unusually rich, but for other reasons having more to do with the lyric. I usually shun narrative or see how little I can get away with. I'm sure this is a preference I hold because of the way my mind works, which is by association and ellipses. I may be condemned to be a lyric poet because I have little tendency to think in narratives or chronologically. For what it's worth, I also think most narrative work goes on too long: few writers can resist starting their narratives too early and ending past necessity.

I agree. Many poets, for example, by attending too closely to a narrative, miss the lyric gesture in the poem.

They may miss the possibility within the poem—what other emotional and metaphysical possibilities there are. Walcott's narrative poem *Omeros* is pure genius. So is Brigit Kelly's "Song." However, I found I had more fluency in the lyric mode when I was writing my Abstractions, even with the first poem "The Past." I wanted to write about the people who owned our old farmhouse in the Otsdawa Valley before we did, but couldn't realize the poem, which more and more seemed to want to talk about some essence of the Past. The narrative seemed to be flattening out my interest in that still ineffable notion. So I tried to write the poem in another way.

Instead of trying to pile up moments in time, I tend to pile up images. I want to see how they collide and what friction or energy can be created through this collision. I have noticed that some readers lack patience for highly metaphorical poems, maybe because they do not trust themselves to understand by association. The associative element in our thinking is so natural that people do not realize that they're doing it, but if a poem is built out of metaphors they become *aware* of their associations and begin to mistrust them, wanting instead a discursive hint or expository sentence that will say how to feel and think about what's going on in the poem. Or some story to mend any sense of time dislocation.

As a reader, there are many ways of understanding a poem. There are other ways of knowing a poem. Interestingly, I've just interviewed Robert Glück, who is associated with the New Narrative writers in San Francisco. You and he could not be writing about more different subjects, but some of your observations about narrative and the lyric are strikingly similar.

When I was a younger writer and feeling a little insecure about my few aesthetic notions—and couldn't have made a fire out of them if I had dried them and put gasoline on them—I was very certain about what I liked and didn't like, and I was afraid of some experimental writing. I started, as many poets of my generation, being taught by poets who had grown up with the New Criticism. That was my bias. But the older I get, the freer I feel to appreciate the sort of writing I may have recoiled from twenty years ago.

In one of Glück's essays on Kathy Acker, another New Narrative writer from the coast, he suggests that the best place for a reader to be is at the point of uncertainty.

I think that's great. I would agree with that. Now, only if readers would.

I notice that your own writing—particularly in the "Voyage to Black Point" poems—has become more experimental.

Now in my 35th year of writing, with a lot more self-confidence, I'm finding that I'm far more experimental than many of my writing students! When I was starting out I was trying to prove to myself that I knew anything at all about writing poems. I was afraid to experiment. Now I think I need to call into question everything I do all the time. Before, I wanted not to have to call things into question, so I wrote poems that behaved. Now, if the poems are going to behave, they're going to do so differently and on their own terms. I'll enjoy the spectacle.

Frost, Carol. "Secrecy." *Love and Scorn: New and Selected Poems.* Evanston: TriQuarterly Books, 2000.

Williams, William Carlos. "The Red Wheelbarrow." *The Collected Poems of William Carlos Williams, Vol. 1: 1909–1939.* New York: New Directions, 1991. (See Permissions.)

Poetry:

Honeycomb, TriQuarterly Books, 2010
The Queen's Desertion, TriQuarterly Books, 2006
I Will Say Beauty, TriQuarterly Books, 2003
Love and Scorn: New and Selected Poems, TriQuarterly Books, 2000
Venus & Don Juan, TriQuarterly Books, 1996
Pure, TriQuarterly Books, 1994
Chimera, Peregrine Smith, 1990
Day of the Body, Ion Press, 1986
The Fearful Child, Ithaca House, 1983
Cold Frame (Chapbook), Owl Creek Press, 1982
Liar's Dice, Ithaca House 1978
The Salt Lesson, (Chapbook), Graywolf Press, 1976

As Editor, a Selection:

Rollins Book of Verse: 1885–2010, with Maurice O'Sullivan, Angel Alley Press, 2010
The Pushcart Prize Anthology, XXVIII, with Martha Collins, Pushcart Press, 2004
The Best of Pushcart Prize Poetry: Selections from the First 30 Years, with others, The Pushcart Press, General Editor Joan Murray, 2006
The Start of Something: An Anthology of Young American Poets in Australia, Picaro Press, 2002

Abandoning the Middle Distance: An Interview with Robert Glück

Robert Glück's books are the intimate, uncensored confessions of a master storyteller. In prose that transcends traditional genre identification (Glück insists his writings are neither fiction nor prose poetry nor memoir but prose pieces or simply stories), the reader's psychic life becomes the stage. "That's the power of being a writer," Glück explains. "You enter other people's psychic lives and stage a drama. Even if the drama occurs on a formal level, it's still a drama." With Bruce Boone, he began the now legendary West Coast-based New Narrative movement. (See the introduction to Kevin Killian.) "We were fellow travelers of Language Poetry and the innovative feminist poetry of that time," Glück writes in his essay "Long Note on New Narrative," "but our lives and reading led us towards a hybrid aesthetic, something impure." This aesthetic was informed as much by an embrace of "high" and "low" culture as it was by Marxist and Feminist theory and practice. It was also informed by a desire to embrace narrative to explore the dynamics of narration itself while telling stories. Currently a Professor at San Francisco State University, he has received a San Francisco Arts Commission Cultural Equity Grant and a fellowship from the California Arts Council.

For a voice level, say something.

"My heart aches, and a drowsy numbness pains / My sense."

Keats?

Yes, the first line of "Ode to a Nightingale."

I would not have expected you to quote one of the Romantics.

Keats is where I got my start. He's my guide in a sense: his enameled surface and below that the longing and loss. That combination of polished language and harsh emotion—I have never abandoned it. Words resoundingly in place—with a sense of inevitability even, that nineteenth-century idea of Poetry—and loss and incompletion riding underneath. For me, that's what Keats is. In high school, I memorized Keats's poems and then wrote them out, just to see how it feels to be writing those lines. It was a gestural experience.

That you were calling the poems to you.

That's right.

Were your earliest writing attempts in verse?

Oh, yes, entirely. My first poem was a sonnet. I had the classic wonderful high school English teacher who got me reading and writing poetry, Marjorie Bruce. For me, poems were something to be fabricated. I started with the sonnet not because I felt that I had something important to say, or that I had to burst out and tell the world my feelings. Rather, I wanted to make a beautiful object with language.

Has that impulse been sustained in your work?

What beauty might be seems more complex, but I still think of my books as three-dimensional objects, globes, and in fact, at the end of the novels there is always something revolving.

At the end of Jack the Modernist *there are a series of heads coming out of a body.*

Right.

And there's a scene in the beginning of the book that is loosely repeated at the end—a scene where the narrator watches Jack hug someone and wishes he could get a hug like that, only to realize when he does it's not what he imagined it would be.

In college, in Edinburgh, I took a year-long Conrad seminar. He thought of his books as spherical. That's where I got the idea. I recognized at once that it applied to me.

More of an understanding that this was your conception for your work all along?

Yes. I am dyslexic and dyslexics tend to think globally, rather than linearly.

Could you give me an example of that?

For a dyslexic, understanding comes in images rather than words or narratives. A lot of dyslexics are visual artists, which I was initially studying to be.

A traditional narrative suggests a syntax of action, a particular order to experience.

Whereas global suggests that experience is one, and that you take it in all at once, even though you can plug into it at different places. I think of my books not as temporal sequences but as incidents that occur on a globe. So it's not as though one goes from one thing to the next thing to the next. Instead, all those moments, images, and tableaux make one object. There may be different elements but they exist in a sculptural relation to each other.

There are two huge groups of dyslexics in society: one in museum studies and visual arts, the other in prison. Trouble with reading will lead you into a visual field, or you become so alienated that your relationship with society is compromised.

The first pieces of literature you produced were verse poems in traditional forms. You say you were consciously trying to make beautiful things. As I look around your house, I see beautiful art pieces. Your connection to the art world is still very much with you, and you often reflect upon it in your writing.

I have a long, complicated relationship with visual art. In some way, I'm a frustrated visual artist whose medium is language. So, that's another way of thinking about writing as an object. Add to this, my boyfriends, for the most part, have been artists . . .

So there's an erotic dimension.

Perhaps a narcissistic aspiration. (laughs)

Often in your work there appears to be little distinction between what some might consider a prose poem, an essay, or a short story. How do you make these distinctions?

I don't. My way of dealing with it is to not make the distinction. But I don't really like the term short story—and yet I have story collections. I simply call them stories. Or pieces. The short story has a history I do not feel especially related to. Other traditions are more important to me.

Such as?

Well, the modernist writer Blanchot made fictions called *contes* (tales). In these *contes,* which I admire tremendously, there's a pressure brought to bear on language itself, and a porousness. By porousness I mean that one sentence doesn't necessarily pick up where the last one left off. So you find a kind of air between the sentences. They can take any direction at any time. It's composition by the sentence. These are things I think about, and one could talk about some prose poetry that way, as well as lyrical fiction.

I teach a class in prose poetry, and I teach the different modernisms through the genre: cubism, négritude, surrealism, symbolism, and so on. This inspired me to write my own prose poems, as opposed to what I call prose pieces—those one paragraph prose blocks.

The world of the short story is a world of psychological insight. The classic short story hunkers down into certain plot moments. I want to be lyrical, I want to draw away into historical perspective, or move closer into an intense sensory event. I have nothing against moments of psychological insight, and I hope plenty of them occur in my writing, but that's not the sole purpose of my work.

Do you see yourself as an eclectic?

I assemble as much as I write. It's rare for me to just sit down and write something from beginning to end. My old boyfriend Nayland Blake had a retrospective in New York. He asked me to be part of a night of readings where writers respond to his work, so I sat down and wrote what I felt was the trouble with our relationship. My piece was about bunnies—he uses bunnies in his work—two bunnies who are both bottoms sitting in bed not knowing what to do. They love each other but they don't know what to do . . .

They want to fuck like rabbits but can't?

That's right! And I talk about diffidence, or even nausea, before the act of creation. I weave those two concerns together.

I get a sense of that weaving in your novel Margery Kempe, *where Margery's story is occasionally interrupted by the story of Bob and L. There are startling juxtapositions between the two contexts.*

If my books have plots they're usually borrowed. The plot of that book was lifted from Margery's autobiography, whereas the story of L. is really just a frame for her story. It would be hard to put together Bob's relationship with L. Those interruptions keep reframing Margery's story. But you couldn't make anything out of Bob and L.'s story on its own, you could say the exploration and development of their story exists in the Margery sections.

As a reader, I thought Margery's story was framing—and/or informing—Bob's relationship with L.

Of course it goes in both directions. I thought about Flaubert when I was writing that book. Flaubert's reply at the famous trial. Who is this woman Mme. Bovery?—*C'est moi.* Well, okay, I did the same thing. I said Margery, *c'est moi*. But I included the activity of projection inside the matter of the book. It took me a long while to decide whether to include or edit out Bob and L, because it would have been a purer book to eliminate them. And I wanted the book to be a jewel, I wanted it to be beautiful.

It would have been much more of a meditation. I remember reading the book and thinking the Bob and L. sections were pushing the book in unexpected directions.

In the end I wanted to make a book that could not be closed, that couldn't be a unit. Both my novels end when life becomes more reversible because obsessions are subsiding. Bob and Margery are no longer so obsessed.

Things are also potentially more chaotic, too.

Yes, when you're obsessed, your priorities are strict.

There are other ways in which I try to make my books open and porous. *Margery Kempe* is basically a collaboration with Margery. The sentence in that book is half hers. And there are all these notes—I asked men and women to write about their body. I put them in the book too. And there's Bob, who is a person in the world. Bob lives in the same world as the reader, so there's a way the book cannot close because you can't close something or someone in the same world as you. In *Reader,* I collaborate with the different authors; in *Jack* I give the book to Jack and he rewrites sections.

In the sense that each of your books is assigned some genre title and your work chafes against certain conventions of those genres, you are collaborating with the readers of your books as well.

Yes, insofar as the audience will act as witness.

Given your interest in collaboration, I'm surprised you didn't dramatize the fact that Margery dictated her book to a priest. That could have been an opportunity to show the collaborative relationship between them.

I would have had to back up too far to show what dictating to a scribe meant in her period, which is very different from somebody working with a ghostwriter today, or even from someone dictating today. In the first place, her scribe was a priest, which gave her work some credibility. Their relationship was like confessor and priest in a confessional. In the second place, it was not unusual to write this way. Masterpieces like Julian of Norwich's *Revelations of Divine Love* were written in the same fashion. And people often had books read to them, even if they were literate. Books were read out loud, even if the reader was standing alone in a room. A book was a script, it was not real until it was spoken. But in the end, I didn't think all of that material would fit into my book. There were tons of things I could have included.

Do you ever feel you haven't yet exhausted Margery, that there's another book in you about her?

Oh, no, I have exhausted Margery and Margery has exhausted me! We have exhausted each other.

Why did you turn to her in the first place?

Well, I first learned about her in 1966 in a Medieval Studies course in UCLA. At that point she wasn't well known and we read only a few pages of her book in an anthology. Her book had been lost until it was discovered in a castle library in 1934. Before then, all that existed were a few prayers. When it was discovered, people were hopeful that here was another great English mystical text. In fact, her first editor, in his preface, kept referring to her as "poor Margery," since she was so disappointing—in her vulgarity and self-aggrandizement. It's not a lofty piece of piety. Even then I thought there was something in her story for me. I felt her book was a comedy, like Patrick Dennis's *Little Me,* in which Belle the starlet continuously brags about herself, but you realize through her bragging that she is a flop. I felt that Margery was the *Little Me* of the fifteenth century. I liked the fact the she didn't seem to understand her own experience. I felt that she lived at a time when that would have been hard to do because the paradigm itself was changing—just like today. Only a few years after I was introduced to her, I did a junior year abroad in Scotland and I was hitchhiking around Northern Europe looking at the Flemish masters, looking carefully at the Van Eyck altarpiece in Ghent, the Hans Memling museum in Bruges . . . so that period has always been important to me. In a way, writing *Margery Kempe* was the fulfillment of that interest.

In the early 70s I tried to turn Margery's story into a musical comedy. I even wrote songs for it. I liked the idea of a musical comedy that ends with the crucifixion. I liked the clarity of her lust. She's clear about that at least. She wants the manhood of Jesus. Poor John—it's his story in a sense. But then it hit me: here I was, a hippie in San Francisco: what did I know about getting a musical comedy produced! Later, during a midlife crisis, I became so obsessed with a man that I found my way back into her story. I couldn't write about her before, because the story would have been crass. When I became crazy in love myself, I could enter her experience.

I think her story resonates with a lot of gay men insofar as we too lust for the divine in other men.

There are all sorts of ways into her story: the desire for a complete and authentic experience, understanding sex and romance as a way to be safe. Gay men are generally—for good reason—fearful, and some parts of gay culture offer ways of achieving safety. For Margery, Jesus was safety, a way to escape death.

Some feminist critics have argued that she used her divine relationship to Jesus as a way of avoiding the marriage bed.

It's possible, though John seemed to go along with practically anything. And she did buy her way out of the marriage. It was an era when woman could own property apart from their husbands—an era that soon came to an end. She didn't need Jesus to escape her conjugal duties.

Back to your composition process. You said you often compose by the sentence. Could you talk about this?

My palette is a sentence. Each next sentence can start at a very different place and so that makes for a kind of porousness, which is a quality I want.

There are spaces between the stitchings.

And dissonances.

Many writers will map out where they want their narratives to go and the sentences lead logically from one incident to the next. In composing by the sentence, are you discovering where your piece needs to go as you write it?

Well, possibly. I generally know what a work is going to do before I start. The question is what pattern will it take. How is it going to be organized. In that sense, I give myself more elbow room than many other writers. In prose, when you are telling a story, two things have to happen at once: one event has to follow another with a sense of inevitability; but you also want to create a field of possibility in each moment. I try to pressure that proposition by increasing the possible directions in which a story or a next sentence can go by creating a larger view, say, a long view, or a too-intimate close-up, or I jump to the subject of story telling itself, or to the reader—I abandon the middle distance.

Explain what you mean by that.

Most narrative takes place in the middle distance, which is basically what someone can see. So, Tony walks into the room: He walks into the room, he sits down at the pine table, he wears a green blazer and a fedora with a green feather. Working on this level, I create a kind of guided daydream. Readers project into it and make a story-world in their brains. But why? The naturalism this method supports is a set of conventions that leads to the status quo. The more "normal" the convention, the more it supports the status quo. We take this kind of writing as natural but Chaucer would not have, or Sappho, or some tribal writer. Since I'm the writer, and I can include anything I want, what has made me confine my work to this small palette? Why don't I say, Tony walks in and relives the orgasm he had that morning. I could say how much money Tony has in his wallet or bank account, as Balzac might have done. I could say what Tony will be thinking about tomorrow, what he will dream tonight, how he emerged from his mother's vagina, how English torques his brain, what he knows subliminally, Bob's smell perhaps. I could say how a flu virus is commencing but not yet experienced, how Tony is going to die. I could talk about Tony's grandfather's journey to America. A human being is large and complicated, and the middle distance diminishes him or her.

It also dictates the expectations a reader will have for a text. It tells us what a "good" story "should" have.

Yes, so in a vile MFA fiction workshop, all this would be read as excess. To put pressure on the expectations of the middle distance is a kind of politics. Anything that reorients the reader and writer is political, because organizing a reader's mind and psychic life involve power.

And such conventions came about through sociopolitical contexts.

In genre literature, the conventions are emphatic, and they generate pleasure and feeling. I am not the enemy of the middle distance or other writing conventions. I want to understand them and use them consciously.

Frost, in his very folksy way, said when we write poems we go a-sentencing. When you go a-sentencing, is there a certain kind of sentence to which you are prone?

Not that I know. In each book I spend everything. By the time the book is done, the cistern is empty.

So any one book of yours is a reflection of who and what you were when you wrote it?

After both *Jack* and *Margery* I didn't even know how to write a sentence. I had used those sentences up, especially the sentence from Margery. I didn't know how to begin again.

So it sounds like you're saying there is a typical kind of sentence within each particular work.

Yes, I think there is.

Could you give an example?

In *Margery*, the sentences have a lilt that derives from Margery's prose, an attractive flat-footedness, a beat that asserts itself again and again. The Bob and L. story has a different rhythm, which is part of the reason why those sections are so jarring.

L. is my object in the prose sequence "The Visit" as well. We had taken a trip to Portugal together and those prose poems are about that visit. That sentence is more of a whisper.

With the stories I'm writing now about Ed, my former lover who appears in *Elements of a Coffee Service*, part of the text comes directly from his journals, and another part he wrote for me. I asked him to write about the day that he was diagnosed and I composed a section by reforming what he had written. He left me his dream journals as well. So, even though this book is being written after his death, it's a collaboration.

It's fascinating that you have access to his dream journals.

Well, I started him writing them when we were together in the early 70s. Ed was such a great dreamer—every morning he would relate dream after dream to me in great detail going backwards into the night. I used to pillage them for my poetry.

So, you have been collaborating with Ed for a long time.

We were artists together. He would draw me, I would write poems about our relationship, first how good it was, then how fucked up. I plan to make all the weather in the book come from his dreams. He was always watching the sky and painting the sky and so I think it will be good to have all the atmosphere come from his dreams.

In doing so, you're creating an interesting formal constraint for yourself. Do you do such things in most of your books?

In *Margery*, for instance, all the birds are real, even in her visions of the Holy Land, the right birds appear where and when they should. All the clothing is accurate. Other things are purposely anachronistic. Also, four words appear again and again throughout the book. I wanted the book to hang off them, as though the book were a longer version of those words: *exalt, exasperate, abandon, amaze*. I wanted the novel to be four words, as well as the longer version.

The prose poem "Mexico" from The Family Poems *is a fascinating piece. It could have easily appeared in a collection of stories.*

I suppose I'm proposing them all as poems, even though the stories are very much stories. My goal was to put narration back into poetry. My first book, *Andy*, was verse but it could have been recast as a story. I was using Chaucer's *Canterbury Tales* and other texts for models. What I'm working on now, "I, Boombox," is an autobiography. It's made up of my misreadings, which for me are like dreams, dreaming on the page. Put all these dreams together and you have a pretty complete autobiography.

What does misreading mean to you?

I fashioned this project so that I can recuperate something from my loss, because I make tons of errors. In the activity of misreading there is a kind of creative energy.

An instance when the subconscious is being pushed to the fore.

Pushing itself to the fore. I also like the idea of writing the poem until I die, like the Modernist long poem that is only interrupted by the author's death. So, my catalogue of errors is my version of the Modernist long poem. It's a disjunct autobiography. I need some disjunction and fragmentation in order to make writing recognizable to me as it describes the times and my own life, and as it is writing that knows itself as such.

In Family Poems, *you often use the ampersand instead of writing out "and." Why?*

I liked the way it looked on the page. It created an interesting energy. Also, I see those poems expressing a kind of exasperation; I just want to push it, make it jumpy, and the ampersand is part of that.

You like to include personal material in your work. Have you ever said to yourself, "I can't write this; it's too personal"?

Many times, but that's not reason enough to stop. Sometimes I will wonder quite a bit if I should keep something in. And it's not what you would think. I don't really care about sexual things—though combining sex with the abjections of age gives me pause, but not enough to press delete. In the novel I am working on, I talk about getting rejected by a certain press and how the rejection flattened me. Writers published by that press and the editors are still around. Now *that's* embarrassing.

Reader *still stands as your most substantial contribution to verse. It also seems very much a unified book.*

Originally, all the pieces were called "Learning to Write" and I was quite a ways into the book before I abandoned that title.

I wanted to return to the freedom of being a student, just trying things out. I was imitating and in a sense becoming those many writers, and each took me in a different direction, which staved off the pressure to produce work of high quality—or even more, to produce original work. That was the first idea for the book.

The book also seems like a collection of homages.

It explores the way one is taken over in the act of reading. Each poem is an instance of possession. When you read someone in a deep way your thoughts and your rhythms are taken over.

Then the book appears to explore the paradox that reading at once empowers you and disempowers you. In one sense you are learning a new vocabulary and becoming more knowledgeable; in another sense you commit to someone else's style and vision.

Extends may be a better word than commit because you extend into somebody else's world. Writers use your psychic life as a stage to enact whatever they wish. That's the power of being a writer: to enter other people's psychic life and stage a drama. Even if the drama occurs on a formal level, it's still a drama.

Are you cognizant of this when you are writing?

It's a structural part of the process. But I might want to foreground the reader-writer relationship.

Like the end of "Mexico" where you ask the reader, "Tell me, given the options, where would your anger have taken you—where has it taken you?" I was no longer a voyeur in the narrator's experience.

Yes, the direct address to the reader brings the relationship between reader and writer into the drama, which is one of the basic tenets of New Narrative.

Back to Reader, *I was really moved by the prose poem "Hitler."*

There's a bit of the Holocaust in all of my books—I don't know why—and the effect Hitler had on the Jews. In *Denny Smith* I talk about his Americanizing the Jews. The prose poem "Hitler" was my attempt to record a moment of understanding: Hitler's treatment of the Jews was not a punishment, it was to make something beautiful—that was his impulse.

Through cancellation—

A terrible minimalism. He was attempting to make what he thought was beautiful: a pure race. Before this revelation, I could only understand the camps as a kind of punishment.

Punishment suggests a certain kind of intimacy Hitler did not seem to have with the Jews. One punishes to redeem. When you punish someone you are invested in them.

I realized that was not the case for Hitler.

Were the earliest poems in Reader *the ones you wrote for Kevin and Dodie?*

No. The earliest ones were aimed at the grandest historical writers, Wordsworth and Basho, for example.

How do these poems work when you read them to an audience?

Some I have only recently attempted, like the double-columned one about Jack Spicer.

Do you share with Kevin an obsession with Jack Spicer?

My obsession is nothing compared to his obsession. Still, Jack Spicer was ours in a way. He was a local writer, almost tribal in spirit, who happened to be great. Spicer addressed our concerns, yet there's plenty in him that will remain obscure. He grapples with the largest issues, and he expresses what one often feels as a gay man.

Your comment about portions of Spicer's obscurity is spot on. Reading his work, I've often felt he was writing about something private he didn't want to share.

Some of it was not meant to be understood; otherwise, he would have written it differently. He also liked to travel in the direction of nonsense—nonsense was an important ingredient.

Did you carry some of that into your own work, perhaps writing private or obscure things that either a small group of people or no one could understand?

Let me put it this way: there may have been a small group who would have understood most of his personal references. He was kind of a court writer. There's very little in my work that my smallest audience wouldn't get. The obscurity in it is obscure to me too.

In your essay in Biting the Error, *you talk about how critical theory was very important to you when you started out. You would, in your own word, "pillage" the texts of critical theorists to work through some of their ideas in your writing.*

Oh, certainly, yes. Theory in the 70s meant Marxist theory for the most part. That's a huge treasure house of critical writing that the world has. Walter Benjamin, the Frankfurt School, Theodor W. Adorno, Lukács, Sartre. And then came Feminist Theory and to a lesser degree Gay Theory.

I was looking for ways to expand my own little point of view. These critics were giving me a larger frame. Here's Georges Bataille talking about how sex, death, and community function all together. Who was talking about these things? Sex went from one's local comedy to an event in the species, to the way our whole society is organized, to loss, to death. And so, without self-aggrandizement, I could see myself in a larger frame. I could hitch up to the largest economic forces, the largest cultural forces. What do we take for granted? How does power work in an intimate relationship? The feminists were talking about that. You understand how power works between classes, then you come home and mistreat your mate. All these shifts in scale created a different concept of what autobiography could be.

Elements of a Coffee Service was written under the spell of Walter Benjamin, his essays are both thinky, lyrical, and intimate—Bataille and Barthes too. Bataille was a revelation for me. A few others have been as well. It felt like I'd been given a ladder to see over my wall. I don't know them rigorously—I couldn't teach a course on Derrida right now. I basically use these writers to help me understand my own experience. If they don't give me access to my own experience, I'm not interested. I don't need to know them like an academic who learns his subject rigorously. Bruce Boone is more like that; he's a completist.

It sounds as if what Bob Glück is at any given moment is very permeable.

I certainly hope so! The best reading is an uncertain reading. In an essay on Kathy Acker's work I talk about this. We are educated to think that we should be able to know the meaning of a piece of writing, but what if the intention of the writing is to throw us into confusion, induce a state of wonder, and unravel the basic tenets of our experience?

Glück, Robert. "Mexico." *Family Poems.* San Francisco: Black Star Series, 1979.

______. "Long Note on New Narrative." *Biting the Error: Writers Explore Narrative.* Ed. Mary Burger, Robert Glück, et al. San Francisco: Coach House Books, 2004.

Poetry and Prose:

The Dead, (with Sarah Schulman), Bella Donna Series, 2008
Denny Smith, Clear Cut Press, 2003
Margery Kempe, High Risk, 1994
Reader, Lapis, 1990
Jack the Modernist, Sea Horse, 1986 (reissued: High Risk, 1995)
Elements of a Coffee Service, Four Seasons Foundation, 1982
La Fontaine (with Bruce Boone), Black Star Series, 1982
Family Poems, Black Star Series, 1979
Metaphysics, Hodypoll Press, 1978
Marsha Poems, Hodypoll Press, 1973
Andy, Panjandrum Press, 1973

As Editor, a Selection:

Biting the Error: Writers on Narrative (with Camille Roy, Mary Burger, and Gail Scott), Coach House Press, 2004
Saturday Afternoon: Poems and Stories by Older Writers, Black Star Series, 1985

Polysemous Poetry: An Interview with Arthur Sze

Although a second-generation Chinese American who has absorbed the language and culture of his ancestors, Arthur Sze is very much an American poet writing within and responding to a tradition specific to American poetry. His earlier poems and many translations of Chinese poetry suggest a strong identification with the concise, elliptical imagery of classical Chinese poets as well as Japanese haiku; however, the legacies of Walt Whitman and Wallace Stevens are perhaps even greater influences upon Sze's more recent work, which is serial in nature, often expansive, and syntactically-dense. His vision is also informed by a unique synthesis of Eastern/Western ideas: "If you inscribe Emerson's beliefs in one circle, and Zen beliefs in another, as in a Venn diagram, they overlap extensively; and the circle of my beliefs would overlap them both." But no amount of description can prepare one for the uniquely rich experience of reading Sze's work, which also incorporates Native American myths and the language of science into a texture that is both sensual and rigorously intelligent. "I'm keenly interested in creating a polysemous poetry," he explains below. "To accomplish that, depth and layering are important." Indeed, Sze's work is as involved and multilayered as an expertly woven tapestry—the product of patience and insistence. He has earned many honors, including the Lannan Literary Award for Poetry, the Lila Wallace-Reader's Digest Writers' Award, a Western States Book Award for Translation, and an American Book Award. The first poet laureate of Santa Fe, he has taught at a number of prestigious universities, and is currently a Professor Emeritus at the Institute of American Indian Arts.

At the end of your poem "The Living Room," you write, "I close / my eyes, feel how in the circumference / of a circle the beginning and end have no end."

Similarly, the ending of the sixth section of "Inflorescence" also refers to circles: "And what appears to be up close a line / becomes by air, the arc of a circle." These are just two among many instances in your poems where references to circles emerge. Moreover, many of your poems are circular in form, insofar as they begin with some image or phrasing that is echoed in the final lines. Can you discuss the importance of circles in your work?

Geometries of space—point, line, web, and circle—are significant motifs in my work. I'd like to start by quoting from Emerson's essay "Circles," in which he asserts, "Around every circle another circle can be drawn." Each circle implies a series of ever-expanding concentric circles and is an image of the expanding cosmos. Emerson also asserts circles are "the highest emblem of the cipher of the world." Here I'm more interested in "cipher" than in the hierarchy of "the highest emblem," and I read "cipher" as zero, emptiness, and mystery. From an Eastern perspective, the *enso*, or Zen circle, can represent void, totality, or even enlightenment. If you inscribe Emerson's beliefs in one circle, and Zen beliefs in another, as in a Venn diagram, they overlap extensively; and the circle of my beliefs would overlap with both.

Two examples from my work might be helpful. First, at the end of "Streamers," I mention a circle as "a dot that must enlarge into / a zero, a void, *enso*, red shimmer, / breath, endless beginning, pure body, pure mind." In many poems, I play with scale, and here the circle appears, at a distance, to be a period, to put finality and closure on things; but, if you look up close, what appears to be a period may actually be a circle that contains emptiness. The dot, then, is a circle that incorporates red shimmer, breath, endless beginning, pure body, pure mind; so the circle is not a static one-dimensional symbol but rather, emptiness rich in possibility, a three-dimensional force actualized in breathing.

I want to add that circularity often involves returning to see or experience something again for the first time, and it doesn't have to enact closure. "Because a circle opens in all directions," it enables connections to form in an infinite array. Point, line, spiral, web, and circle all connect. In a second example, "Labrador Tea," I begin with the image of "labrador leaves in a jar with a kerchief lid." The poem moves through a series of associations and comes back at the end to "leaves clothed underneath with rusty hairs / suffuse a boreal light glistening on tidal pools." I cite this poem, because the circling motion does not enact formal closure. Instead, when the return takes place, I hope the reader discovers that the poem occurs during the time that labrador leaves have been steeping—the tea is now ready to drink.

In an outstanding interview you did with Eric P. Elshtain for Chicago Review, *you state: "I believe the poetic sequence is the form of our time . . . I have been drawn to the poetic sequence because it enables me to develop a complexity that intensifies as well as enlarges the scope and resonance of a poem." That interview was published in 2004 shortly before the publication* Quipu *(2005), which, though not mentioned there, features many poetic sequences. The same goes for* The Ginkgo Light *(2010). Although you explain your reasons for using the poetic sequence in that interview, I was wondering if you could discuss them again—a task that will require some repetition, of course, but, considering your persistent and extensive use of the form since then, some enlargement as well.*

I still believe the poetic sequence is the form of our time. In 2004, I mentioned several important factors: I could (a) "develop a complexity that intensifies as well as enlarges the scope and resonance of a poem," (b) "make juxtaposition a more active structural principle," and (c) "braid lyric, dramatic, and narrative elements and utilize them simultaneously." I continue to affirm these points but want to add that the enormous flexibility of the sequence is one of its greatest strengths. Unlike a narrative that relies on a fairly linear unfolding in time, with a sequence, I can more easily change location or character, shift focus and tone, vary rhythm, and radially amplify thematic concerns.

In writing sequences, I'm still very interested in exploring the relationship between part and whole, and my conception of fragmentation inside of sequences has shifted between the *Chicago Review* interview and today. In my sequences through 1998, I often conceived of fragments as shards of a pot. I liked the jagged edges and how the stillness between them suspended narrative motion. When I wrote *Quipu*, I began to conceive of fragments as carded but unspun fiber—in weaving, one cards or aligns fibers before spinning them into a one-ply yarn—where images and thematic concerns were visible and unharnessed. In *The*

Ginkgo Light, I conceived of fragments more as line segments than uncarded fiber, and only occasionally as shards. In any case, when sequences incorporate fragments inside of a larger whole, they are not merely complex. A sequence is most cogent if it integrates the one and the many, so that it is complex and simple at the same time.

To give an example, I'd like to discuss "Spectral Line." After teaching for twenty-two years at the Institute of American Indian Arts, I wanted to write about some of my experiences there but found that a single narrative line wasn't capacious enough to respond to the complexity of cross-cultural tensions. The definition of a spectral line—on small scale, a particular wavelength of light corresponding to an energy transition—gave me the "one" which I could amplify into "many" manifestations. As I wrote, I found that, in addition to a loose narrative that harnesses incidents from the Institute, it was important to add a second narrative where a speaker journeys to China. I initially conceived of these two narrative strands as continual points of comparison and contrast. Then one day a third narrative unexpectedly entered the poem. A character, Robin, appears in the second line, where she adjusts the saddle on a horse. She disappears for much of the poem and then reappears in section seven, where a reader learns that she quit her job in the telecommunications industry after her coworkers were terminated, and now she grooms "the horses she loves." This is the barest of narratives, but it applies psychological pressure to the situation at hand. Robin's narrative radially amplifies the issue of how people treat each other, and, in writing a fluid sequence that wasn't tied to linear narration, I was able to let her enter, exit, and reenter without difficulty.

Finally, I want to add that I find the gaps between sections of a sequence supremely useful. A new section can start far from where the last section ended, create tension and surprise, though ultimately it has to connect and become part of the essential fabric.

One of the most salient features of your poetry since Dazzled *(1982) is its simultaneous accessibility and difficulty. On one hand, the poems do not pose too many linguistic challenges. There is, in fact a disarmingly direct and unadorned simplicity of utterance. Many of your poems, for example, braid to-*

gether a series of basic grammatical structures: "I gaze . . . I notice . . . you stare . . . they walk . . ." On the other hand, the poems require a considerable amount of intellectual rigor to be adequately understood, partially because of the subtlety of the juxtapositions, partially because you are grappling with complicated ideas, and partially because you dramatize complicated moments of perception. Can you talk about these tensions between accessibility and difficulty in your poems?

As you say, the basic grammatical structures in my poems are often direct. In addition, I value clarity, and that gives my imagery and descriptive language broad accessibility. Yet I also employ a wide vocabulary, and many words from different disciplines—quipu, *omega minus*—and different languages—*dhyana*, *xun*—can be a hurdle. In addition, my syntax and sentences were simpler in my early work, but, as evidenced by the increasing use of semicolons, dashes, and colons, they've become more nuanced. Juxtaposition is another difficulty for some readers, because rather than a linear narrative where B follows from A, A and B are placed into simultaneous interaction with each other without resolution.

Here I want to add that I am not writing to be difficult: I am writing the poems I need to write, and I'm keenly interested in creating polysemous poems. To accomplish that, depth and layering are important. I like to invoke the Japanese aesthetic term, *yugen*: the two characters have been translated as "subtle," "profound," "mysterious," and, in the words of a former Japanese student, "almost disappearing." The *yu* character is, in one etymology, derived from indigo dyeing. In that art, a dyer dips a skein of spun white silk into an indigo vat, soaks it, and pulls it up into the air. When indigo comes in contact with oxygen, it chemically reacts, and the yarn turns greenish-blue. After repeated dippings, the yarn changes in color from greenish-blue to blue to deep blue to blue-approaching-black. At this last stage, it arrives at that state of mystery, subtlety, and profundity.

I hope that the depth and multiplicity in my poems strike a reader immediately, even though he/she cannot immediately articulate what is happening. I also hope that initial shock leads to a vibrancy that impels a reader to come back again and again. In this process of engagement, I hope that some of the initial disorientation or difficulty that my poems cause are experienced as necessary steps or stages toward experiencing a new totality, and that, as the poems reveal themselves over time, this experience is enriching and compelling.

You are a second-generation Chinese American who has strong geographical and cultural ties to the American Southwest—particularly New Mexico and the Native American tribes there. How have you absorbed both the Chinese and Native American traditions into your work?

I have absorbed the Chinese literary and cultural tradition through translation and through my family. When I was a student at UC Berkeley, I approached Ts'ai Mei-hsi, an instructor in conversational Mandarin, after class, and showed him my translation of a Tang dynasty poem. I asked Ts'ai if he would respond to it, and he got excited and said he loved Tang poetry. He offered to meet me at the Oriental Languages library, and, there, he checked the accuracy of my translations and also looked up geographical and historical references. Our meetings were never part of a class, but, with his help, I translated twenty-nine poems by Li Bo, Du Fu, Wang Wei, and a few others. A decade later, I translated poems from other time periods, by such poets as Tao Qian, Li Qingzhao, Ma Zhiyuan, and Wen Yiduo, who broke from the classical tradition and wrote in the vernacular. A decade after, I translated a third set of poems and collected all of my translations in *The Silk Dragon* (2001).

I thought my work as a translator of Chinese poetry might be over, but then, from 2002 to 2008, I was invited to China, Taiwan, and Hong Kong for international poetry festivals and met many of the leading poets. I decided to translate a fourth set of poems by Xi Chuan, Chen Li, and Yang Lian. Then in 2009, Ed Hirsch invited me to edit *Chinese Writers on Writing* for the Trinity University Press *Writers on Writing* series. Instead of selecting writings from across two thousand years, I decided to focus on modern Chinese poetry and fiction. I selected all of the writings and, with the help of many translators, assembled a collection of essays by 41 Chinese writers from 1917 to 2009. So, over time, my work as a translator and editor has enabled me to absorb a large part of the Chinese literary tradition.

In terms of cultural tradition, I've drawn extensively from my family background as well as travel in China. My parents were immigrants and spoke Mandarin and English at home. My father had, in his library, such classics as the *Lao-zi, Zhuang-zi*, and *Yi Jing*, and I remember, as a teen, puzzling over them. In 1985 I traveled for a month with an uncle in China and visited my mother's family's home outside Beijing and also sailed, before the dam was built, a thousand miles down the Yangtze River. My uncle introduced me to friends and relatives; he and an aunt were particularly interested in Chinese history, and I learned a lot from them.

I also have a long connection with Native American culture. After I graduated from UC Berkeley, I moved to Santa Fe and worked as a poet in the schools. I conducted workshops at a number of Indian pueblos and met Ramona Sakiestewa, a Hopi weaver, through the New Mexico Arts Division. We were married from 1978 to 1995, and our son, Micah, is an enrolled member of the Hopi tribe. During those years, I experienced the gritty as well as the sacred in contemporary Native life.

In addition, from 1984 to 2006, I was on the faculty at the Institute of American Indian Arts. During those years, I worked daily with students from over 200 tribes across the United States and was privileged to teach and learn from them. Many of my former students have become writers, and they include Sherwin Bitsui, James Thomas Stevens, Allison Hedge Coke, Jennifer Foerster, Irvin Morris, Orlando White, Layli Long Soldier, Santee Frazier, DG Okpik, Cathy Rexford, Sara Ortiz, and Eddie Chuculate. Over time, my experiences at the Institute greatly widened and deepened my understanding of Native culture.

Despite your many links to Chinese and Native American cultures, you are an American poet. How would you situate yourself in the tradition of American poetry?

My links with Chinese and Native American cultures are significant influences and sources of inspiration, but, yes, absolutely, I am an American poet. I hope it is not too presumptuous to invoke Whitman, Williams, Pound, and Stevens to say I am in conversation with them. With Whitman, I share an interest in the possibilities of the poetic sequence, an impulse to inventory and catalog and make a living record, and I share his inclusive vision and desire to put worlds inside of poetry. With Williams, I share "deep noticing," an interest in dispassionate presentation of the thing itself, and in harnessing luminous particulars. Ezra Pound's imagism drew on the primacy of the image in classical Chinese poetry and drove it deep into American modernism, and, with Pound, I share a keen interest in the poetic image, the use of juxtaposition as an active, structural principle, and the braiding of cultures. With Stevens, I share an abiding interest in the relationship between the mind/imagination and the world, a search for "what will suffice," and in meditative duration. I share his belief that "poetry must resist the intelligence almost successfully."

Certain concepts—such as expansion and contraction, loss and retrieval, recollection and transformation—are revisited throughout your work. Certain images reemerge as well: acequias, arroyos, blood, mushrooms, candles, moons, gates, light. Never are these repetitions repetitious. Instead, I see you writing, in the interests of clarity and rediscovery, the same poem again and again, inscribing your signature upon a constellation of themes in new and fresh ways. In this way, your work reminds me of Whitman's. Would you agree or disagree with this, and can you explain how it is true or not true for you?

I'd like to begin by responding to the issue of repetitions. Anthropologists assert that repeating patterns and images are not mere repetitions but are "forms of insistence," and that these forms of insistence reveal the very fabric of a culture. In a similar way, my repeating images and patterns are variations that widen, deepen, and enrich the meanings of a poem. On a micro-level, in "Quipu," I use the word "as" twenty times, but I am utilizing different denotative meanings so that each time the word recurs, a new layer and resonance is added. Eventually this process is explicitly revealed when the poem asserts, "as: to the same degree or amount; / for instance; when considered in a specified // form or relation; in or to the same degree / in which; as if; in the way or manner that; // in accordance with what or the way in which; / while, when; regardless of the degree to which; // for the reason that; that the result is."

I'd also like to propose that the view that I am "writing, in the interests of clarity and rediscovery, the same poem again and again, inscribing [my] signature upon a constellation of themes in new and fresh ways" is a helpful point of departure but is ultimately limiting, because it doesn't fully allow for progression. Like Whitman, I am indeed interested in a constellation of themes, but my style, as well as thematic concerns, has shifted from book to book. From *Dazzled* (1982) to *River River* (1987), you can see a significant enlargement of scope and imaginative command. In *River River*, I wrote my first sequences, and there have been significant changes since then. *Archipelago* foregrounded part and whole, while *Quipu* foregrounded linguistic experimentation. Also, there's an erotic charge in the section of new poems in *The Redshifting Web* that carries over and informs *Quipu*. If I've shifted my scientific interest from physics in *River River* to living biology in *The Ginkgo Light*, from inquiries into the nature of the cosmos to considering the immediate challenges of our imperiled world, I believe this change is no longer about putting my signature upon a constellation of themes. Instead, the poems become landmarks on a journey.

Finally, I'd like to add that currently I'm collaborating with Susan York, an artist here in Santa Fe. After spending hours in her studio, discussing her graphite sculptures and drawings, and seeing how she incorporates a "record of labor" into her art, I've written a new sequence, "The Unfolding Center," in eleven sections. Sections three and eight are monologues in different voices, and, as the speakers talk, they revise what they say, and these passages are visually marked with strikethrough lines. The two voice-driven sections create key points of tension with some of the more image-driven sections, and this creative tension is elevated and incorporated into the very fabric of the poem. I believe this is a new achievement, so the notion of writing the same poem again and again, or writing with a constellation of themes in mind is no longer adequate to describe the progression in my work.

In a 1977 interview with Christopher Busa, Stanley Kunitz said, "The vocabulary of modern science is fascinating . . . but, by and large, [it] remains exclusive and specialized." Such terminology, he insisted, should be as common to us as myths were to the ancient Greeks. I mention this to you because your writing engages the language of science—be it physics, astronomy, botany, or other branches of science—more thoroughly and deeply than any poet I can think of. And your use of such terminology, though precise, is never dry or merely technical. It does what Kunitz felt the language of myth did for the ancient Greeks: it gave them a language with which to grapple with the mysteries of the world; it gave them a language—however imperfect—with which to make sense of space and one's place in it. How did you develop the richness of your scientific vocabulary and how do you see its place in your poems?

I've mentioned in other interviews that I started to write poetry at MIT. I spent my first two years of college there and then transferred to UC Berkeley. During my freshman year, I took the usual courses in physics, calculus, and organic chemistry, but if my knowledge of science had stopped there, it would not have become very interesting. Years later in New Mexico, I met Dick Slansky, a physicist who became the director of the theoretical physics division at Los Alamos National Laboratory. Conversations with Dick sparked my interest in what physicists were working on, and he inevitably discussed string theory and other issues. Through him, I met other physicists, including George Zweig and Murray Gell-Mann, the Nobel laureate. Conversations with Dick, George, and Murray widened and deepened my understanding and helped me develop the richness of my vocabulary in science. From Murray, I learned about complexity theory, and, he, in turn, titled his book *The Quark and the Jaguar* after a phrase from one of my poems. In addition, over five summers, Micah and I took a mushroom identification class with naturalist Bill Isaacs, and we learned how to identify many species, as well as their habitats.

It's a delight to read your excerpt from Stanley Kunitz's 1977 interview, and I am in agreement with him. Although scientific languages are specialized, I find their vocabularies and structures helpful to talk about the world. Unlike scientists, I think of these terms as contemporary languages of myth. For instance, who knows if string theory will provide a breakthrough or be relegated to the dustbins of scientific history, but, for now, it's an engaging vision, and it gives us a vehicle with which to grapple with the mysteries of the cosmos. When I was writing *The Ginkgo Light*, I became fascinated by the biology of the ginkgo leaf: the initial vein bifurcates and each subsequent vein bifurcates so that, instead of a web, the veins branch endlessly. When I did further research and discovered that a ginkgo tree survived the atomic blast at Hiroshima and flowered a week later, I found an image of nature pushed to the brink, and also a mythic response. So scientific inquiry has informed, strengthened, and even inspired my poetry, but I do not feel bound by it.

I want to add that I like using the structures of science to give underlying rigor to the poem and in that sense they can help shape it. I don't want to hit a reader over the head with "look, here is science." I liken the scientific motif to a thread that appears and disappears, that reappears and disappears. By not calling attention to itself, a reader who doesn't know the science can still experience what is happening in the poem. I like poems that have mystery and surprise: poems that you have to read and reread and that reveal themselves over time. I never want to feel like a reader has to have certain sets of knowledge to be able to appreciate the poem I am writing. I just want the reader to come to my poems with open eyes, to read with their nerves, so to speak, to be open to experience.

Reading with their nerves, that is interesting.

Reading a poem is a visceral experience. Emily Dickinson said, "If I feel physically as if the top of my head were taken off, I know that is poetry." I like that intense visceral reaction. And I use "nerves" because when I'm reading someone else's poem I might not know where I'm going or what's going to happen. I'm sensing with my nerves a multiplicity of effects in language; it's imaginative and it's emotional. That's why I proposed reading with one's nerves. It is not only intimate and vulnerable but also electric and powerful.

A poem that takes one's head off would more likely appear in a compressed poem, a single movement. Given the serial nature of your poems, and that you often write poems that are spread over pages, do you want the reader to have an "it takes my head off" reaction the whole way through, or do you feel there are moments of intensity that are followed by a certain slackening, and then intensification, and so forth?

That's a wonderful question. If it's a compressed poem, I sometimes hope the reader has that experience at the end. But in a sequence, spread over many pages, I wouldn't want that to happen again and again; in fact if it did, if you repeatedly and deliberately try to startle or stun a reader, I believe it would have a diminishing effect. I am more interested in—well, it's always back to Whitman, right?—incorporating worlds, utilizing different tonalities and textures, and having moments that jolt or stun a reader. These moments do not happen in easy succession or all at once; instead, they are moments or flashes a reader might not quite understand—"Oh! What is that?"—but a reader is going to feel like "I want to understand this more, I'm going to come back." Unlike a short poem, a sequence keeps unfolding, and, yes, there will be slacker moments, more narrative moments, lyrical moments, dramatic moments; they will be woven together, and *then* the reader is going to say, "Hmm, I need to reread this again, I want to understand this more." And hopefully each time, more emerges.

When I'm reading your longer poems, I do have those moments when I am startled or surprised. And the reaction is visceral. But I never know where this is going to happen. These shocks, for example, do not always happen at the end of a poem.

Absolutely. If I said I wanted the end of each section to stun or startle a reader, that intention becomes programmatic. And, in writing, one would then confine the possibilities of the poem, because one would have the need to go in a certain direction, whereas for me one great thing about poetry is I'm always discovering, I'm shedding where I think the poem is going. I might start with an impulse and then find, "this isn't it at all, the real poem is somewhere else." And so I'm constantly discovering. I want those shocks to be there, but I myself writing them don't quite know where they are: they get discovered along the way.

I'm looking at a book like Quipu, *which is really a mix of shorter, one-page poems and longer poems. Do you know in advance which poems will be shorter, concise movements and which ones will be serial pieces? Or does the serial poem come about because along the way you think, "I haven't said everything I wanted to say yet"?*

I don't plan out in advance. I sometimes write a short poem and think, wait a minute, the end is just the beginning. I liken it to a stone from an archipelago that is beginning to emerge above the surface, and I often intuit there's much more below that I need to mine and explore and develop. Although I don't sit down and say, "Now I'm going to write a sequence," sometimes I feel enormous inner pressure and guess that I will write something long. At other times, I will write several poems and find they're interconnected, and then those poems become the core to something larger. When I wrote "Apache Plume," I really just had this outpouring of emotion, and then, after writing many separate poems, I laid them out on the floor and thought, "They're all interconnected in ways I could not have envisioned beforehand; they should be moved together." And when I wrote the tenth and last poem, the other nine poems were already there.

You have a tendency in some of your other serial poems to include sections that might not hold up at all on their own. Such as some of the listing poems.

That's right.

Are such poems like interludes that corral some of the themes and imagery in the longer poems?

I think different principles and rationales are at work and it's hard for me to articulate it from the inside out, but I'm interested in—and I'm thinking of the list of endangered species in "The String Diamond"—suspending narration. I love the sounds to those plants. I had a list of 500 endangered species from *National Geographic* and played with the names, and it became an articulation of pure sound. From one point of view, it was an elegy, mourning species that are vanishing off the face of the earth, but, from another point of view, each one of these species is unique, is still here and still exerting its presence. And where that moment of revelation can happen in a poem is endlessly fascinating to me. If "The String Diamond" sequence started with the list, it would have no narration to suspend, but having set in motion a game of go, it's as if the naming—creating a litany or spell or incantation with language—is also trying to suspend time.

Oddly—and I'm not trying to be contrary here—I think that list section of "The String Diamond" reads like an independent poem. You could have titled it and it would have been able to stand on its own. A reader can deconstruct those names, too, to see if they are leading somewhere.

That's interesting. I certainly had not envisioned that. One thing that interests me is how you can have an enormous disparity between the intention and the effect. And that's actually a good thing. When I was writing the list of names in "The String Diamond," I was thinking, "This is like placing stones along a line on a go board; it's like linear thinking and you're doomed." But you're saying it's a complete poem in itself, and hearing you say that, I agree, though I had not thought of this before.

This poem was not what I was thinking of when I mentioned that in your serial poems you tend to include pieces that really only make sense when contextualized with the larger sequence. I was thinking of section five of "Kaiseki," where you begin, "They searched and searched for a loggerhead shrike." I don't think this would stand alone as easily as the list poem of the names of endangered plants.

Yes, sure. The fragments in section five of "Kaiseki" can't stand alone; they require the larger context of the sequence. And yet it's fascinating how some sections of a sequence can have a large degree of autonomy, while others can't. I think it has to do with the relationship between part and whole, but it's still mysterious.

Yet you appear to have quite a handle on the things you're trying to achieve with your poems. I get the sense, for example, that when you are citing certain scientific and cultural references in your poems you are aware most readers will find them strange. The fact that you supply notes indicates that you're aware of this.

Right. There are bare, skeletal notes, but at least they are like pointers or directions to pursue. I don't want the allusions or references to other disciplines and other endeavors to become too much of an obstacle. I'm trying to negotiate that sense of inviting the reader to stretch a little bit, hoping they will make that effort, because I believe it's rewarding in the end. You asked that wonderful question about balancing accessibility and difficulty and I do try and approach the poem with the understanding that I don't want the reader to necessarily have knowledge of contemporary physics or mycology—in some ways that knowledge might actually be a hindrance. Without knowing anything, you can be more open and discover and experience more.

So, in introducing the reader to the unfamiliar you're trying to get that reader to pay attention to the act of reading and the apprehension of reading.

Absolutely.

One of my favorite poems of yours is the aforementioned "Apache Plume." In the third section, "The Names of a Bird," you write, "If you know / the names of a bird in ten languages, do you know // any more about the bird?" That gave me pause. I felt it to be true and not a little sad. Could you discuss this passage, not only in terms of its place in the poem but in relation to the rest of your work?"

I consider "Apache Plume" a suite rather than a sequence. Each section, with a subtitle, is autonomous, unlike a numbered section in a sequence. In "Apache Plume," I wrote ten love poems to my wife, Carol Moldaw, and the third poem, "The Names of a Bird," explores the relationship between "I" and "you." In the passage you've quoted, the speaker is exploring the possibilities of knowledge, connection, and intimacy. If someone names a bird in ten languages, that naming is a lateral motion: it doesn't bring the namer any closer to what is named, and so connection and intimacy are not possible. If the poem ended there, it would indeed be sad, but the speaker instinctively recognizes this impasse and proceeds to personalize experience through memory, "I recollect how you folded a desert willow blossom // into a notebook . . . I know what it is to touch the mole between your breasts." Here the speaker arrives at a place where contact and intimacy are possible. He does not yet verbalize it—it will happen at the end of section seven with, "I know this instant moment which is ours"—because his intelligence doesn't fully comprehend it. This moment that communicates before it's understood is about poetry as well as love.

The passage about naming birds in ten languages is important in relation to the rest of my work, because it raises the large issues of naming, knowledge and connection. I've already asserted that in "The Names of a Bird," a lateral motion of naming would not help the speaker gain any knowledge about the bird itself, but what if naming enacted a vertical rather than a horizontal motion? In section three of "The String Diamond," I created a vocalization of imminent loss. And in section five of "Spectral Line," I list 40 American Indian tribes. Here the list embodies the names of students I had the privilege to teach at the Institute, and the procession of names is a roll call. If "The String Diamond" and "Spectral Line" contained only the sections of names, they would go nowhere, but context is crucial. In "The String Diamond," nonlinear connections form webs and allow meaning to accrue, while linear connection arrives at a dead end. So I believe the passage of lateral naming in "The Names of a Bird" reveals the limitations of impersonal knowledge. As a poet, I find that I zigzag between objective observation and subjective experience and need to "personalize the way" so that the poem can become a living force.

In the fourth section of your poem "Before Completion," you begin with a startling juxtaposition: "a poet describes herding pigs / beside a girl with a glass eye and affirms / the power to dream and transform. Later, / in exile, he axes his wife and hangs himself." Your poems are filled with such juxtapositions that, at first, shock and then, upon further inspection, seem less shocking than true—and possible. Could you talk about your use of juxtapositions?

Juxtaposition is an essential tool at my disposal. It can surprise, intensify, suspend, disrupt, or reinforce, and I'd like to make a distinction between juxtaposition in stillness (space) and juxtaposition in motion (time). Juxtaposition in stillness occurs where two fragments or segments are placed side by side. Here I liken the effect to magnetism: the two pieces can attract, repel, or undergo varying degrees of attraction or repulsion. A series of fragments can create a disorienting, even bewildering, field of energy, but this experience may be a necessary stage. Juxtaposition in motion occurs when a narrative is telescoped or when two or more narratives are spun together and converge. I liken juxtaposition in motion to moments in a Shakespearean play where a subplot throws light on and exerts psychological force on the main plot. Juxtaposition in stillness is like the moment on stage when charged silence fills the air. In either case, juxtaposition has a dramatic value; it involves tension and coexistent fields of energy.

In other interviews, I've mentioned that Chinese characters are created through juxtaposition and that these juxtapositions create rich and mysterious effects. If you write the character "sun," and then, to the right, the character "moon," you create the character "bright." If you write the character "field," and below, the character "heart/mind," you create the character "think." Notice how physical thought becomes in this language system: to think is to put your heart and mind into a field. In contrast to the juxtapositions inside of Chinese characters that frequently connect and clarify, my juxtapositions are frequently jarring and dissonant; yet, I am, in my own way, also searching for deep connection.

In the passage you quoted from "Before Completion," the lines are shockingly true. In 1985, I met the Misty poet, Gu Cheng, in Beijing, and we became friends. During the Cultural Revolution, he and his father herded pigs in the countryside. Years later, after Tiananmen, in exile in New Zealand, he axed his wife and hanged himself. In the poem, I telescoped many years and juxtaposed the early incident with the later one to compress and intensify the tragic story.

In that same section you write: "Do the transformations of memory / become the changing lines of divination?" Elsewhere, such as in "Aqueous Gold" from Quipu, *you refer to how the memory can "batter and renew," how it is impoverished, and, perhaps most stunningly, how "thoughts inch through" it "the way maggots do a cèpe." Do you have a theory of memory? How does memory function in one to transform and, possibly, transcend?*

I don't have a theory of memory, but I'm interested in how memory is a living force within us all. Memory is a way of unfolding and processing human experience, and it's also invention. Who we are in the present is significantly related to our past, and the wider the range, and the greater the emotional depth and imaginative power to recreate those experiences, the richer, more various and creative we are and can be. As we tap into deep memories, we live more fully in the present. In addition, if one has lived through tragedy, struggling with memories often becomes a process by which one works toward reconciliation and peace. If one dwells too much on these memories, one can become trapped, and then "thoughts inch through / memory the way maggots inch through a cèpe"; but when memories have singularity, they can also be Wordworth's "spots of time" that nourish and sustain.

"Aqueous Gold" is one of my favorite poems of yours. I particularly admire the ways you explore memory there.

To me "Aqueous Gold" is an exploration of desire and memory. Those are two axes in my poetry. One thinks one's going forward in desire, but that can be illusory; one thinks one's going backwards in memory but memory is also invention.

In its references to air and water, I see portions of "Aqueous Gold" as linked to pre-Socratic thought.

Pre-Socratic thinking is a huge influence upon me. I see all of those philosophers as poets: Thales, Parmenides, etc. From a scientific point of view we can say their views of the world—that the world is air or the world is fire—are ridiculous. And yet you read a fragment of Heraclitus and it's like wow, where did that come from, it's so poetic, it's so original.

Perhaps part of the appeal to this group of philosophers may be that all we have are the fragments, that a complete system of thought is lacking, which enables us to project onto their aphorisms and propositions our own intellectual and creative visions.

I think those fragments are tantalizing and provocative, and a great place for any poet to go to. Plato for me is so fully fleshed out it becomes problematical, there isn't room—whereas, as you say, with the fragments and the gaps, that space is supremely useful. When Thales says, "Earth rests upon water," a scientist might balk, but a poet might think what he's really saying, through metaphor, is that there is no absolute foundation—and this is true and something I can make use of.

Space seems to be an important factor in your compositional methods, too. No matter how much you extend a poem into several sections I never sense your poems are overwritten. In fact, I often leave your poems with more questions than answers. There is a lot of space left.

Thank you. I take this as a huge compliment that you sense that spaciousness.

Is it a challenge for you to create this kind of space?

It is and frankly there are often sections to the sequences that don't make it in to the final poem, because I want the reader to experience that kind of space that keeps opening up. Sometimes there are passages where I realize I was just thinking out some things that are enacted more effectively in other sections, so those passages are removed. I love taking sections and laying them out on the floor, putting blank sheets of paper between them, and asking, What happens if I spread these apart? Could something go here that is unanticipated? Or what happens if I bring them together? So I am constantly testing the spacial relations inside of the poem, which is connected to time, of course, as the poem unfolds, as one reads it.

So even when you've written a poetic sequence that is cohesive or has clear linkages, you often deliberately try to break them, creating further spaces between the links.

That's right.

And yet, ironically, the more you expand your poems the more space appears to be in them.

That is, again, a huge compliment. It's like worlds inside of a world. I want the rigor of the poem to be there. I don't want it to feel like "Oh, this is a book-length project." This is one of the reasons I've resisted writing a book-length poem or sequence, although the temptation is there, and so many poets are doing it. Instead of consciously embarking on a book project, I'd rather write 30 sections and realize later that only 10 can truly work together.

Your use of the couplet seems quite useful in creating that sense of space.

I started to use the couplet when I found my poems were leaping a lot. If the poem was laid out in a blocklike one-stanza form, the leaps were jammed together. When I opened the poem into couplets, the white space allowed more breathing room so that a reader could, at the end of the couplet, not only have the slight pause at the end of a line but also a breathing space before the next leap. I want to add that I have found the couplet form supremely helpful for editing: in a blocklike form, I sometimes have difficulty seeing clunky or overwritten phrases, whereas, in couplet form, it is much easier to spot phrases that need to be cut or reworked. So I find myself writing drafts of poems in couplet form. Sometimes I will compress all the two-line stanzas into one stanza, sometimes the poem requires a different shape, but, frequently, because the couplets are integrated into the process of creation, the final poem stays in that form.

How does gingko light serve as a structural and thematic metaphor for the book The Gingko Light?

The image of the ginkgo appears and disappears throughout the book. In the poem "Chrysalis," it first appears as a fossil image, then some of its history—"once thought extinct, the ginkgo / was discovered in Himalayan monasteries // and propagated back into the world"—is revealed. The history culminates in the passage where, after the atom bomb is dropped on Hiroshima, a ginkgo tree survives and flowers. In our challenged and challenging world, faced with the extinction of so many living species, the ginkgo's response becomes a metaphor for how we might live. In addition, the endlessly branching venation pattern of the ginkgo leaf informs the book: the first vein at the base of the leaf, or, equivalently, at the spine of the book, is the catalog of Native tribes in "Spectral Line." The catalog is not only located at the center of that sequence, but it is also located at the center of the book. But my book is not called *The Ginkgo Tree*. I was after a mythic title, and the phrase, the ginkgo light embodied, for me, the precarious splendor of our world.

As we wrap up, I am wondering if you wish to address anything else.

Well, with reference to one of your earlier questions, I was really glad you asked me how I situated myself in the tradition of American poetry, because so often categories such as Asian-American poetry or Native American poetry get used in ways that aren't helpful. I wondered about raising the issue that all these categories should be seen as aspects of one poetry—American poetry. Maybe one of the difficulties right now is that things are artificially divided up. I don't see why an anthology of American literature, for instance, can't start with the Navajo Nightway Chant.

Clearly you are so much more than an American poet who is cognizant of the poetic traditions of China. In this chat alone you've mentioned Whitman more than once. How do you see yourself as participating in this larger story of American poetry?

I have a significant connection to Whitman, Emerson, Williams, Pound, and Stevens. I believe that—and I'm borrowing another metaphor here—growth is at the edge of a leaf, and that we, as contemporary poets, are hoping to add to the tradition and great richness of American poetry.

Busa, Christopher. "A Taste of Self." *Interviews and Encounters with Stanley Kunitz.* Ed. Stanley Moss. Riverdale-on-Hudson: Sheep Meadow Press, 1993.

Elshtain, Eric P. "An Interview with Arthur Sze." *Chicago Review*: Vol. 50, No. 2/3/4, Winter 2004/5.

Sze, Arthur. "Apache Plume," "Streamers," and "Before Completion." *The Redshifting Web: Poems 1970–1998.* Port Townsend: Copper Canyon Press, 1998.

______. "Inflorescence," "In the Living Room," and "Quipu." *Quipu.* Port Townsend: Copper Canyon Press, 2005.

______. "Chrysalis" and "The Gingko Light." *The Gingko Light.* Port Townsend: Copper Canyon Press, 2009.

Poetry:

The Ginkgo Light, Copper Canyon Press, 2009
Quipu, Copper Canyon Press, 2005
The Redshifting Web: Poems 1970–1998, Copper Canyon Press, 1998
Archipelago, Copper Canyon Press, 1995
River River, Lost Roads Publishers, 1987
Dazzled, Floating Island Publications, 1982

Translations:

The Silk Dragon: Translations of Chinese Poetry, Copper Canyon Press, 2001
Two Ravens: Poems and Translations from the Chinese, Tooth of Time Books, 1984
The Willow Wind: Poems and Translations from the Chinese, Tooth of Time Books, 1981

As Editor:

Chinese Writers on Writing, Trinity University Press, 2010

Acknowledgments

Thanks goes out to the editors of the following print and online publications in which a number of the interviews in *Passwords Primeval* first appeared in slightly different forms:

American Literary Review: "A Glimpse of the Beautiful: An Interview with Scott Cairns";

Arts & Letters: "Writing by Ear: An Interview with Michael Waters";

EOAGH: "Poem as Gesture: An Interview with Kevin Killian," "Poetry Steeped in Intellectual Matter: An Interview with Bin Ramke," and "Abandoning the Middle Distance: An Interview with Robert Glück";

Great River Review: "The Embrace of Everything: An Interview with Gerald Stern";

Gay and Lesbian Review: "A Poetry of Expansiveness: An Interview with Mark Doty";

Kenyon Review Online: "Balancing Images: An Interview with Carol Frost";

Left Curve: "Putting Blood Back into Words: An Interview with Martín Espada";

National Poetry Review: By Way of Play and Accident: An Interview with Karen Volkman";

Sentence: "Horizontal Poetry: An interview with Gary Young";

Xavier Review: "Speaking Through a Second Throat: An Interview with Patricia Smith."

This book could not have been completed without the selfless dedication of all the poets who consented to be interviewed, especially Michael Waters who put me in touch with many of them. I also want to acknowledge BOA Publisher-Editor Peter Conners for taking an interest in the project, and for giving me a pretty long leash. More thanks goes to many friends and fellow writers whose belief in my work helped sustain my interest in it: Michael Alleman, Jeana Bonacci-Roth, Darrell Bourque, Vanessa Crary-Vaille, Nicolas D'Agostino, Steve Fellner,

Roger Freitas, Steve Huff, M. J. Iuppa, Susan Jordan, Michael Klein, Joan Larkin, Noah Michelson, Gary Rainford, Linda Reinfeld, Christopher Phelps, Nicolas Schneider, and Mark Tursi, among others. And I send a big hug to artist Kathleen Farrell, who always knows what I'm looking for.

An enormous thanks goes to several people at Monroe Community College, in particular Professor Emeritus Barbara Lovenheim for invaluable editorial advice; fellow faculty members Maria Brandt and Phil Snyder for their enthusiasm; former English Department Chairperson Bob De Felice for allowing me to jumpstart the project in its earliest stages; current Chairperson Cathy Smith for further support; Carmen Powers and the members of the Faculty Senate Awards and Professional Leaves Committee for rewarding my efforts; and former Dean Chet Rogalski, Dean Kristin Fragnoli, and Academic Provost Mike McDonough, all of whom believed in the work I was doing and generously supported the project in various ways.

Permissions

Several partially cited poems and excerpts from prose texts have been reprinted here in accordance with guidelines for fair use or, in the following cases, with permission of their publishers.

"The Inarticulate" from *Parthenopi: New and Selected Poem* by Michael Waters. Copyright © 2001 by Michael Waters. Used by Permission of BOA Editions, Ltd.

All untitled prose poems by Gary Young, from *No Other Life* (Heyday Books, 1997) and *Pleasure* (Heyday Books, 2006) have been reprinted in full with permission from the author.

Li-Young Lee's "This Room and Everything in It" from *The City in Which I Love You* by Li-Young Lee. Copyright © 1990 by Li-Young Lee. Used by Permission of BOA Editions, Ltd.

"Bakersfield 1969" from *The Book of Men* by Dorianne Laux. Copyright © 2011 by Dorianne Laux. Used by Permission of W. W. Norton & Company, Inc.

"Table" by Edip Cansever. Trans. by Julia Clare Tillinghast and Richard Tillinghast Copyright © 2009 by Julia Clare Tillinghast and Richard Tillinghast *Dirty August: Poems by Edip Cansever.* Trans. Julia Clare Tillinghast and Richard Tillinghast. Used by Permission of Talisman House Press.

Excerpt from "The End and the Beginning" from *Poems, New and Collected: 1957–1997* by Wisława Szymborska, English translation by Stanislaw Baranczak and Clare Cavanagh copyright © 1998 by Houghton Mifflin Harcourt Publishing Company and Faber and Faber, Ltd., reprinted by permission of the publishers.

"Underground Dancing" Copyright © 1977 by Gerald Stern; "Soap" Copyright © 1984 by Gerald Stern, from *This Time: New and Selected Poems* by Gerald Stern. Used by Permission of W. W. Norton & Company, Inc.

"The Picasso Poem" Copyright © 1981 by Gerald Stern from *Early Collected Poems: 1965–1992* by Gerald Stern. Used by Permission of W. W. Norton & Company, Inc.

"Sam and Morris" from *American Sonnets* by Gerald Stern. Copyright © 2002 by Gerald Stern. Used by Permission of W. W. Norton & Company, Inc.

"Someone to Watch Over Me." from *Last Blue: Poems* by Gerald Stern. Copyright © 2000 by Gerald Stern, Inc. Used by Permission of W. W. Norton & Company, Inc.

Excerpt from James Wright, "A Blessing" from *Collected Poems* © 1971 by James Wright. Reprinted by Permission of Wesleyan University Press.

William Carlos Williams. "The Red Wheelbarrow." *The Collected Poems of William Carlos Williams, Vol. 1: 1909–1939*. New York: New Directions, 1991. Copyright ©1938 by New Directions Publishing Corp. Reprinted by permission of New Directions Publishing Corp. and Carcanet Press, Ltd.

About the Author

Tony Leuzzi is a writer and Associate Professor of English at Monroe Community College in Rochester, NY. The recipient of a National Institute for Staff and Organizational Development Award and the Wesley T. Hansen Award for Excellence in Teaching, he has written film and book criticism for a number of academic and small-press publications, co-curated two art exhibits, and received two grants from the New York State Council of the Arts. His second volume of poems, *Radiant Losses,* won the New Sins Editors' Prize in 2009. His third, *Fake Book,* was released by Anything Anymore Anywhere Books UK in 2011.

Index of Names and Titles

BOA Editions, Ltd.
American Reader Series

No. 1 *Christmas at the Four Corners of the Earth*
Prose by Blaise Cendrars
Translated by Bertrand Mathieu

No. 2 *Pig Notes & Dumb Music: Prose on Poetry*
By William Heyen

No. 3 *After-Images: Autobiographical Sketches*
By W. D. Snodgrass

No. 4 *Walking Light: Memoirs and Essays on Poetry*
By Stephen Dunn

No. 5 *To Sound Like Yourself: Essays on Poetry*
By W. D. Snodgrass

No. 6 *You Alone Are Real to Me: Remembering Rainer Maria Rilke*
By Lou Andreas-Salomé

No. 7 *Breaking the Alabaster Jar: Conversations with Li-Young Lee*
Edited by Earl G. Ingersoll

No. 8 *I Carry A Hammer In My Pocket For Occasions Such As These*
By Anthony Tognazzini

No. 9 *Unlucky Lucky Days*
By Daniel Grandbois

No. 10 *Glass Grapes and Other Stories*
By Martha Ronk

No. 11 *Meat Eaters & Plant Eaters*
By Jessica Treat

No. 12 *On the Winding Stair*
By Joanna Howard

No. 13 *Cradle Book*
By Craig Morgan Teicher

No. 14 *In the Time of the Girls*
By Anne Germanacos

No. 15 *This New and Poisonous Air*
By Adam McOmber

No. 16 *To Assume a Pleasing Shape*
By Joseph Salvatore

No. 17 *The Innocent Party*
By Aimee Parkison

No. 18 *Passwords Primeval: 20 American Poets in Their Own Words*
By Tony Leuzzi

Colophon

Passwords Primeval: 20 American Poets in Their Own Words is set in Monotype Dante. First created in metal type in the mid-1950s and digitalized in the 1990s, it is the result of a collaboration between Giovanni Mardersteig—a printer, book designer, and typeface artist renowned for the work he produced at Officina Bodoni and Stamperia Valdònega in Italy—and Charles Malin, one of the great punch-cutters of the twentieth century.

The publication of this book is made possible, in part, by the special support of the following individuals:

Anonymous
Anonymous, *in memory of Greg Lippard*
English Philosophy Department at Monroe Community College
Jonathan Everitt
Anne Germanacos
X. J. & Dorothy M. Kennedy
Jack & Gail Langerak
Katherine Lederer
Barbara & John Lovenheim
Boo Poulin
Deborah Ronnen & Sherman Levey
Steven O. Russell & Phyllis Rifkin-Russell
Rob Tortorella
Glenn & Helen William